To Denise-
Happy Trails
From Our Backyard
To Yours!
[illegible]
Christmas 2016

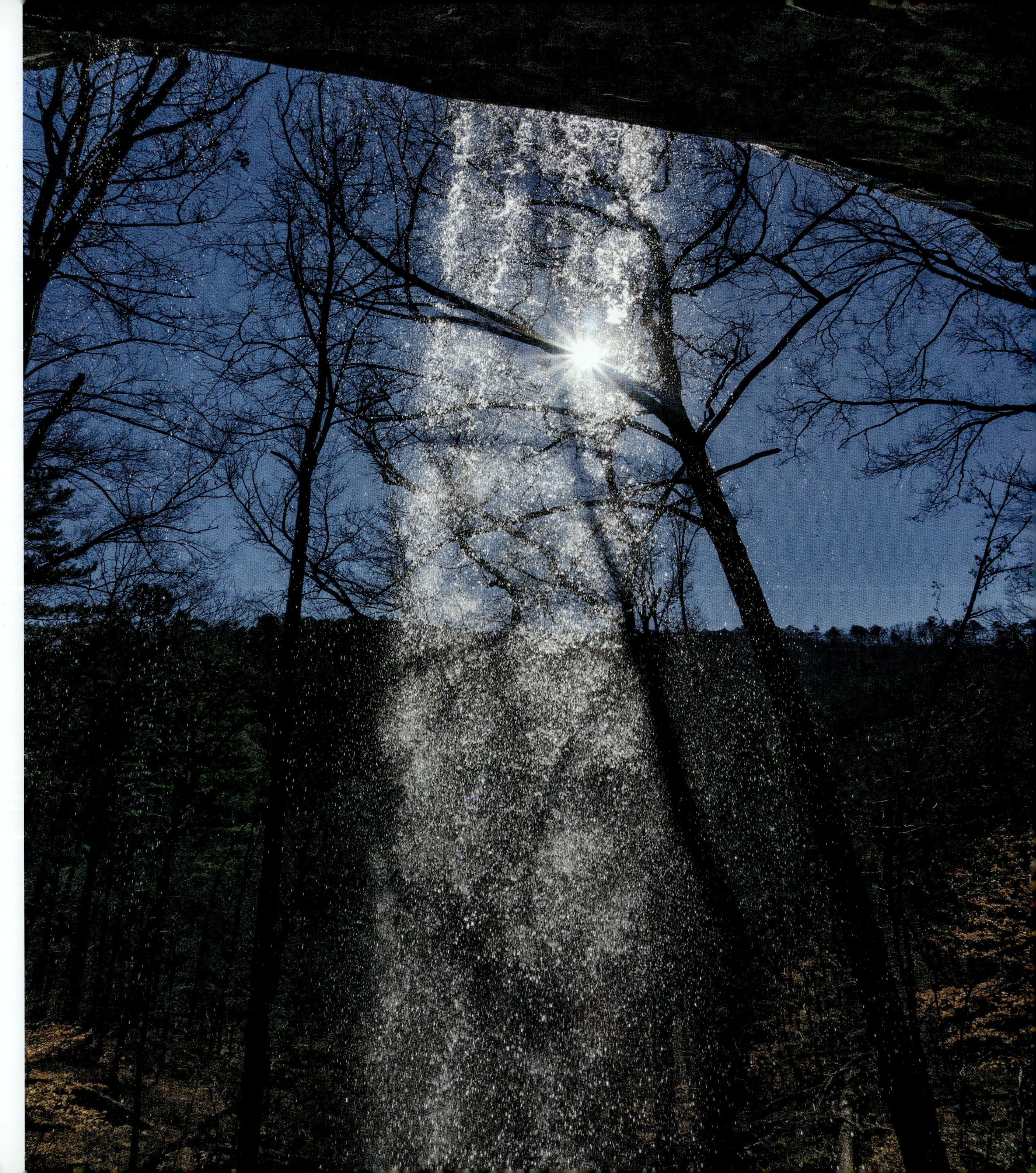

ARKANSAS
In My Own Backyard

by Tim Ernst

Afternoon sun shines through a waterfall in the Cow Creek area, Ozark National Forest (previous page)

Peaceful evening along Big Piney Creek, Ozark National Forest (facing page)

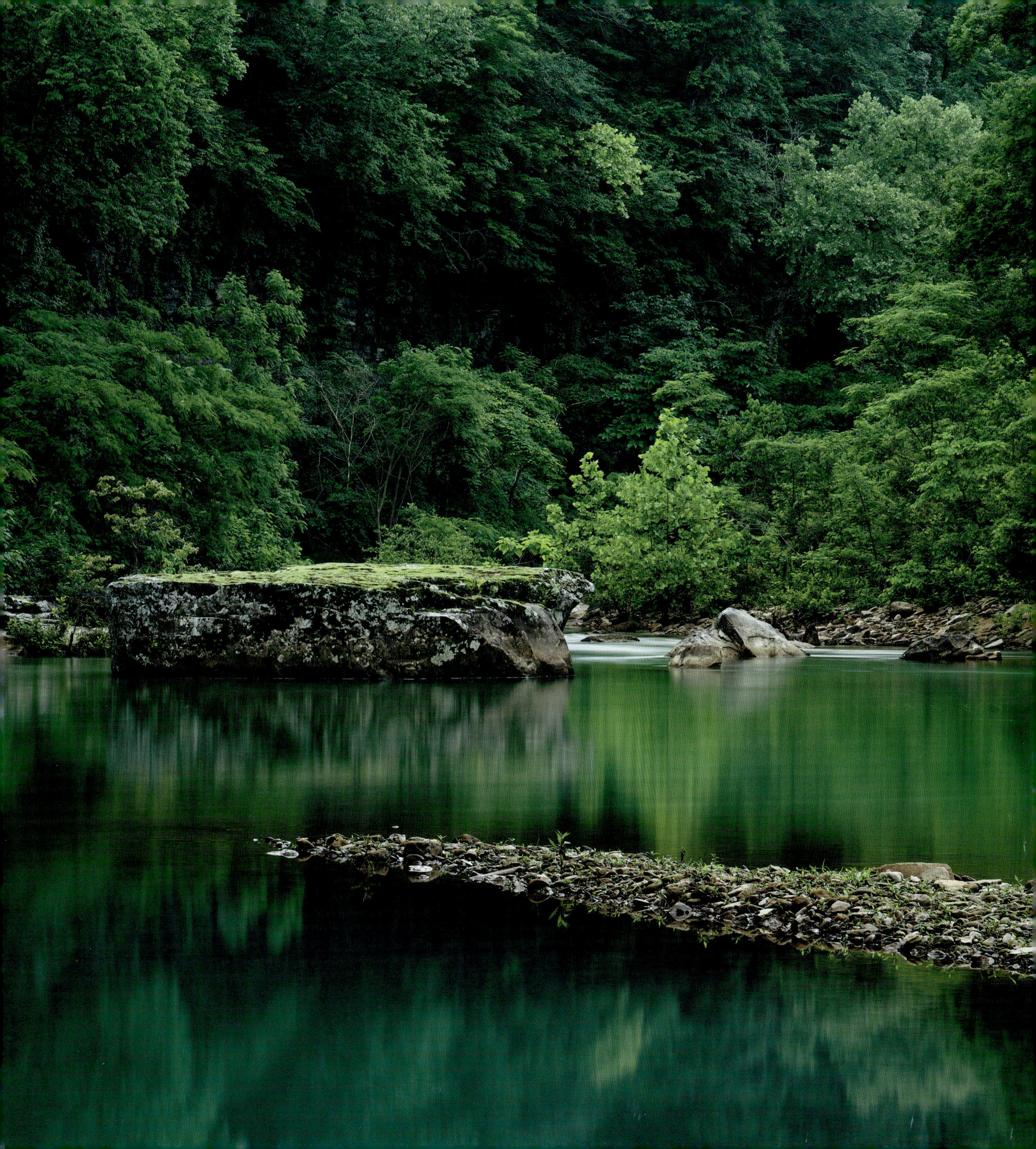

Printed in China
Library of Congress Control Number: 2016911441
ISBN: 9781882906888

Book designed by Tim and Pam Ernst

Clear waters and colorful reflections at Steele Creek, Buffalo National River

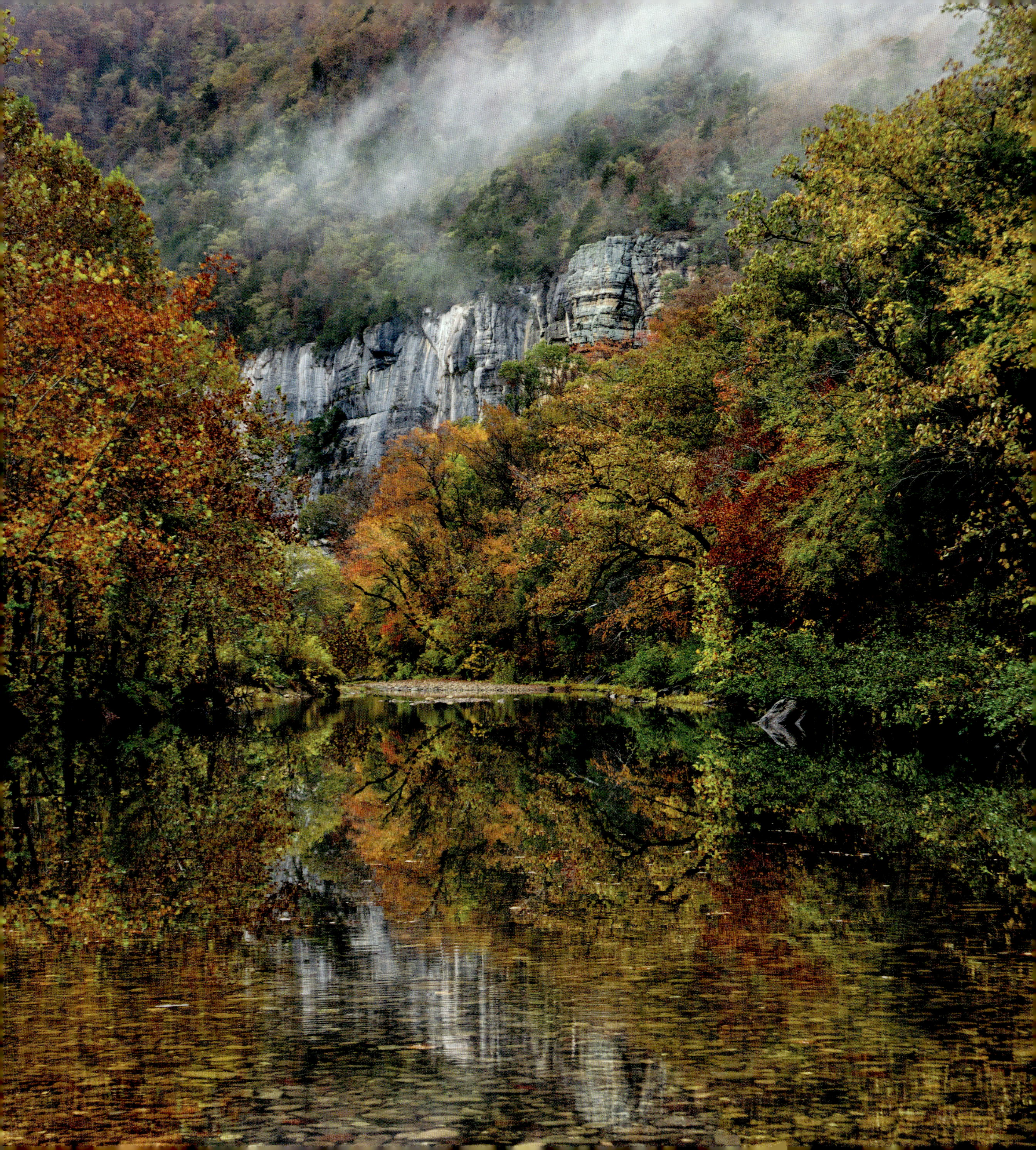

INTRODUCTION

Welcome to ***Arkansas: In My Own Backyard!*** My lovely bride and I have lived in a log cabin in a remote section of the Ozark Mountains of northwest Arkansas for nearly 20 years, at a place we call Cloudland. I've spent a great deal of time working elsewhere during the first 40 years of my nature photography career, and I thought it was about time to stick close to home for this new book. So I got out a map and drew a circle around our cabin a distance that I would be able to hike in one day– 12 miles as the crow flies (or about double that if hiking up and down the hills—I'm old, but I can still hike that far in a day). All the pictures in this book were taken within that 12-mile circle around our Cloudland cabin home.

The circle includes the headwaters of many major river drainages in the Arkansas Ozarks including: the Buffalo River, Little Buffalo River, Big Piney Creek, Mullberry River, Little Mulberry River, Kings River, and the extreme headwaters of the East Fork of the White River.

As luck would have it, we picked a spectacular location for our cabin to begin with, near many of the scenic icons of Arkansas; like Hawksbill Crag, The Glory Hole, Kings River Falls, Sweden Creek Falls, Tea Table Rocks on Home Valley Bluff, Alum Cove Natural Bridge, Eden Falls and Lost Valley, Roark Bluff, and many other beautiful natural and historical areas.

The circle includes hundreds of waterfalls; hundreds of miles of hiking, horseback riding, ATV, and mountain bike trails; hundreds of miles of towering sandstone and limestone bluffs; thousands of miles of pristine creeks, streams, and rivers; the Upper Buffalo Wilderness Area; Kings River Falls Natural Area; Sweden Creek Natural Area; Smith Creek Nature Preserve; the Ozark National Forest; and the Buffalo National River. WHEW! Imagine how difficult it has been for me to get up each day and try to pick a place to go work!

We wanted to include only new photos that had never been published in a book before, so I spent a great deal of time this past year shooting locally—more than 60,000 new pictures. I also went back through the archives and found a few choice images that I'd never published before, including a photo of wild trumpeter swans on the very first day they arrived in Boxley Valley, on Christmas day in 2005! I "forced" myself to revisit some locations I'd been to dozens of times before to get new photos, but also explored some areas near our cabin where I'd never set foot—even some places we could see from our cabin but had never been to before! There are many thousands of acres within that circle that remain pretty remote and wild. My intent was not to document all of this, but rather to simply head out and explore and photograph anything that interested me. And so I did.

The photos in this book are not arranged in any sort of manner—you may open the book anywhere and begin looking. The subjects are whatever I happened to be drawn to at the time and are literally all over the map (well, actually just within that 12-mile circle from our cabin).

One important note that I hope you take away from this book. Many of the scenes I photographed could have been taken anywhere—like the God Beams photo on the right—I just made it yesterday while I was hiking back to our cabin, but it could have been in any forest area or local park. I encourage you to get out and explore ***your own backyard*** and see what treasures you find there. ENJOY!

Tim Ernst

Tim Ernst at Cloudland
July, 2016

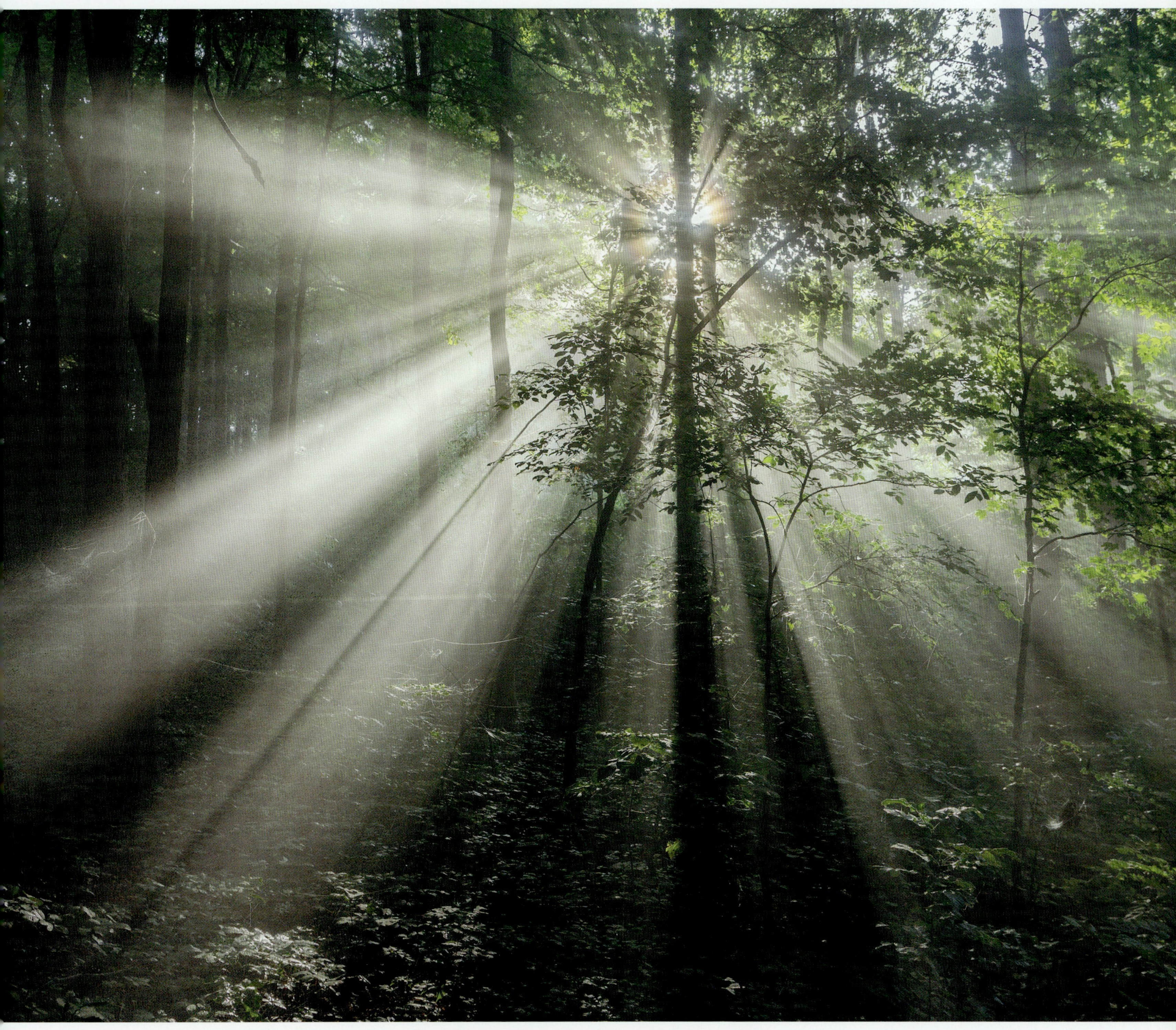

God Beams flood the forest near our cabin

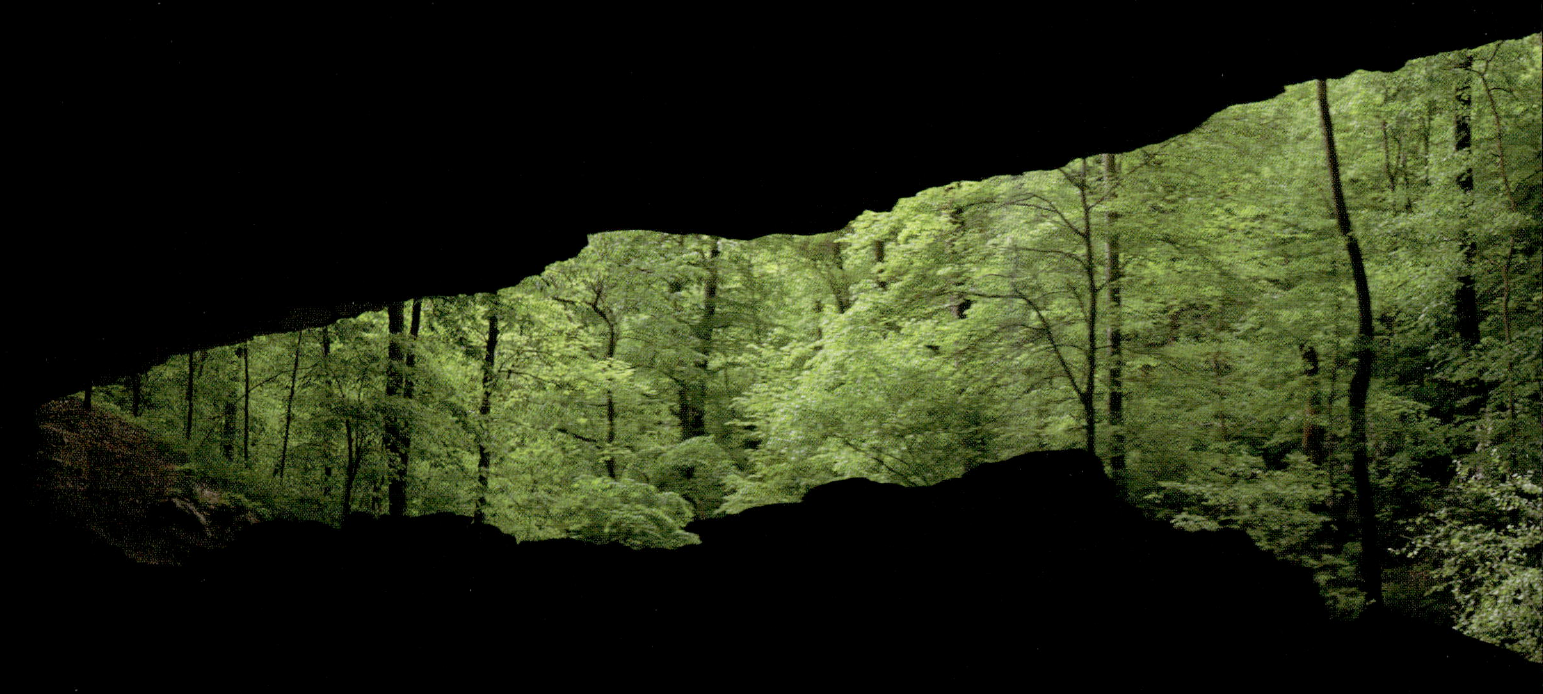

CONTENTS

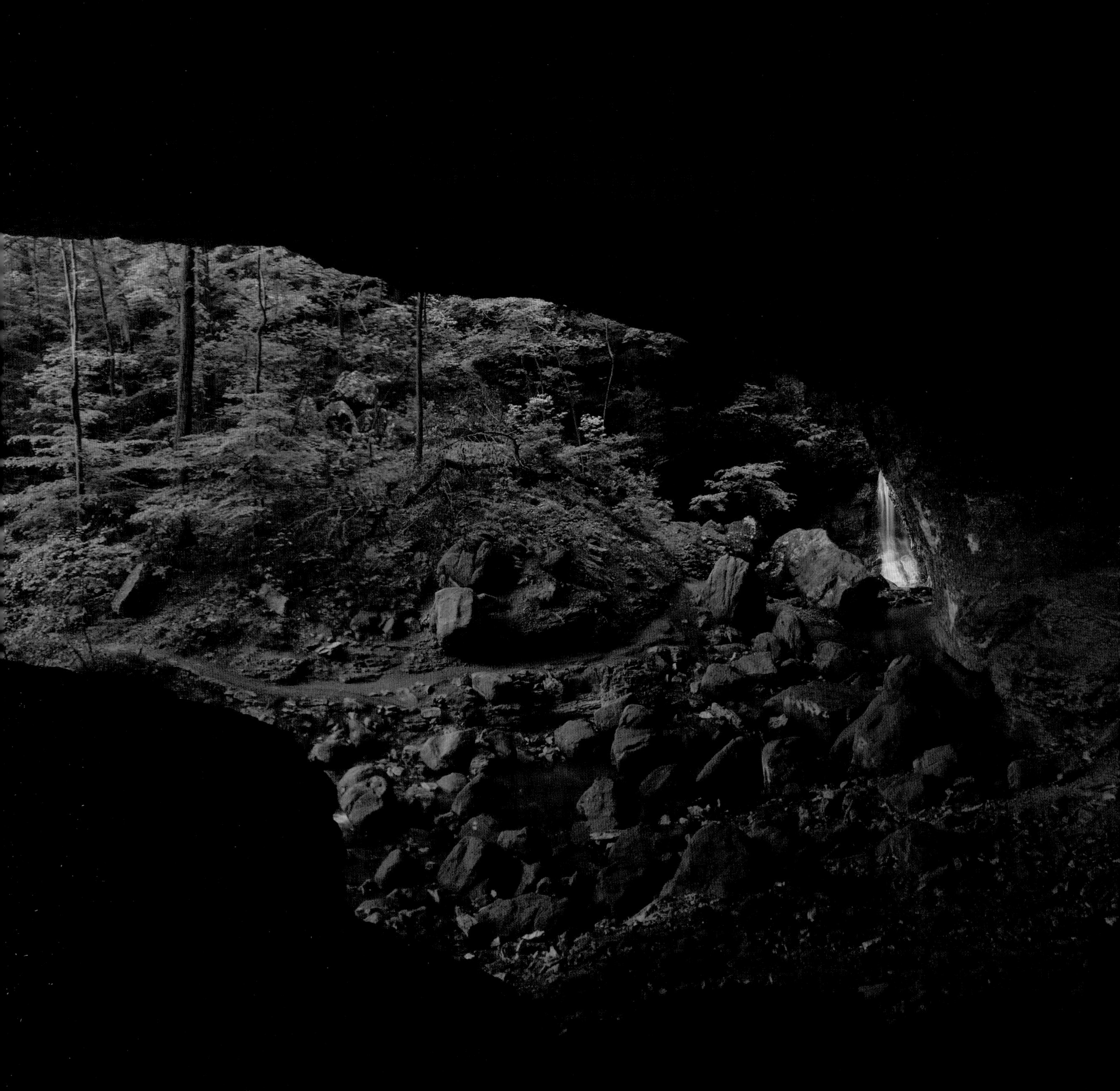

Looking out from Cobb Cave at Eden Falls along the Lost Valley Trail, Buffalo National River

Lichen Falls along the Ozark Highlands Trail, Ozark National Forest

We live in the heart of the best waterfall country in mid-America, which is one reason we live here. There are literally hundreds of waterfalls within our backyard circle. Many famous Arkansas waterfalls are here including: Eden Falls at Lost Valley, Bowers Hollow Falls, Compton's Double Falls, Sweden Creek Falls, and Kings River Falls. There are also countless smaller yet quite beautiful falls in nearly every drainage—often you can find a dozen or more waterfalls while exploring along a single creek, most of the falls remain unnamed. In fact, that is a favorite pastime of mine—find a drainage that is unknown to me, start at the top or bottom and just follow the water to the end.

One of these drainages is Lynn Hollow, which flows into the Mulberry River. The Ozark Highlands Trail (OHT) winds through this hollow and passes Lichen Falls—first you hear it, then you can look right over the edge next to the trail and see the thundering waterfall below. The OHT goes past more waterfalls than any other hiking trail in this part of the country.

Waterfalls from all the major drainages in our circle are included in this book—some great in stature and well-known, others small and unnamed. I hope each one will give you a refreshing blast of visual pleasure.

By the way, it is a medical fact that waterfalls produce negative ions that can have a calming, even euphoric effect on humans. So the more time you spend at waterfalls the happier you will be!

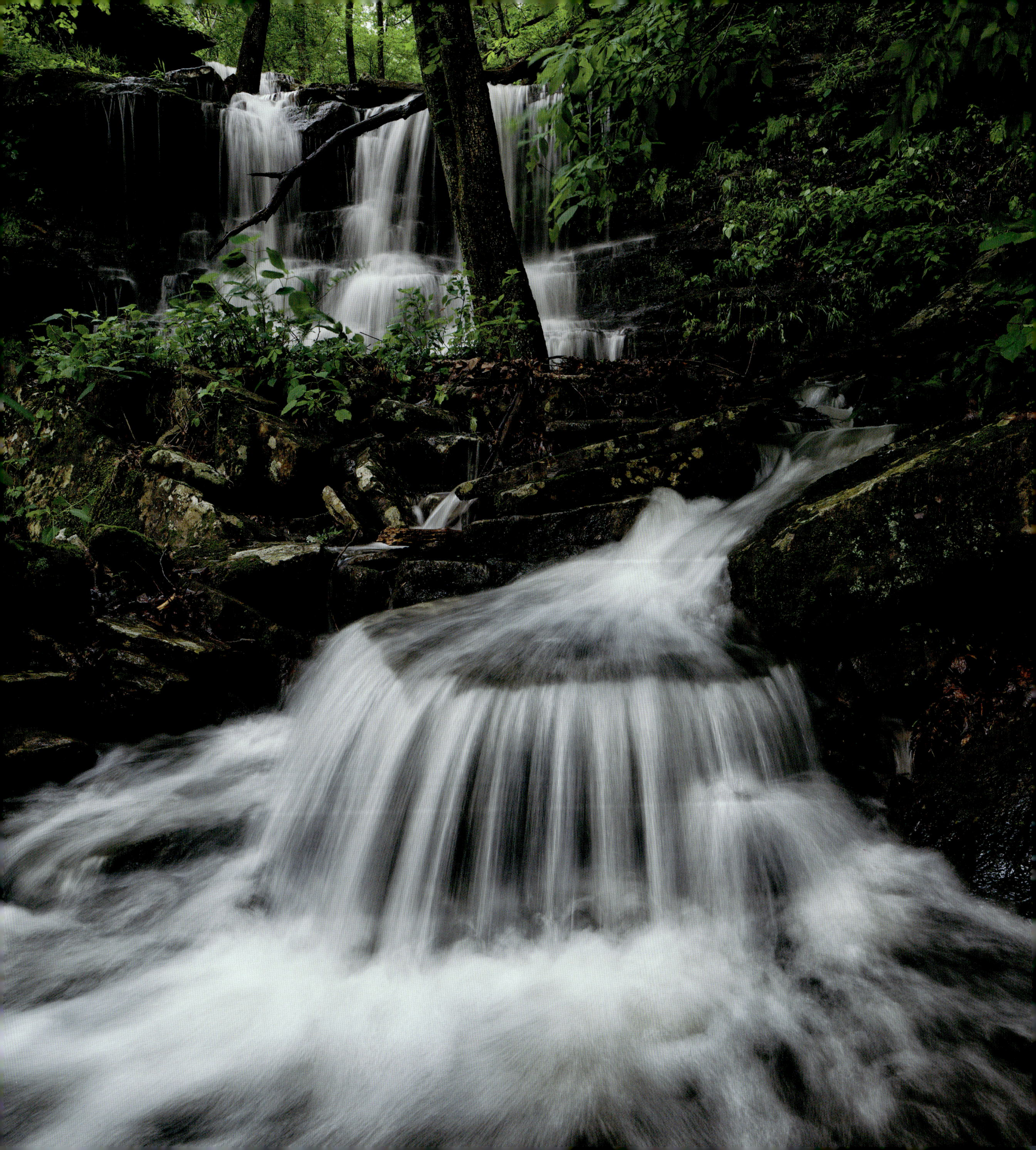

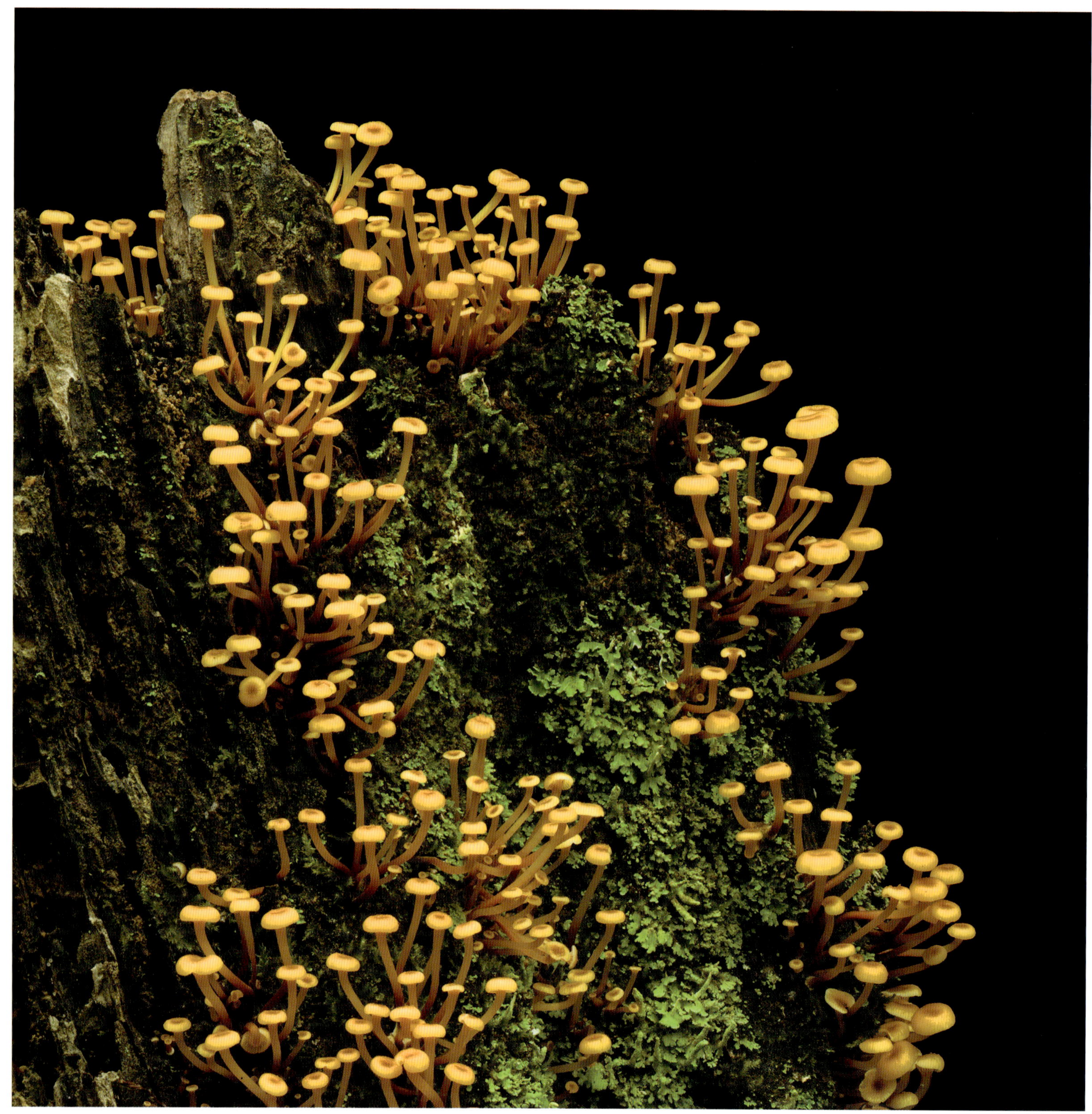

A family of tiny mushrooms, lichens and moss

Chimney and Virginia creeper, Boxley Valley Historic District

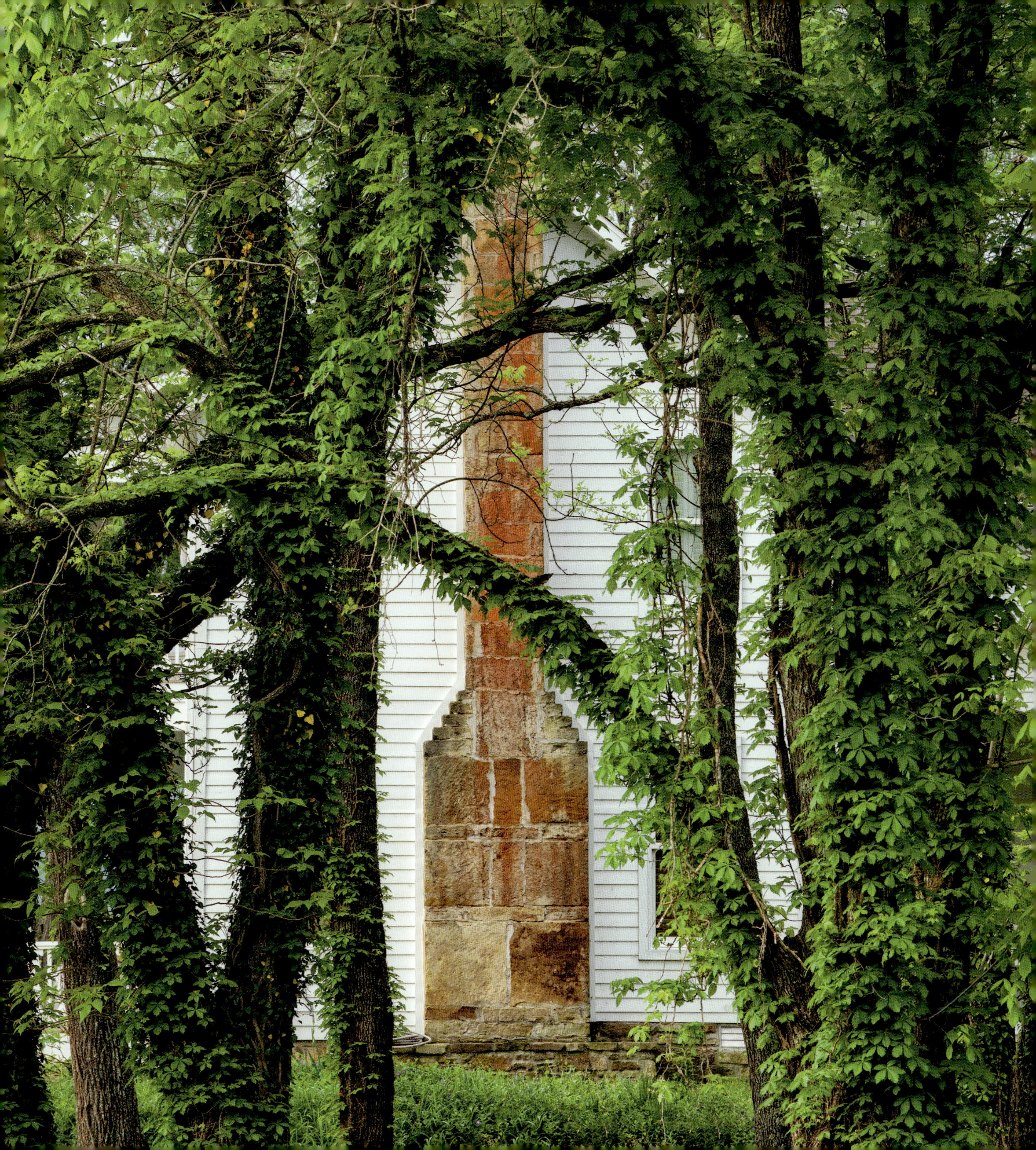

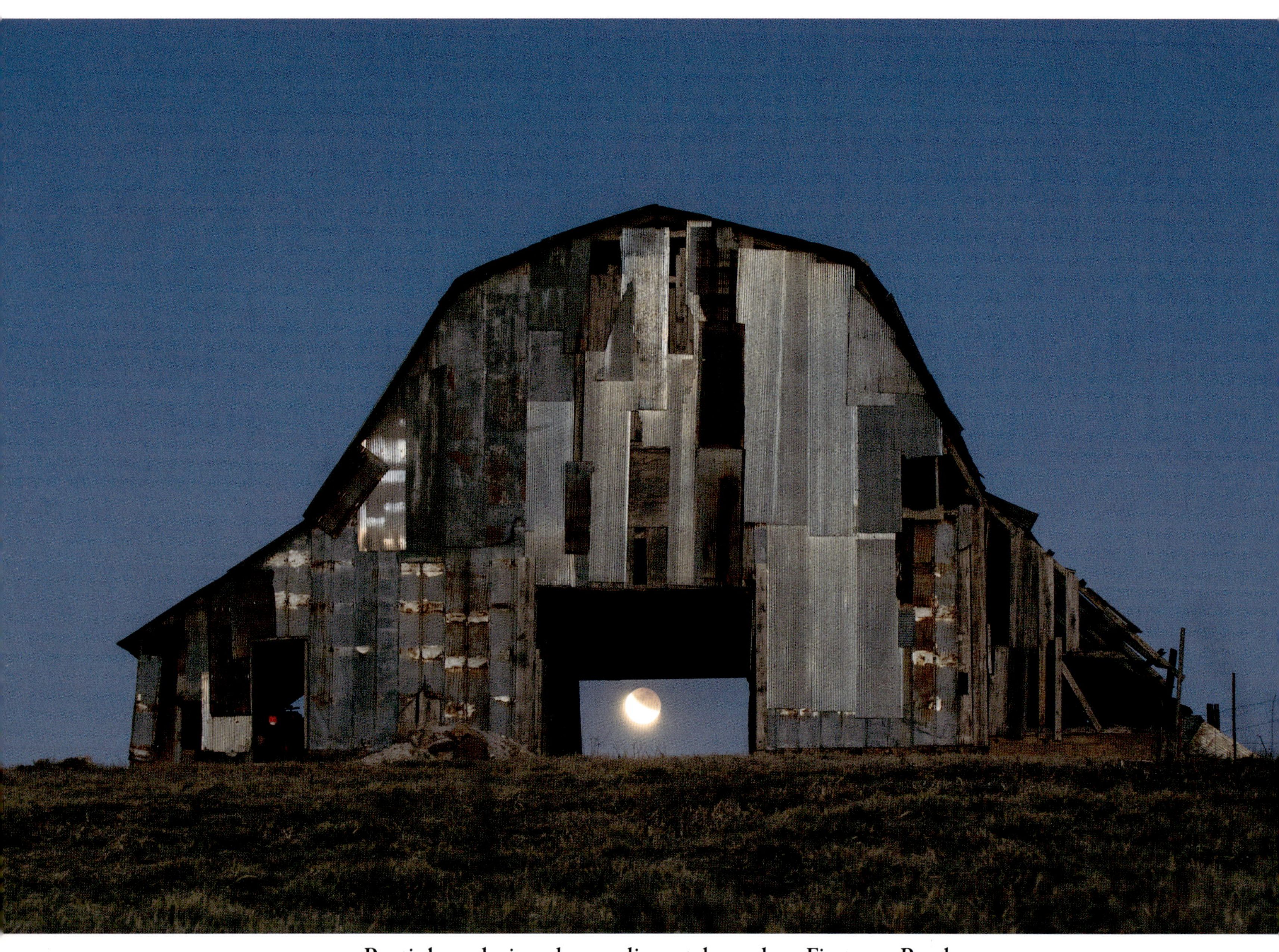

Rustic barn during a lunar eclipse at dawn along Firetower Road

Early October morning on Big Piney Creek, Ozark National Forest

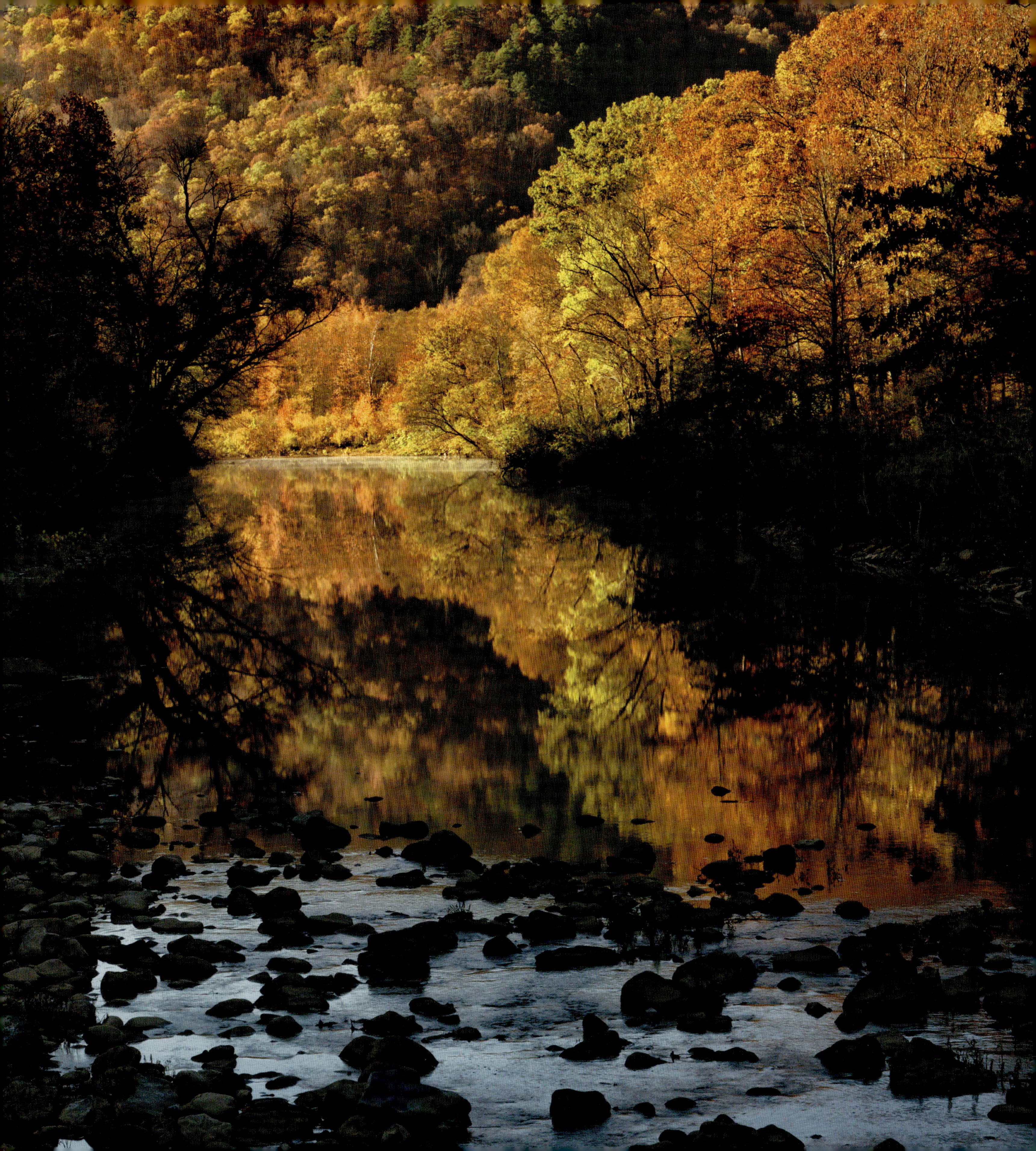

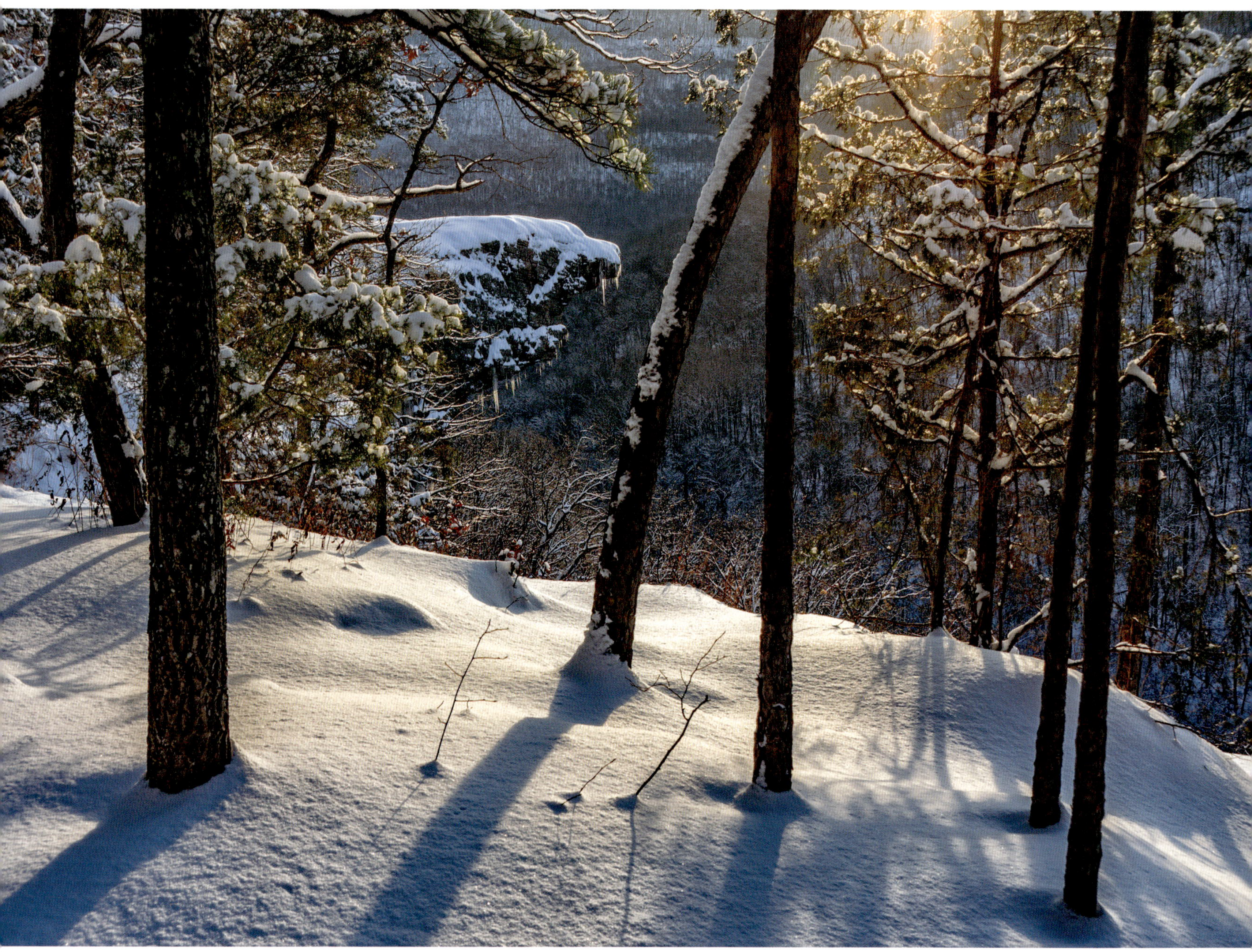

Sunrise on fresh snow, Hawksbill Crag, Upper Buffalo Wilderness Area

The Milky Way, Kings River Falls Natural Area

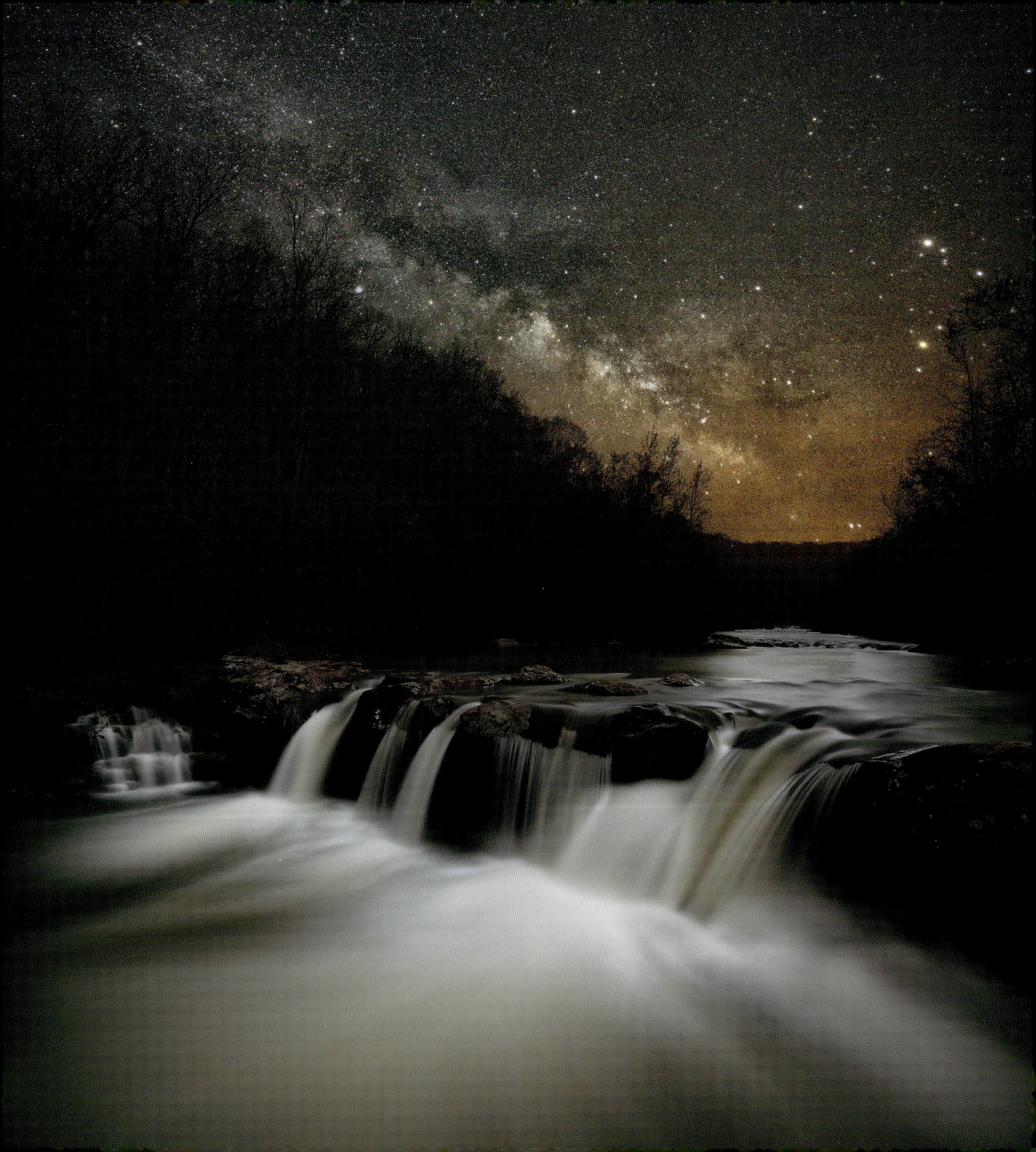

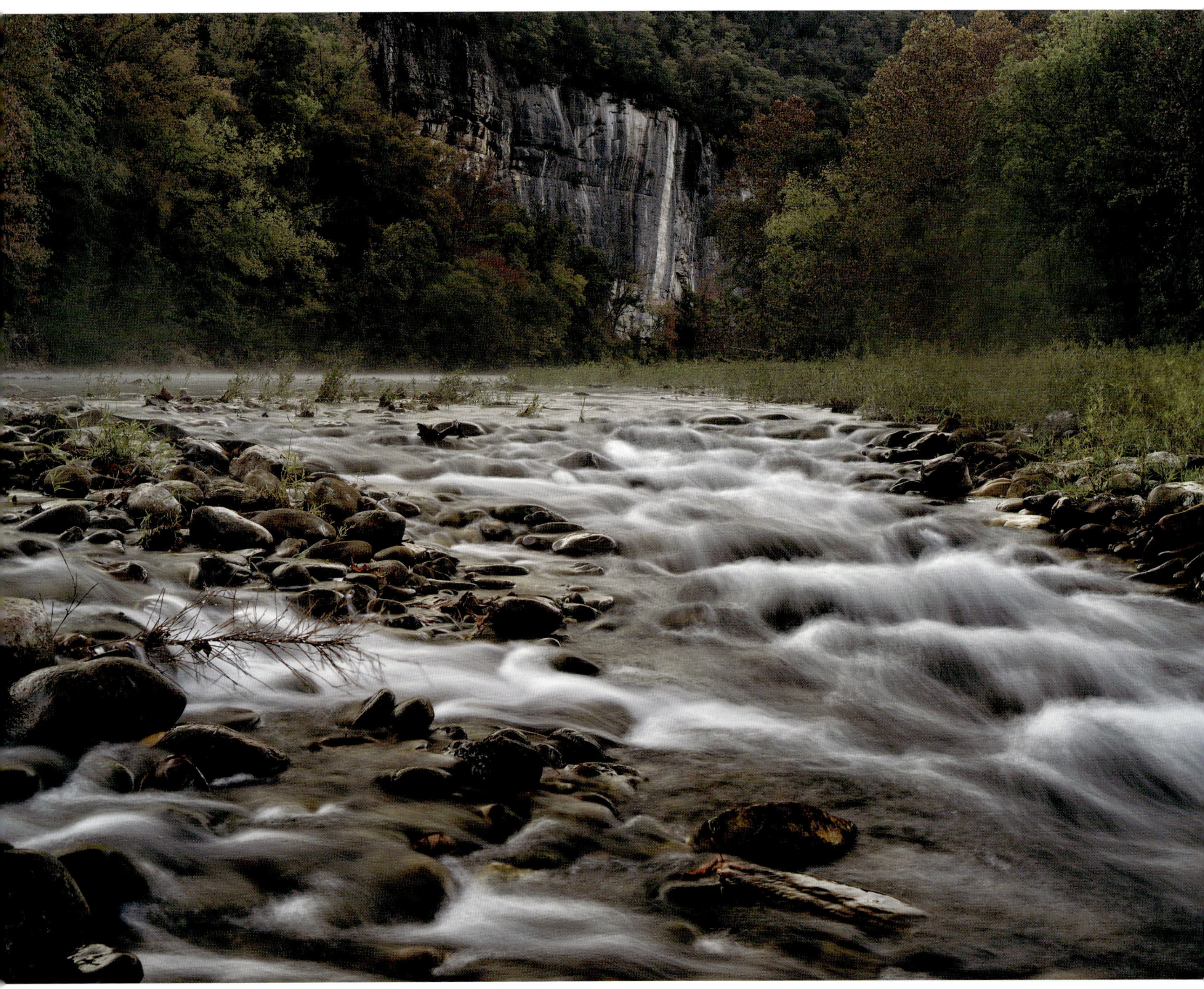

Misty rapids below Bee Bluff, Buffalo National River

Red fox at the watering hole

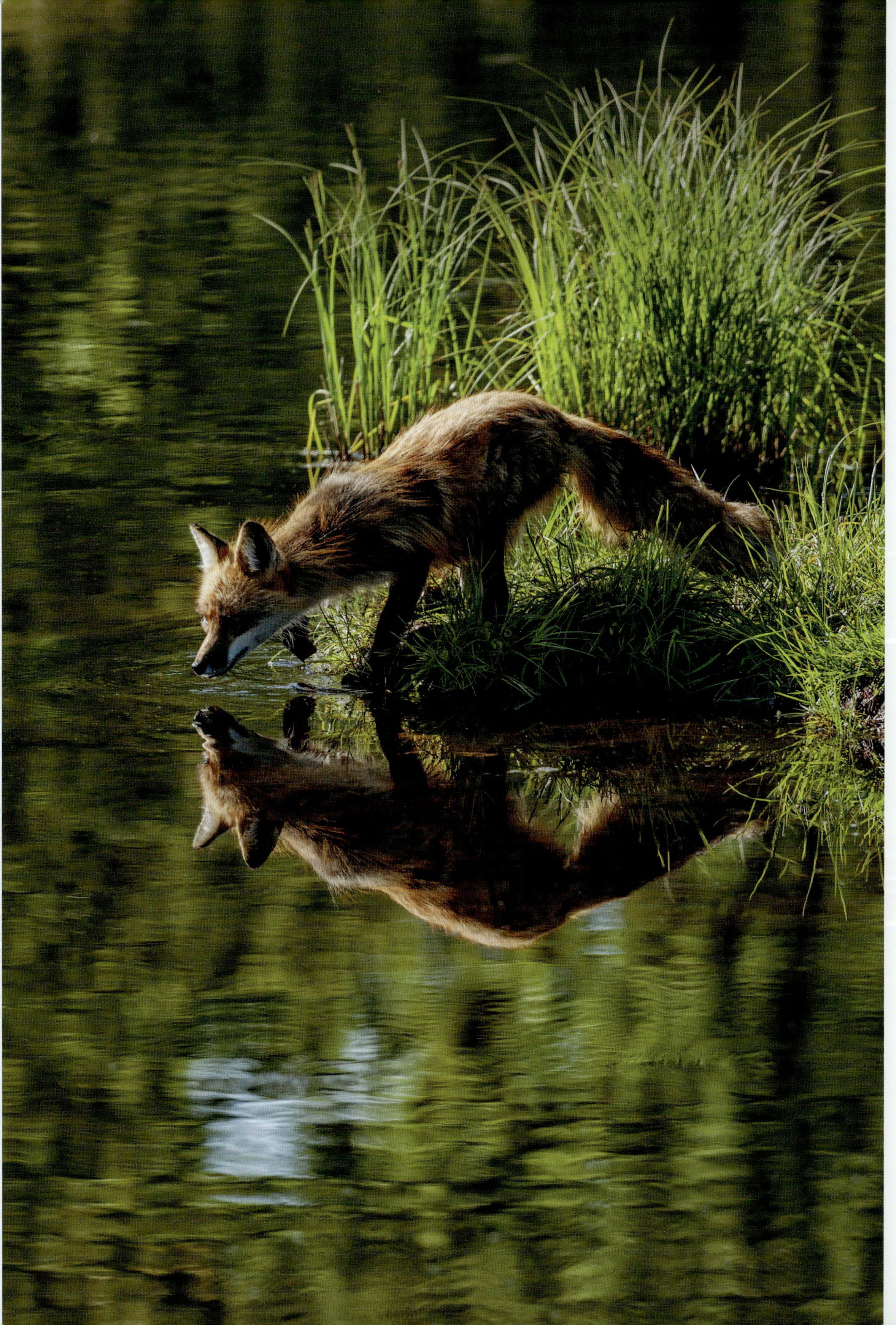

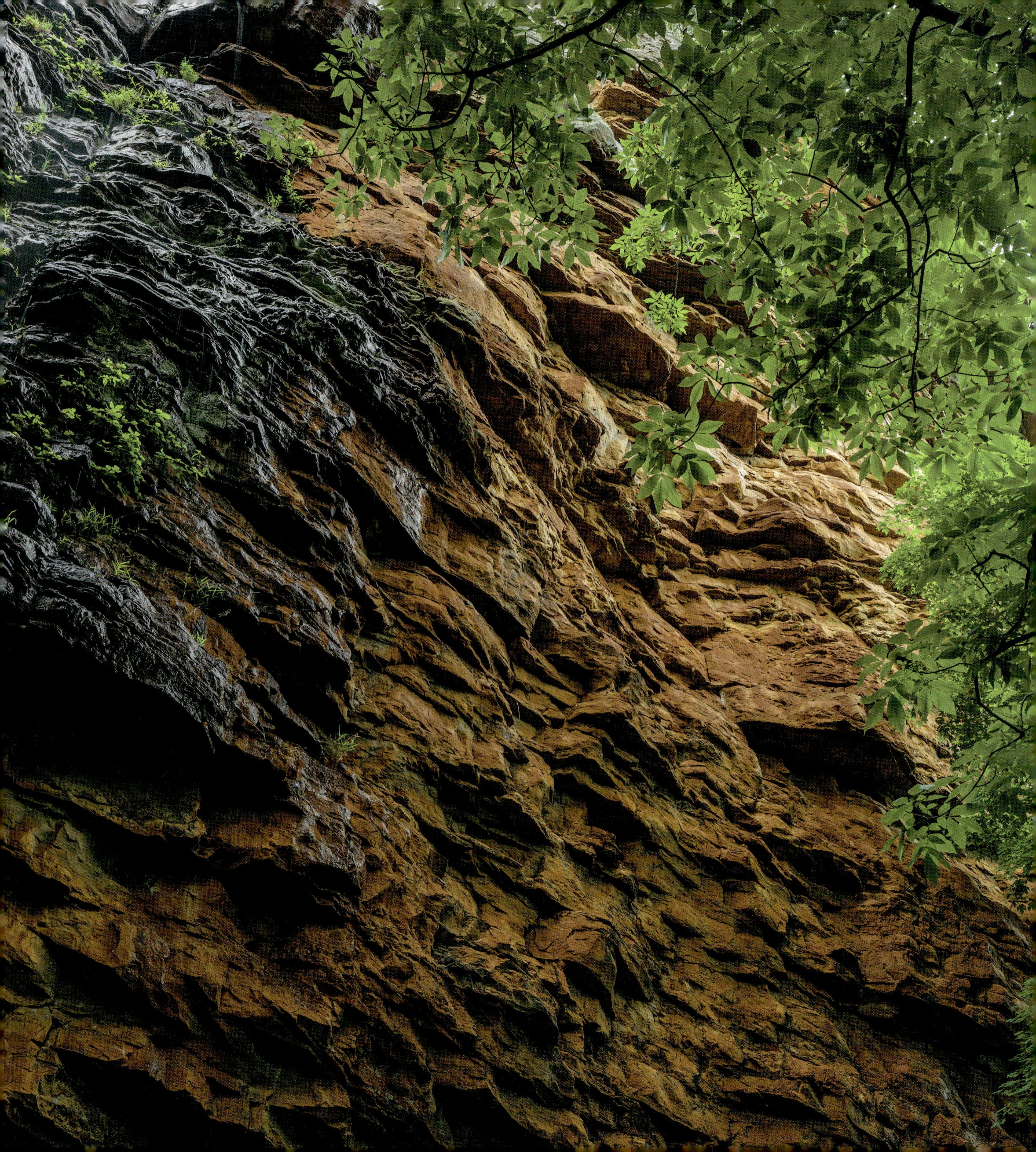

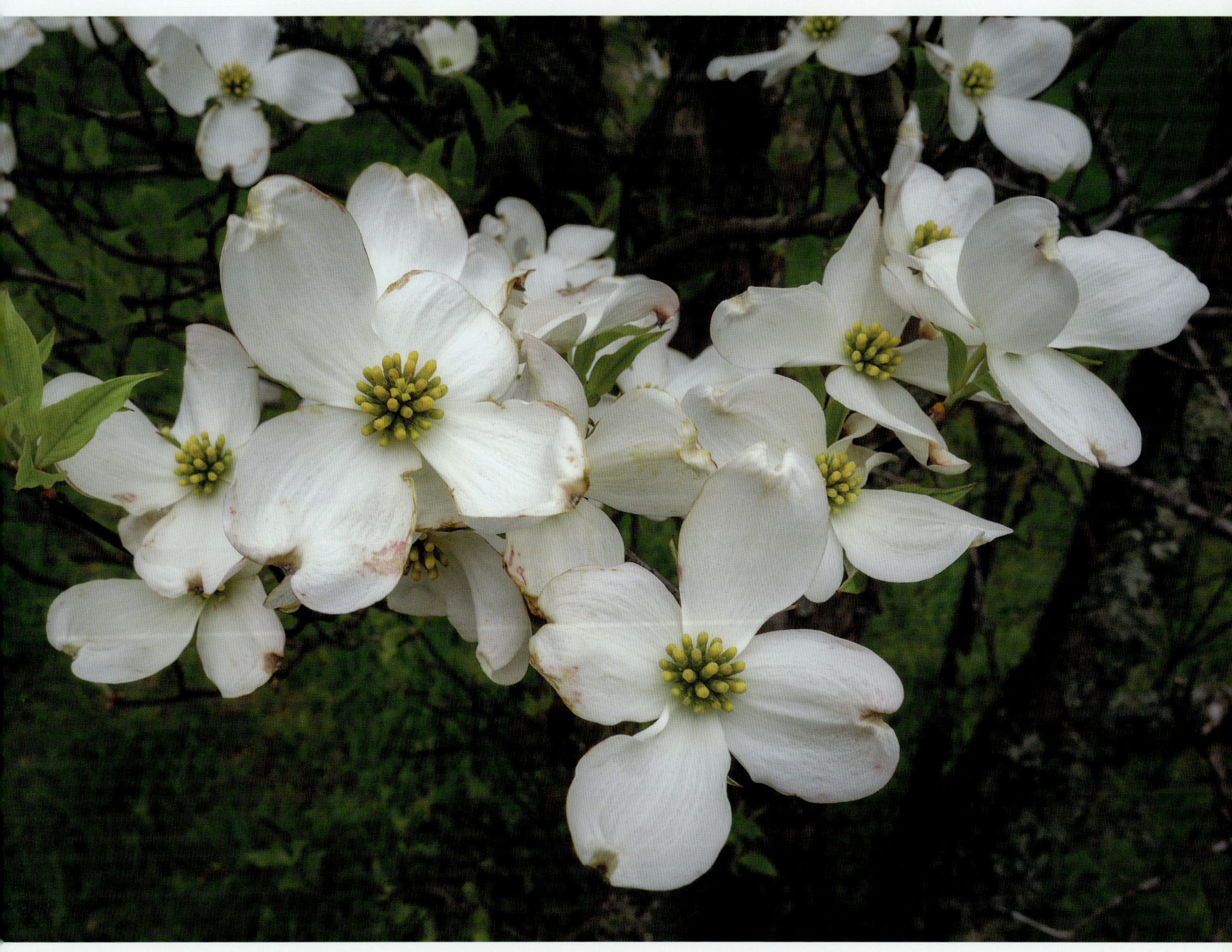

Springtime dogwoods light up the landscape

Colorful layered sandstone, Upper Buffalo Wilderness Area

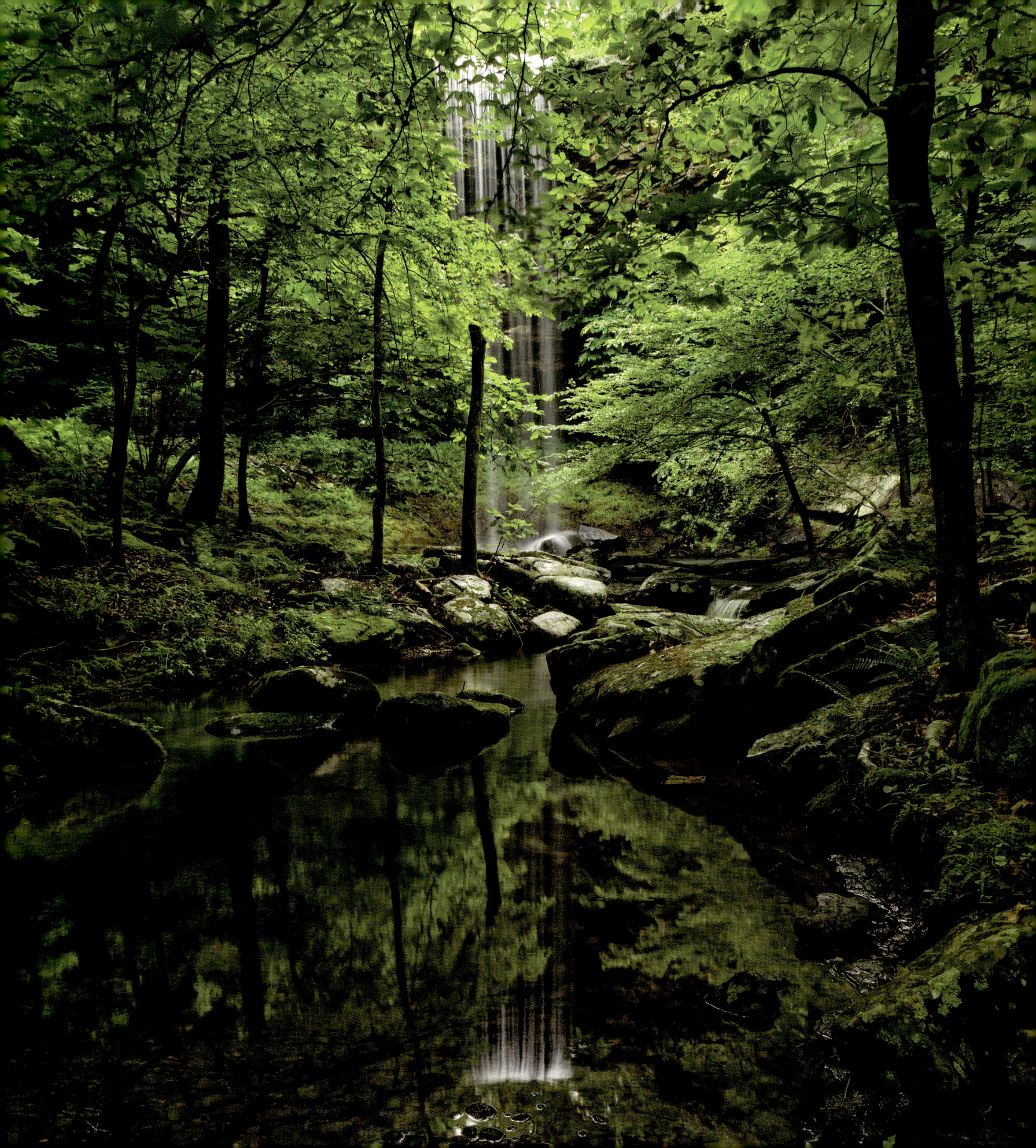

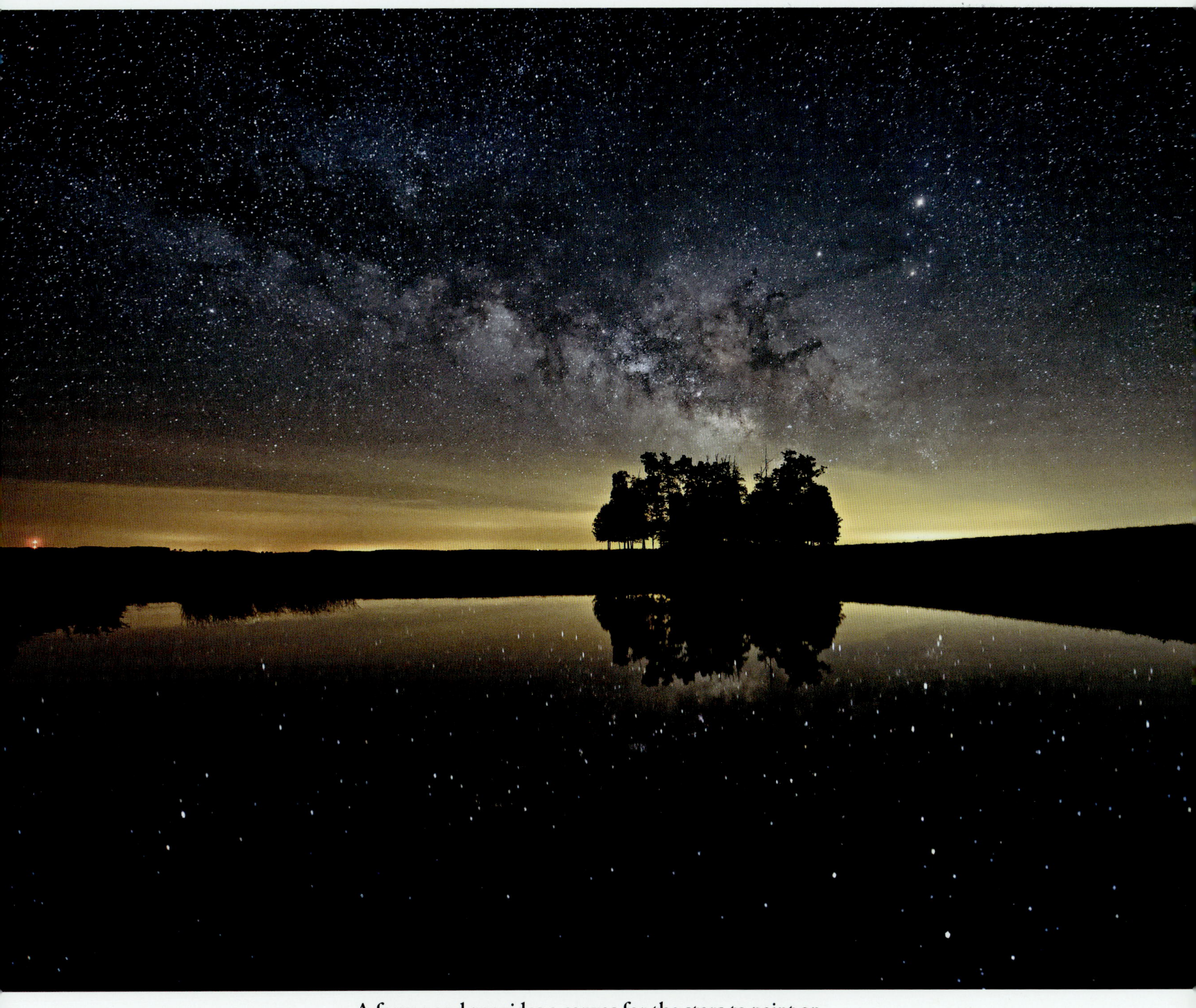

A farm pond provides a canvas for the stars to paint on

Neil Compton called this "The Great Waterfall in Bowers Hollow," Upper Buffalo Wilderness Area

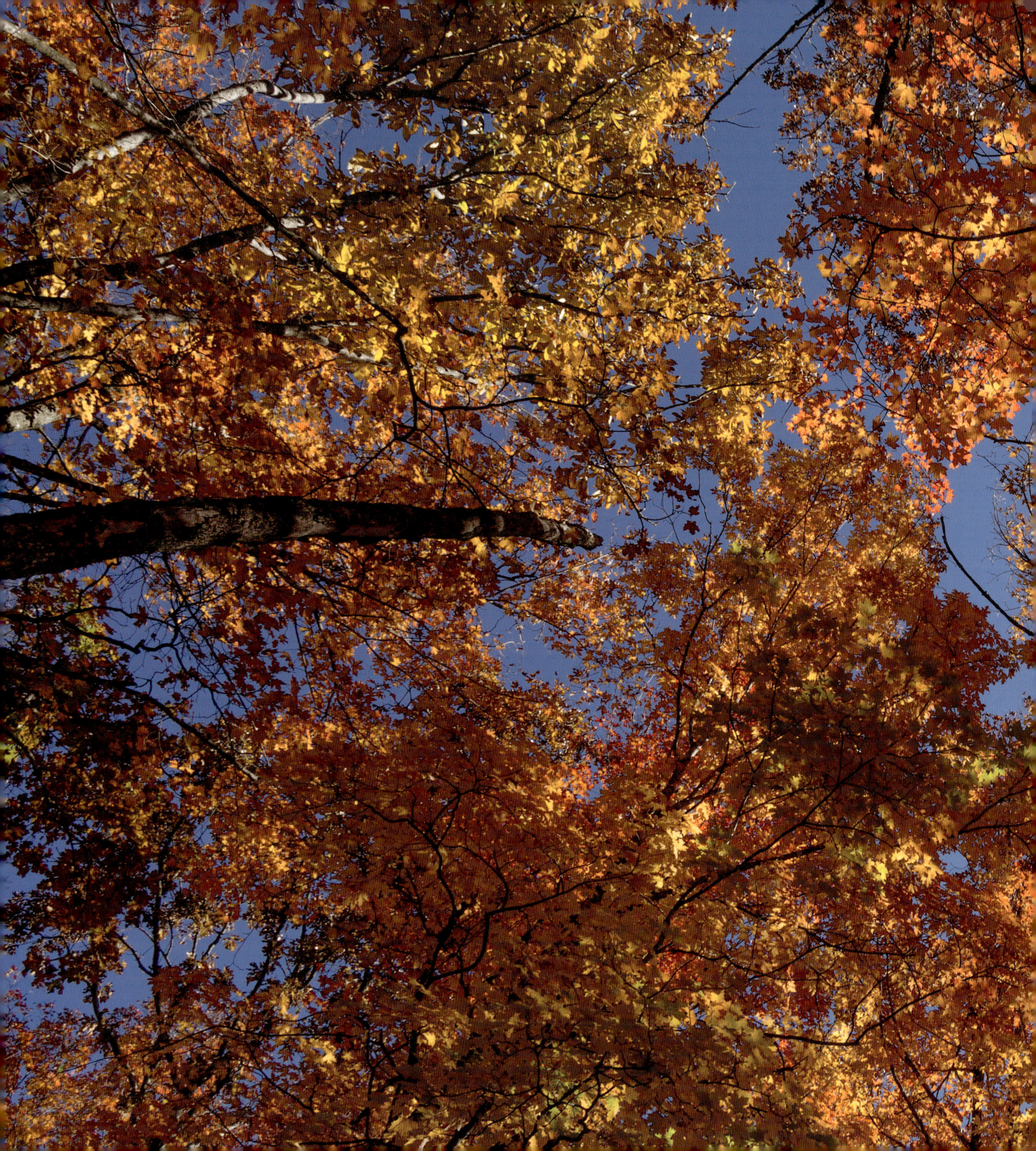

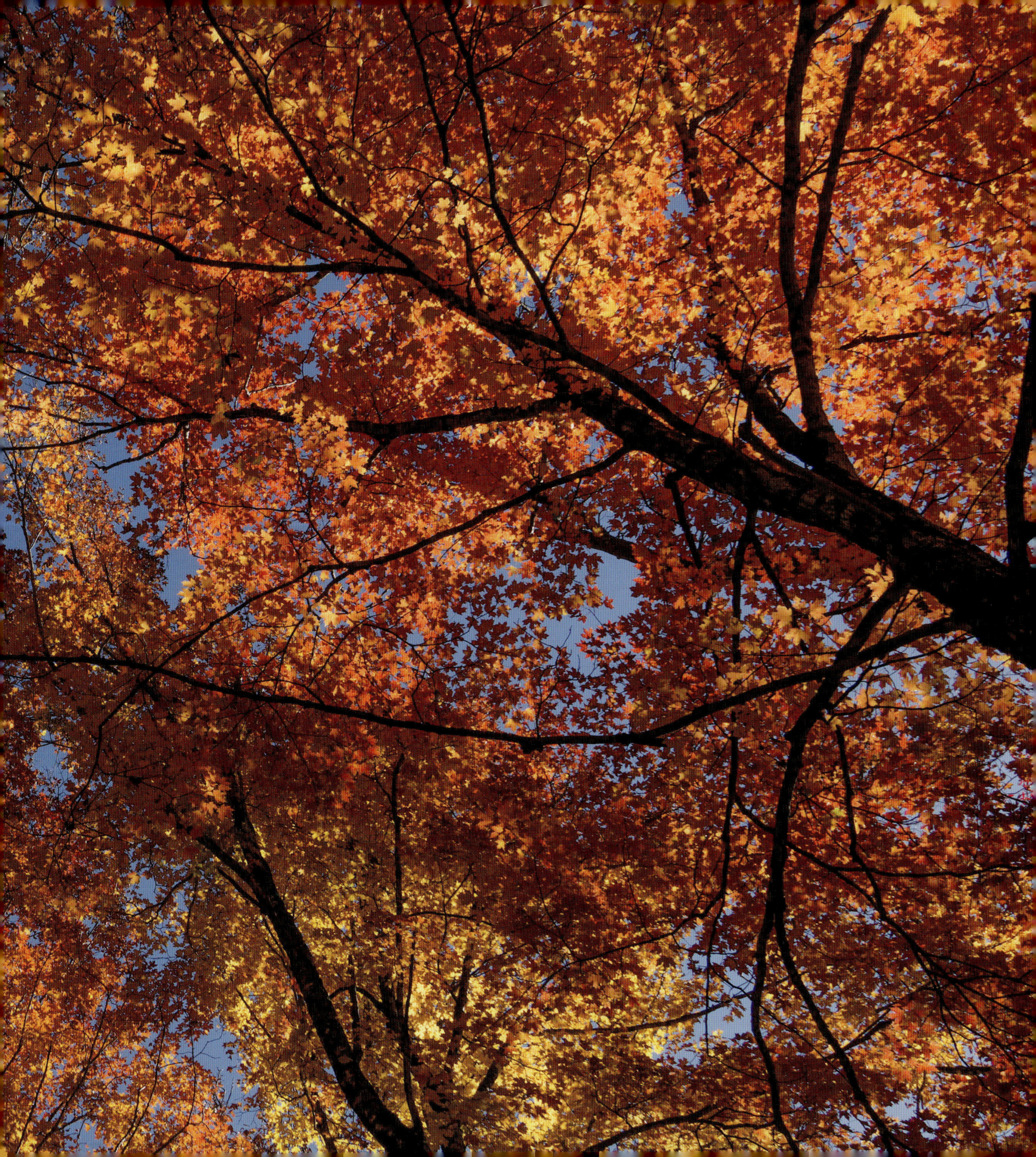

Zen Rocks along the Little Buffalo River

The Ozark Mountains are made up of rocks, layers upon layers of sandstone and limestone. Actually, they are not mountains at all, but rather a plateau that was formed at the bottom of ancient seas. Eons ago that plateau was "uplifted" out of the sea and exposed to weather and the elements, which eroded valleys—some of them more than 1,000 feet deep. So what remains are the flat-topped ridges of what used to be the sea floor, with eroded valleys all around (where the rivers run wild!).

That erosion continues today. Bits of the ancient sea bed up on the plateau break off due to the movements of wind, ice, or water. Over time they make their way down the upper drainages, constantly being washed farther and farther downstream by occasional heavy rainfall. As the rocks tumble in the water they are shaped and polished by other rocks. Think of it as a giant rock-tumbling machine, working year after year. The rocks get smaller, smoother, and I think take on wonderful personalities.

Turns out these polished stones can also be quite colorful when they are wet for long periods. The different colors are caused by minerals within the stones—blue, purple, red, orange, yellow, green—sometimes potholes, stripes, and all sorts of irregular patterns.

I've always been fascinated with these polished river rocks and have photographed them all over the country for decades. I decided to include a group of these stones from each of the different major drainages in our circle. You probably can't tell much of the origins of the stones from these pictures (which drainage they came from), but I think each group has its own characteristics and personality.

Take for instance these guys on the right. They were located near a Buddhist Retreat Center along the Little Buffalo River. I'm not sure if that had any influence on me while I was putting this image together, but when I got home and looked at the photograph, the stones did seem to have a special calm Zen-like feeling about them.

A couple of things about this series of photographs. Yes, they really were these colors—all were photographed while they were soaking wet, and wet stones are saturated and more colorful than dry ones. Remove a colorful stone from the water and soon you'll have just another gray rock, so it's always best to leave them in their own yard.

And secondly, no, I did not place all these rocks. I did place some of them, turned a few over, removed a few, cleaned up each scene a little bit (then left each location the way I found it). I was generally drawn to a particular gravel bar and would often spend an hour milling around (often getting into a Zen-like state of mind), bent over examining the rocks, looking for shapes and colors until I found a group that I liked. Then I would set up my camera tripod and spend some time peering through the lens, studying the scene, refining until it felt just right to me.

So each photo in this polished rock series is mostly Momma Nature, but part me, and part pure karma.

Looking up through a stand of sugar maple trees near our Cloudland cabin (previous pages)

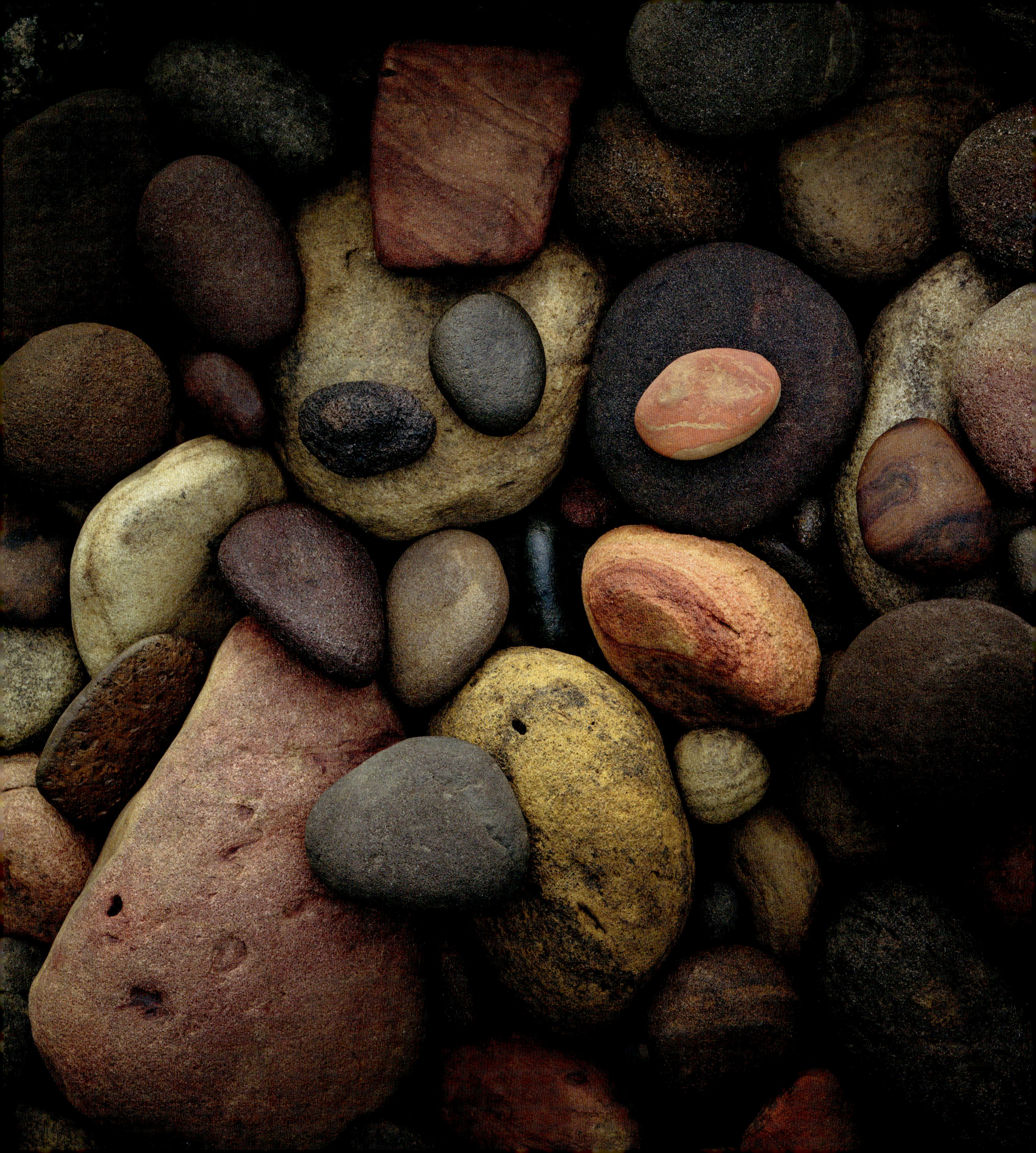

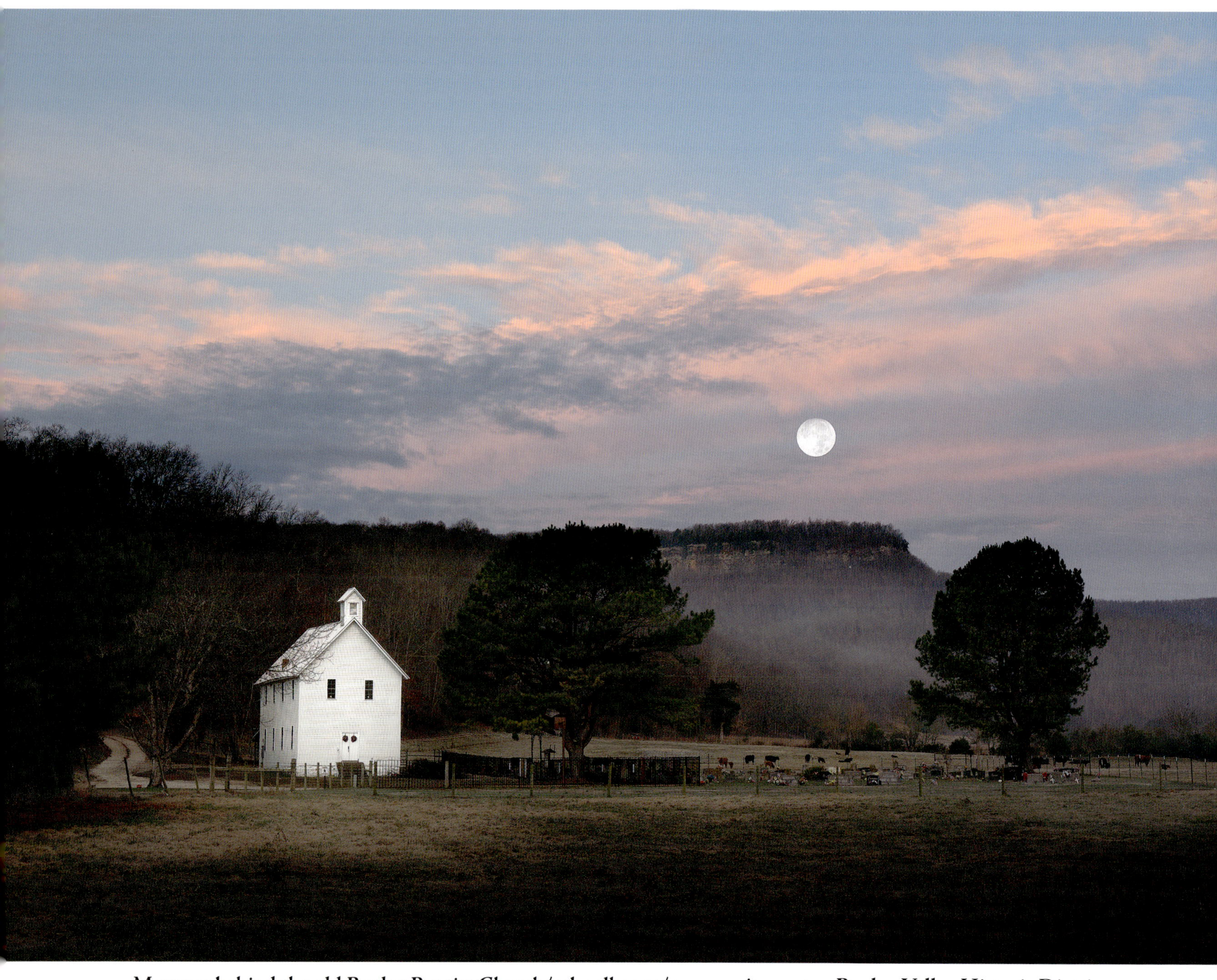

Moonset behind the old Boxley Baptist Church/schoolhouse/community center, Boxley Valley Historic District

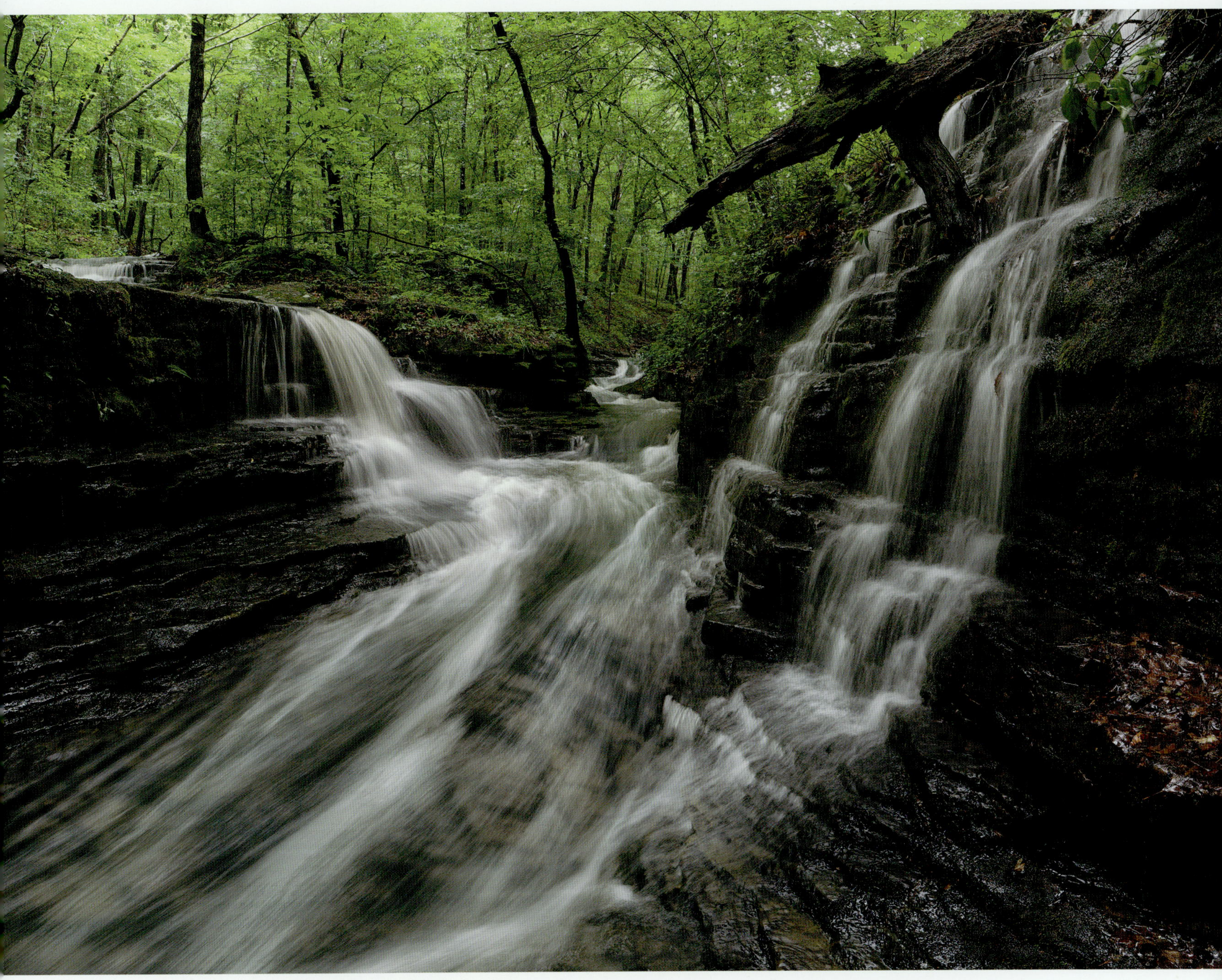

Waterfalls in Lynn Hollow along the Ozark Highlands Trail, Ozark National Forest

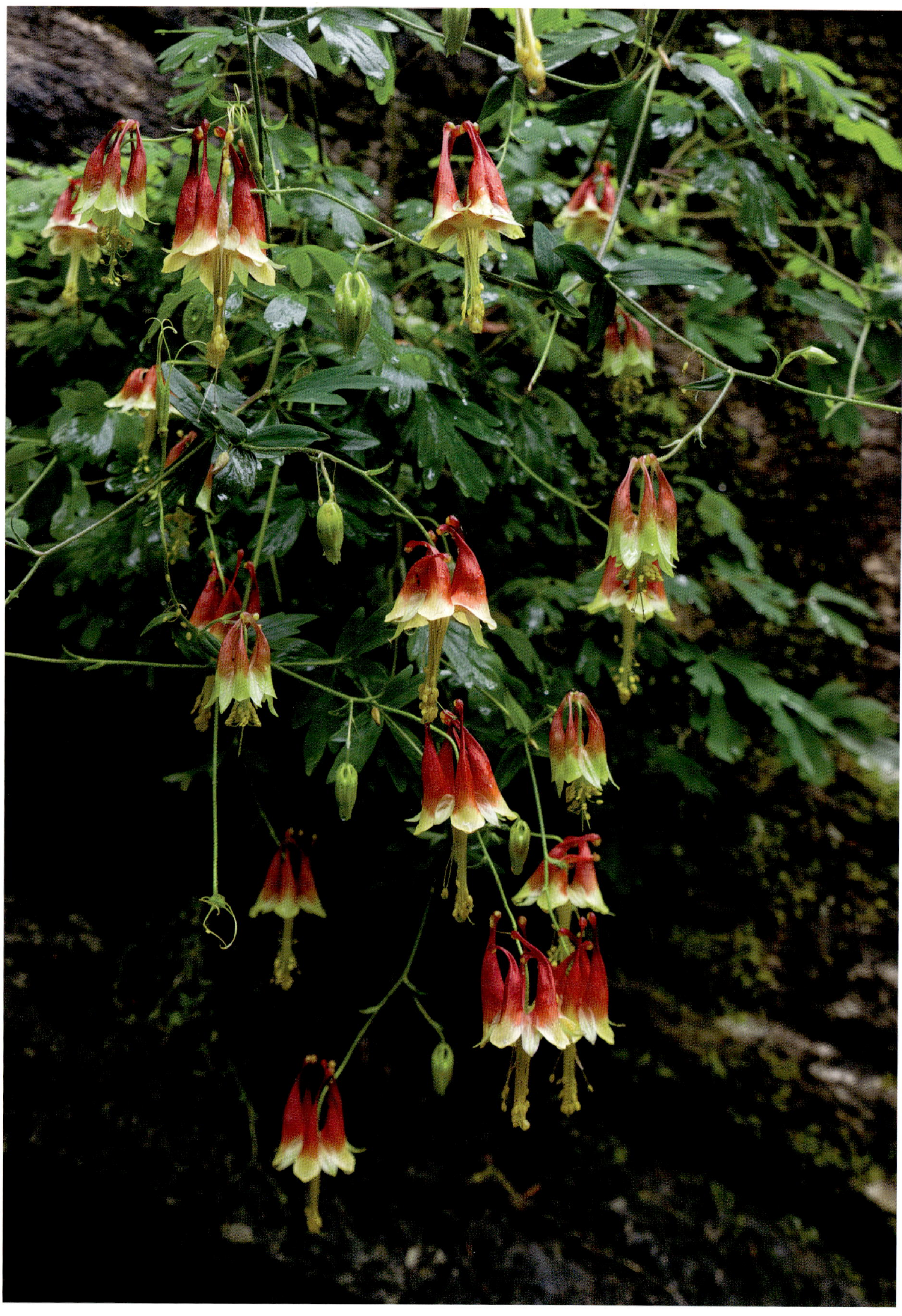

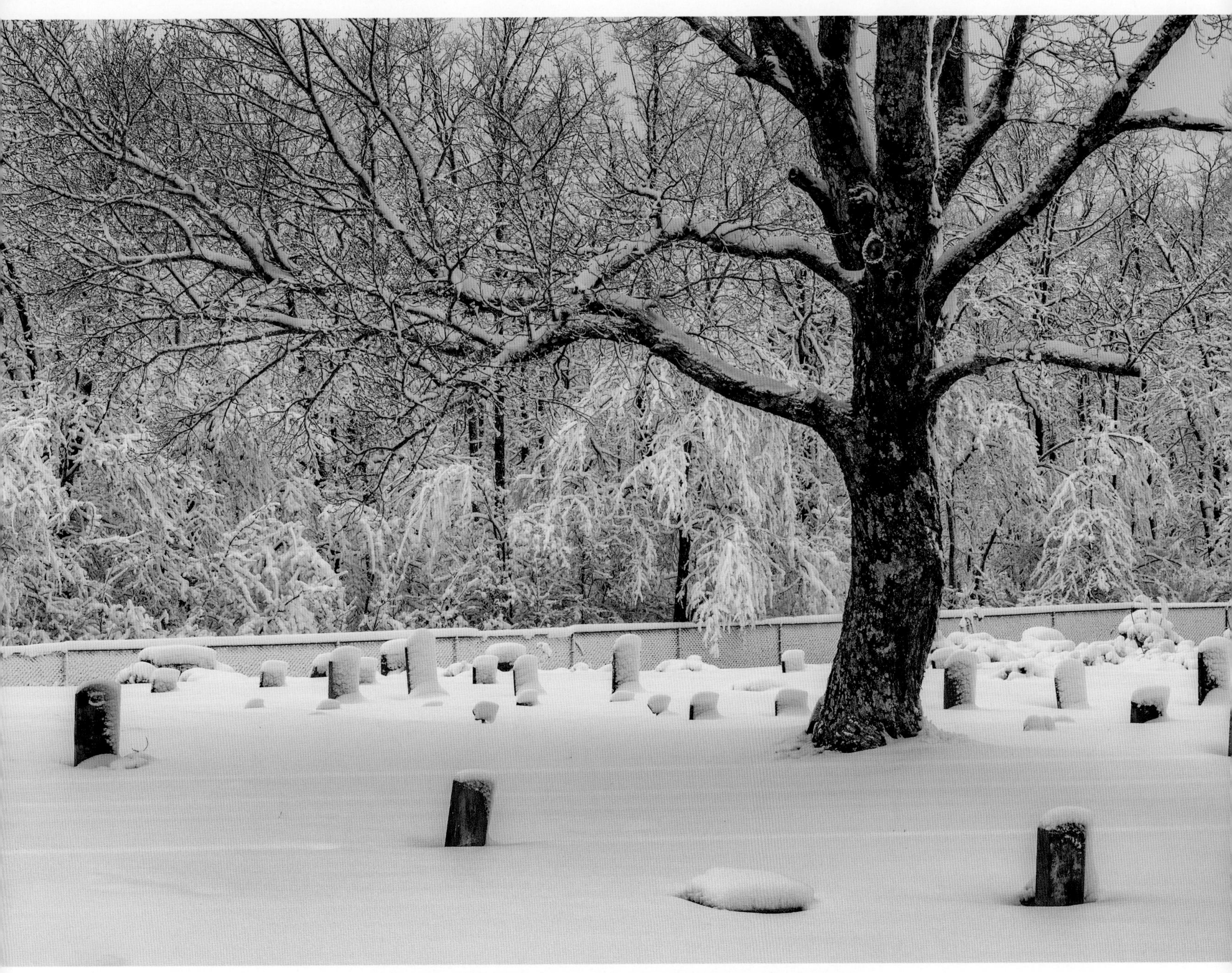

A fresh blanket of heavy snow, Cave Mountain Cemetery

Arkansas columbines

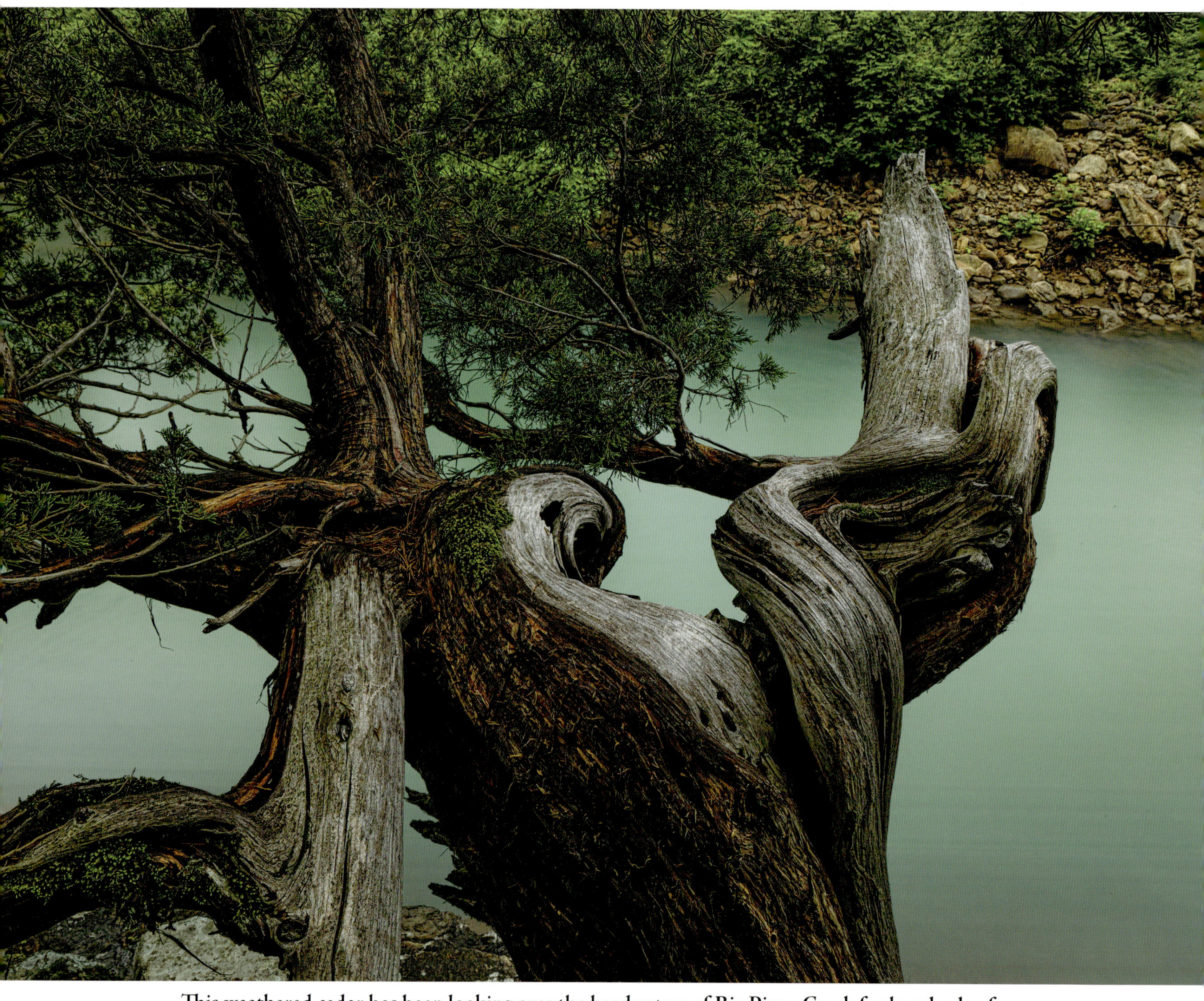

This weathered cedar has been looking over the headwaters of Big Piney Creek for hundreds of years

Sandstone boulders and evening light along the Buffalo River

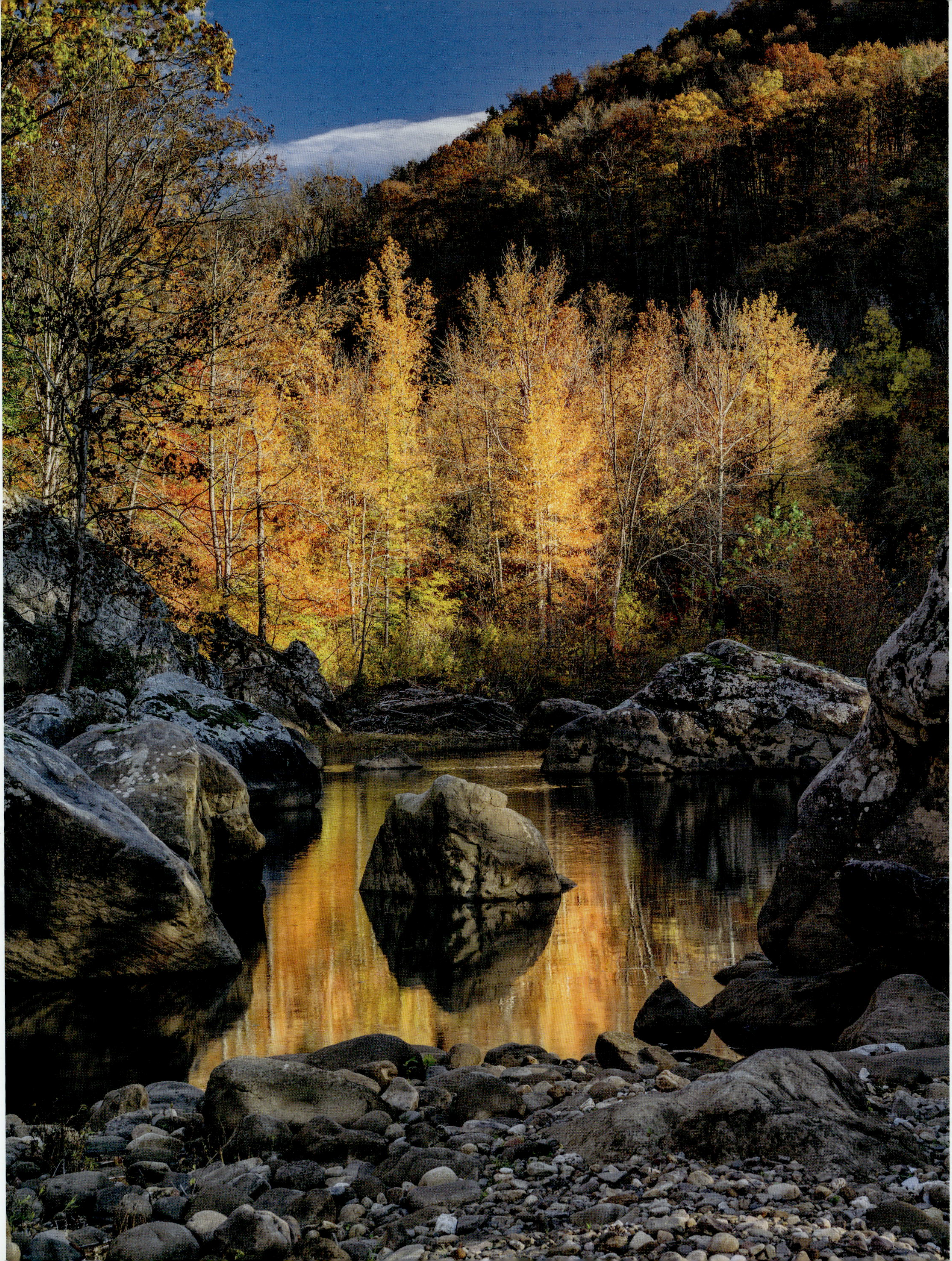

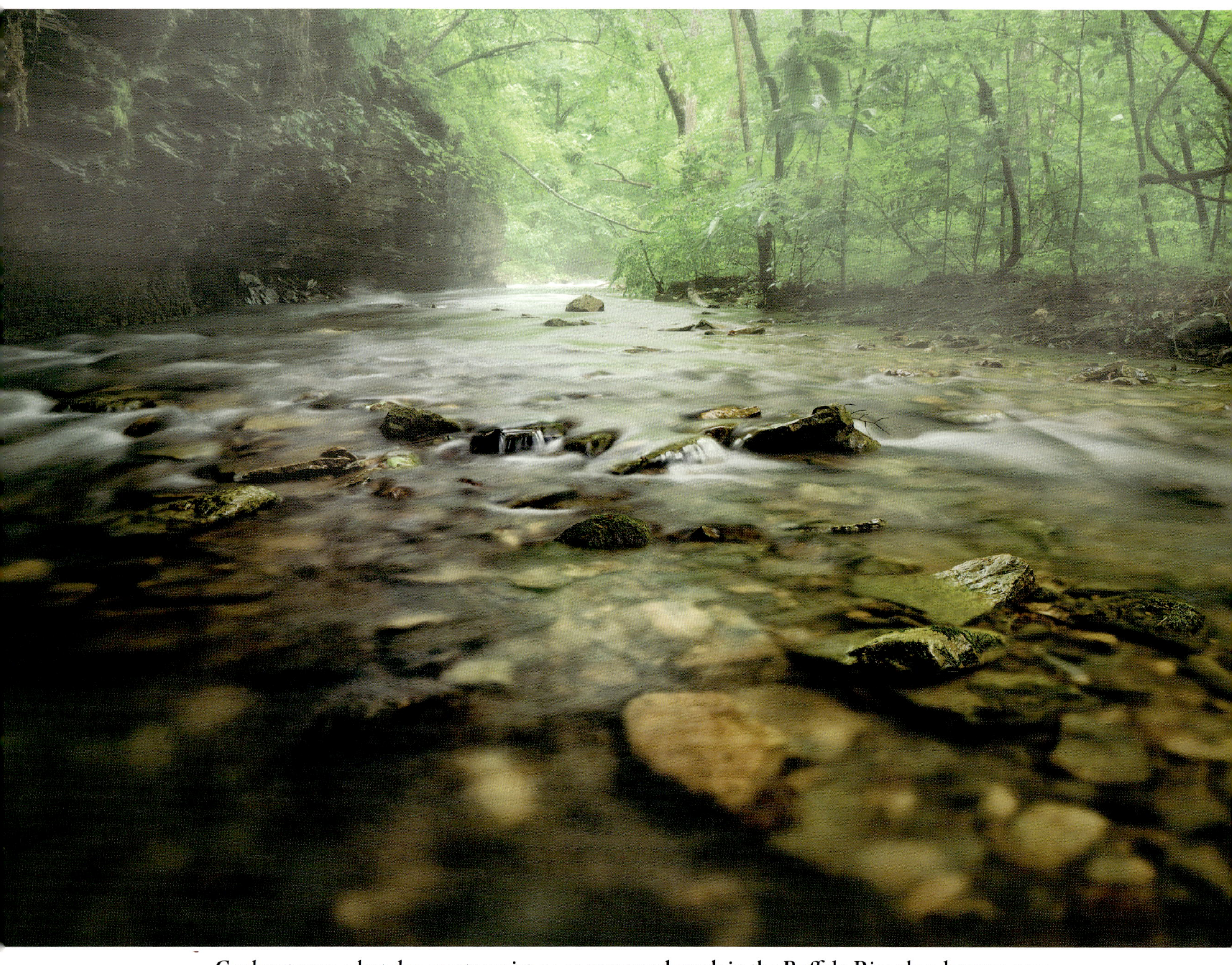

Cool water on a hot day creates mist on an unnamed creek in the Buffalo River headwaters area

Summer Milky Way bids good night to all, Boxley Baptist Church, Boxley Valley Historic District

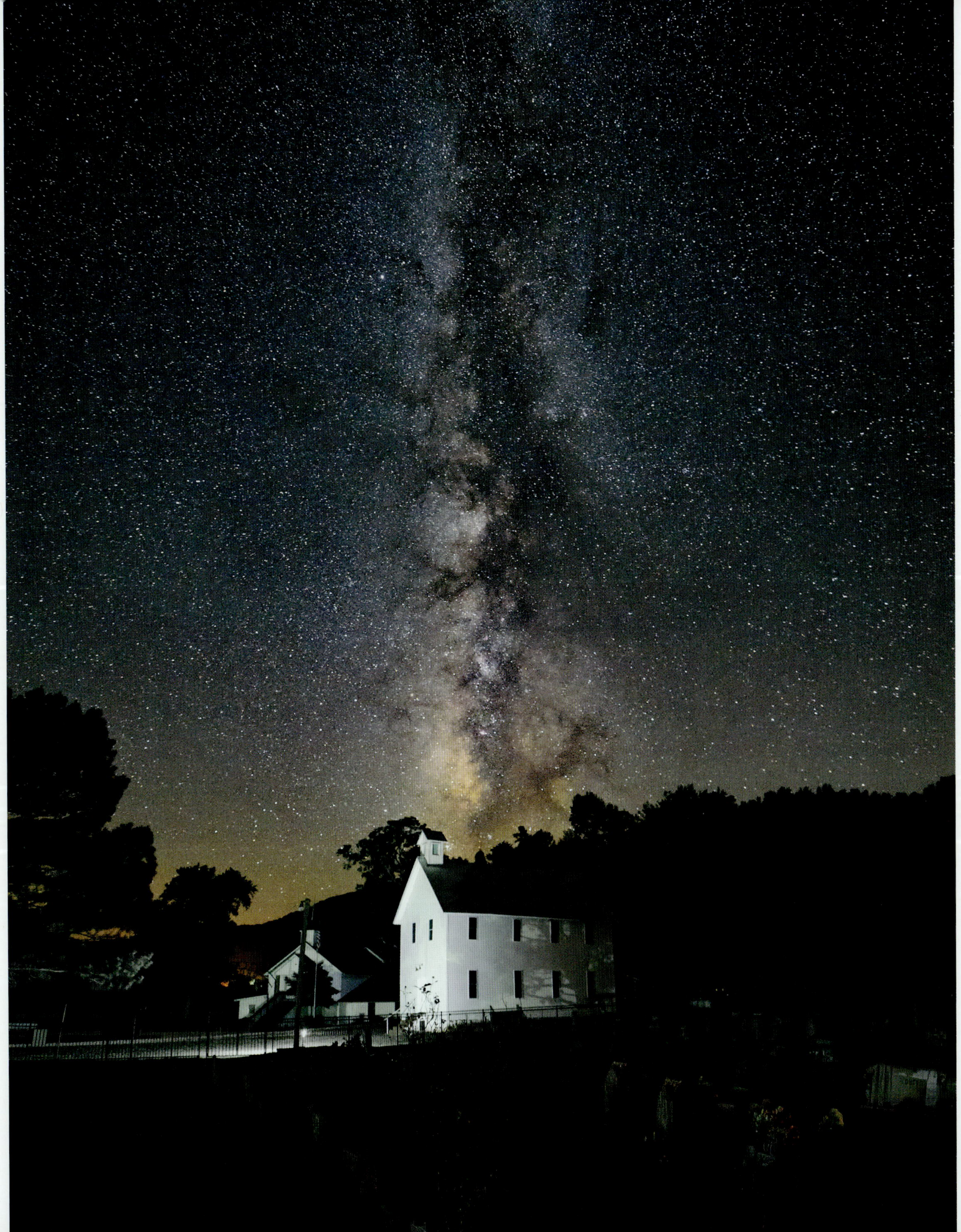

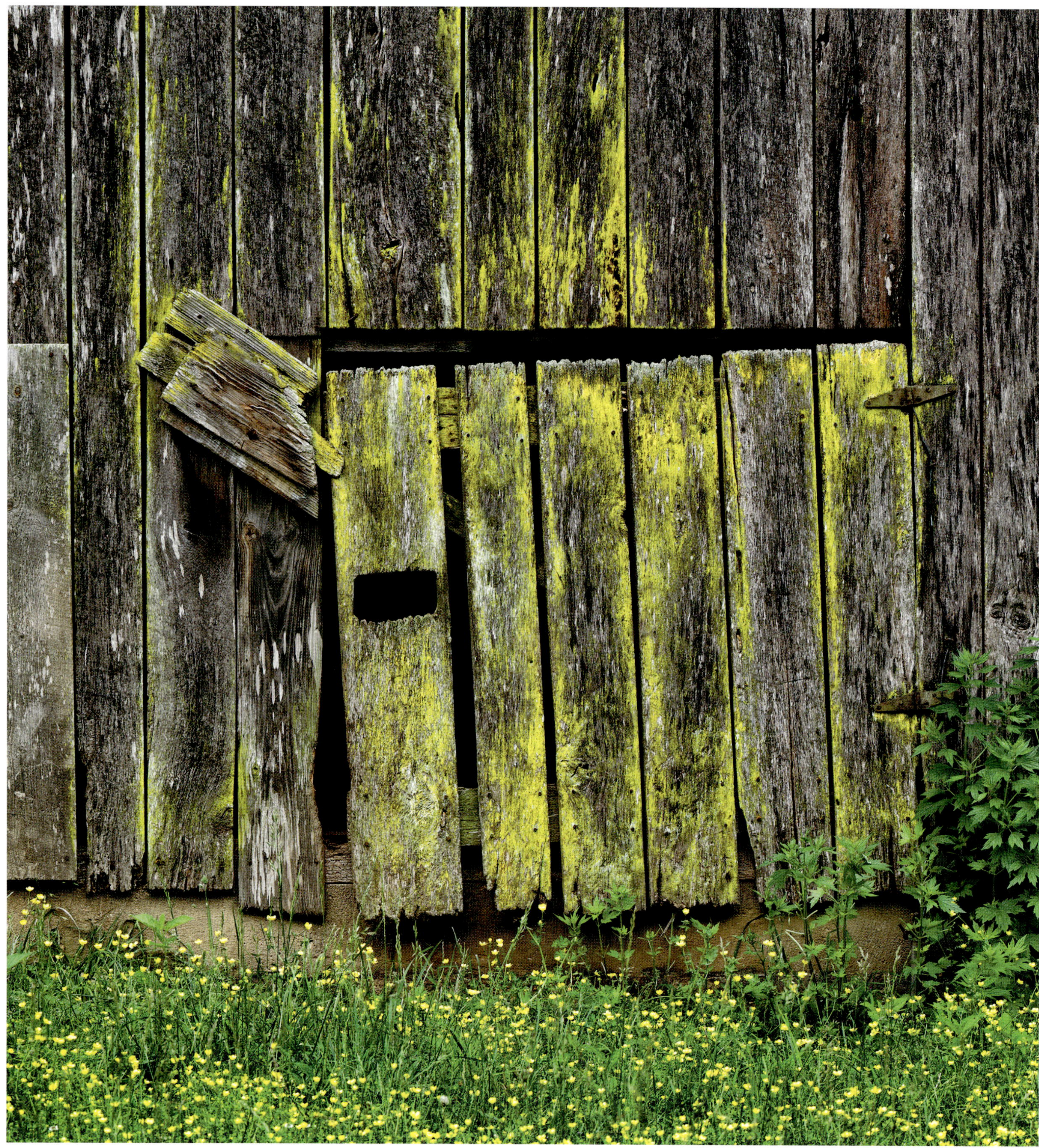

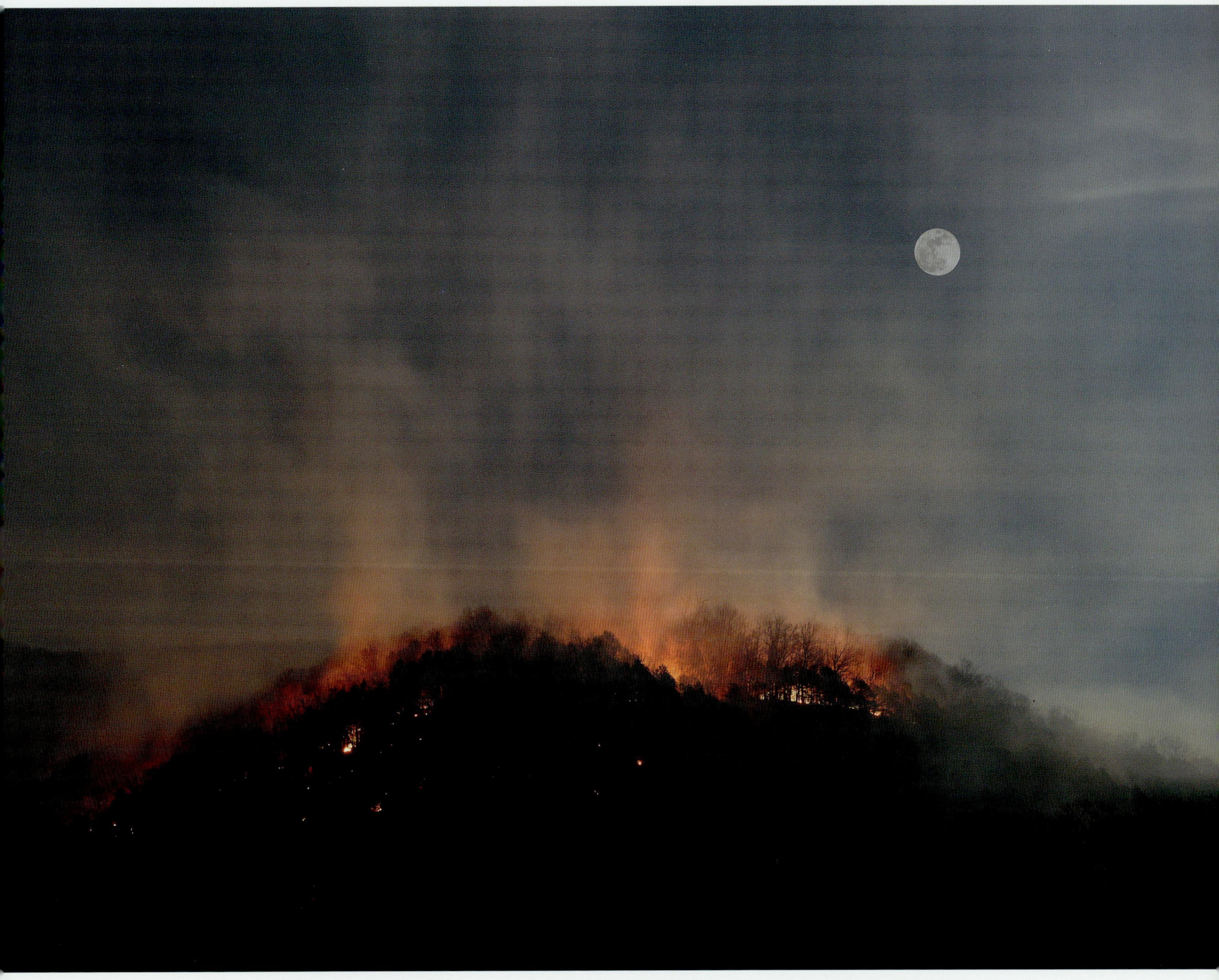

As the full moon looks on, a wildfire burns in the hills overlooking Boxley Valley

Lichen and wildflowers surround an aging barn door in Boxley Valley

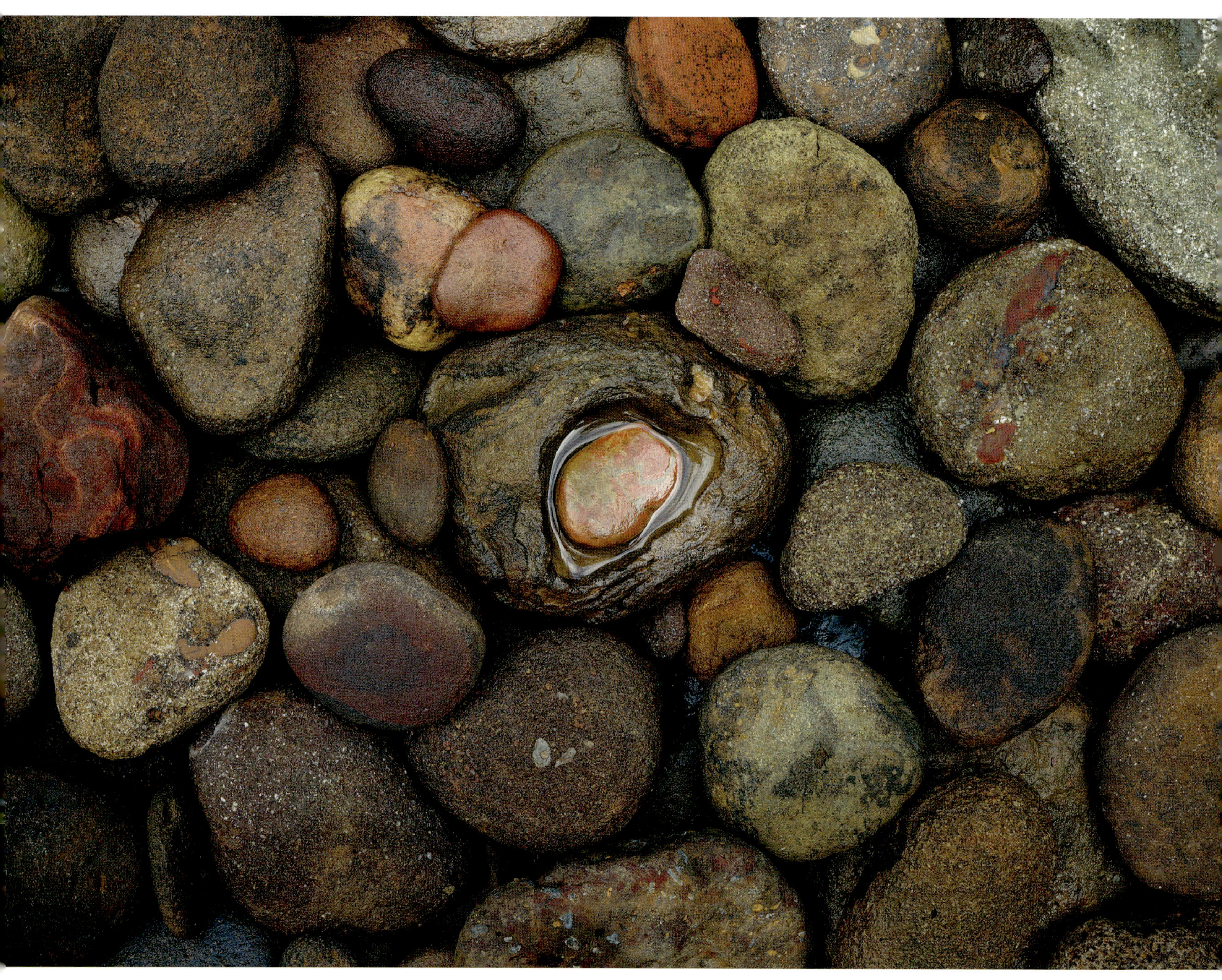

Polished river rocks, Little Mulberry River

Amber Falls on Whitaker Creek, Upper Buffalo Wilderness Area

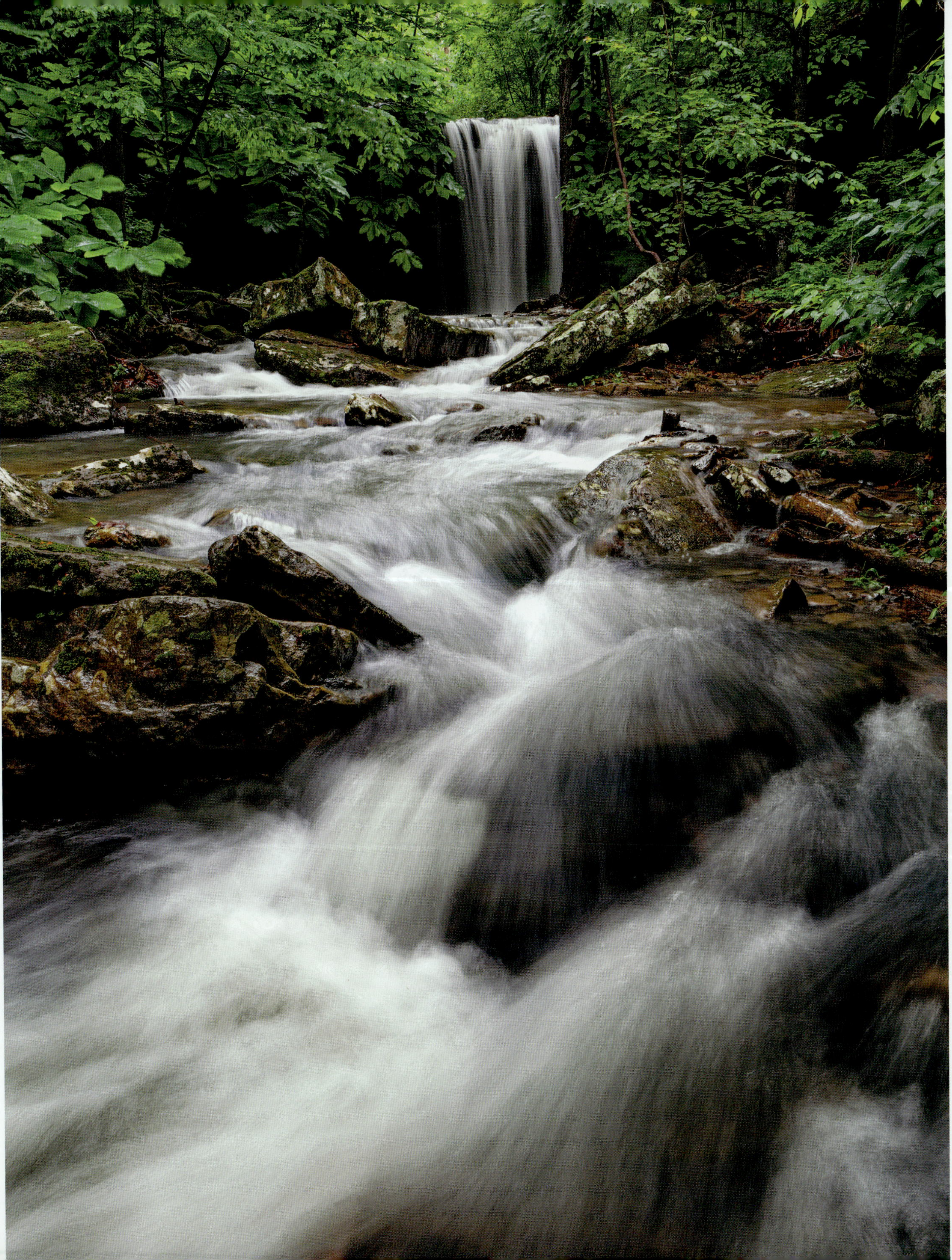

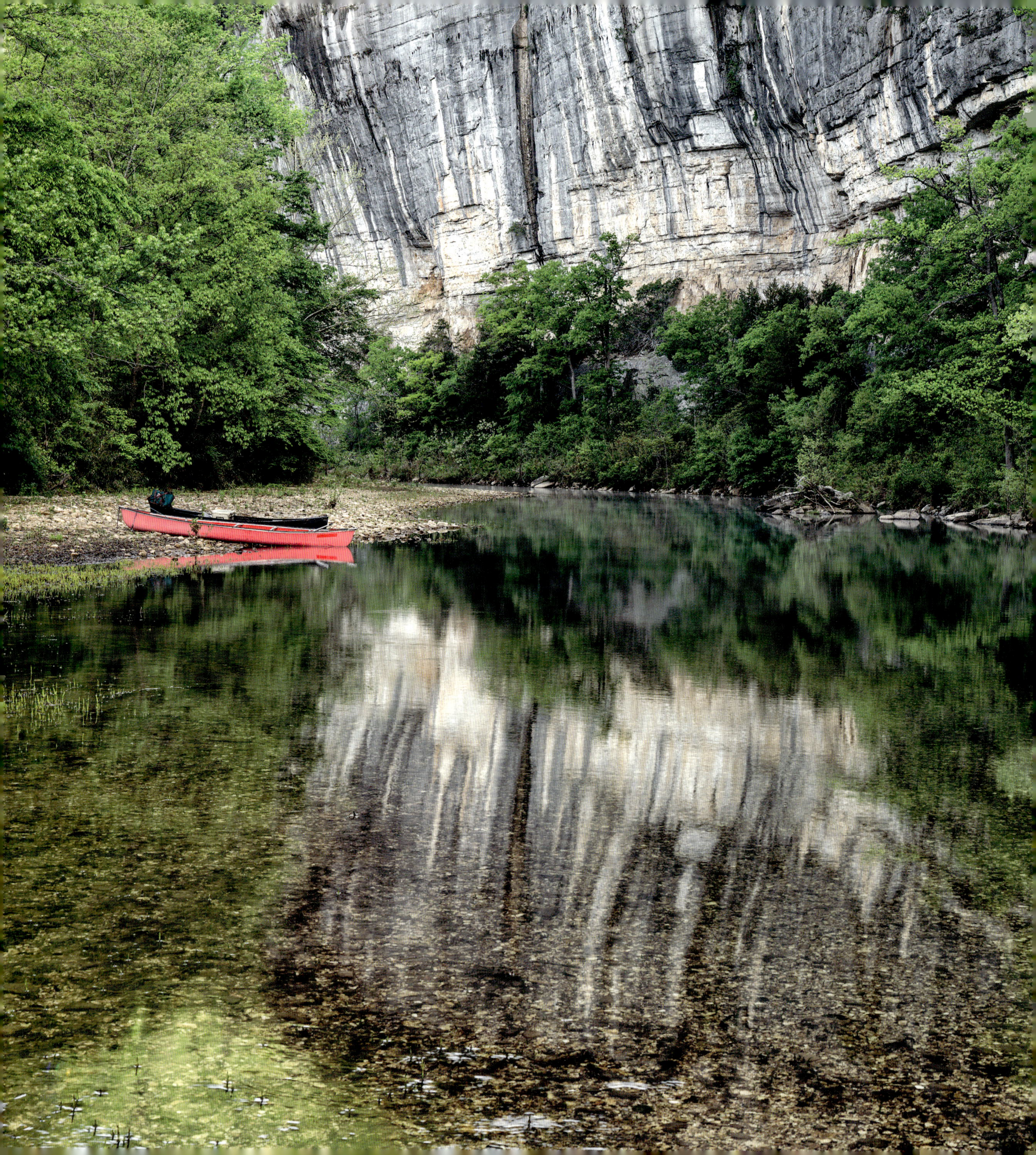

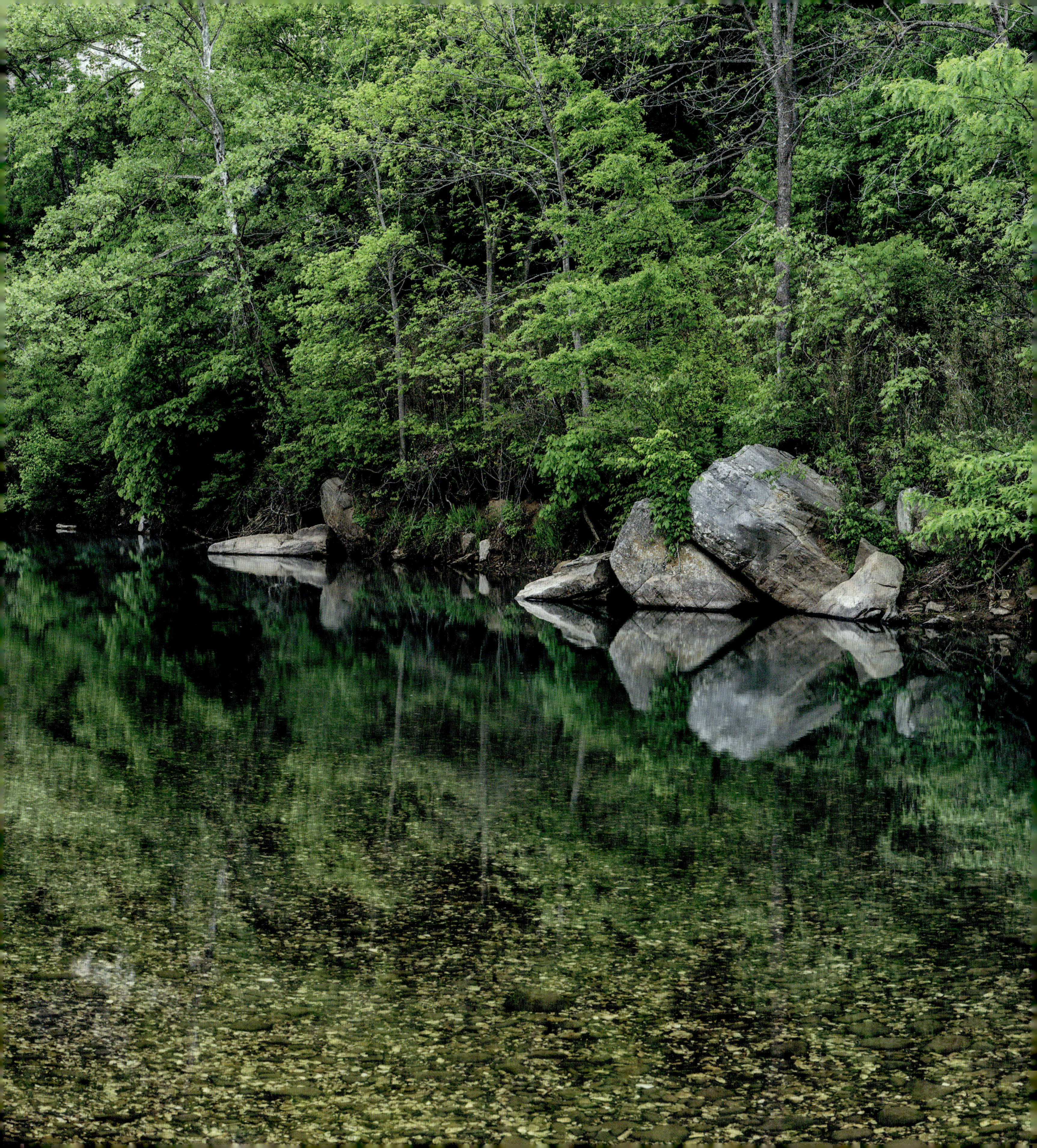

The Milky Way shines over a quiet pool, Buffalo National River

The area around our cabin has some of the darkest skies in the region. The darker your skies are, the more stars you can see. Light pollution from cities continues to expand across the country, but Arkansas is fortunate to be a rural state with some of the best dark-sky areas in the eastern United States.

I got excited about the Milky Way on my very first camping trip when I was five years old. But it wasn't until recently that we could photograph the heavens with the landscape included, thanks to the newest digital cameras that can capture very dim light. I love to take pictures at night as much as I do during the daytime (maybe even more). There is something quite surreal about standing there in the darkness with a scene like this spread out before you (it's really a lot of fun in a graveyard at night too!).

The Milky Way is very dim to the naked eye, but the camera sensor can record a great deal more detail if you know how and have the right equipment. Some nights are much clearer than others, and for the best view you need cool temps, low humidity, and low air pollution. And also, little or no moon—it will wash stars away. You need to be far away from city lights, and then be outside for several hours with no lights of any kind so that your eyes can become adapted to the dark.

Most scenes like this that show part of the landscape illuminated have been "light-painted" with some type of light. In this example, I placed a small light behind a bush on the left out of camera range. The light cast a soft glow across the scene, equal to the brightness of the Milky Way. Moonlight can also light up the landscape, but too much moonlight will wash out the stars, so it has to be a crescent moon.

If you use an exposure several hours long, the rotation of the earth will produce star "trails." And if you point your camera at the North Star and let it run all night, those star trails become circles (see page 48).

I enjoy finding a structure (barn, church) or natural feature to light up in front of the stars, and have included several in this book. There is no limit to the amazing things you can see and photograph at night.

Canoe camp at Roark Bluff, Buffalo National River (previous pages)

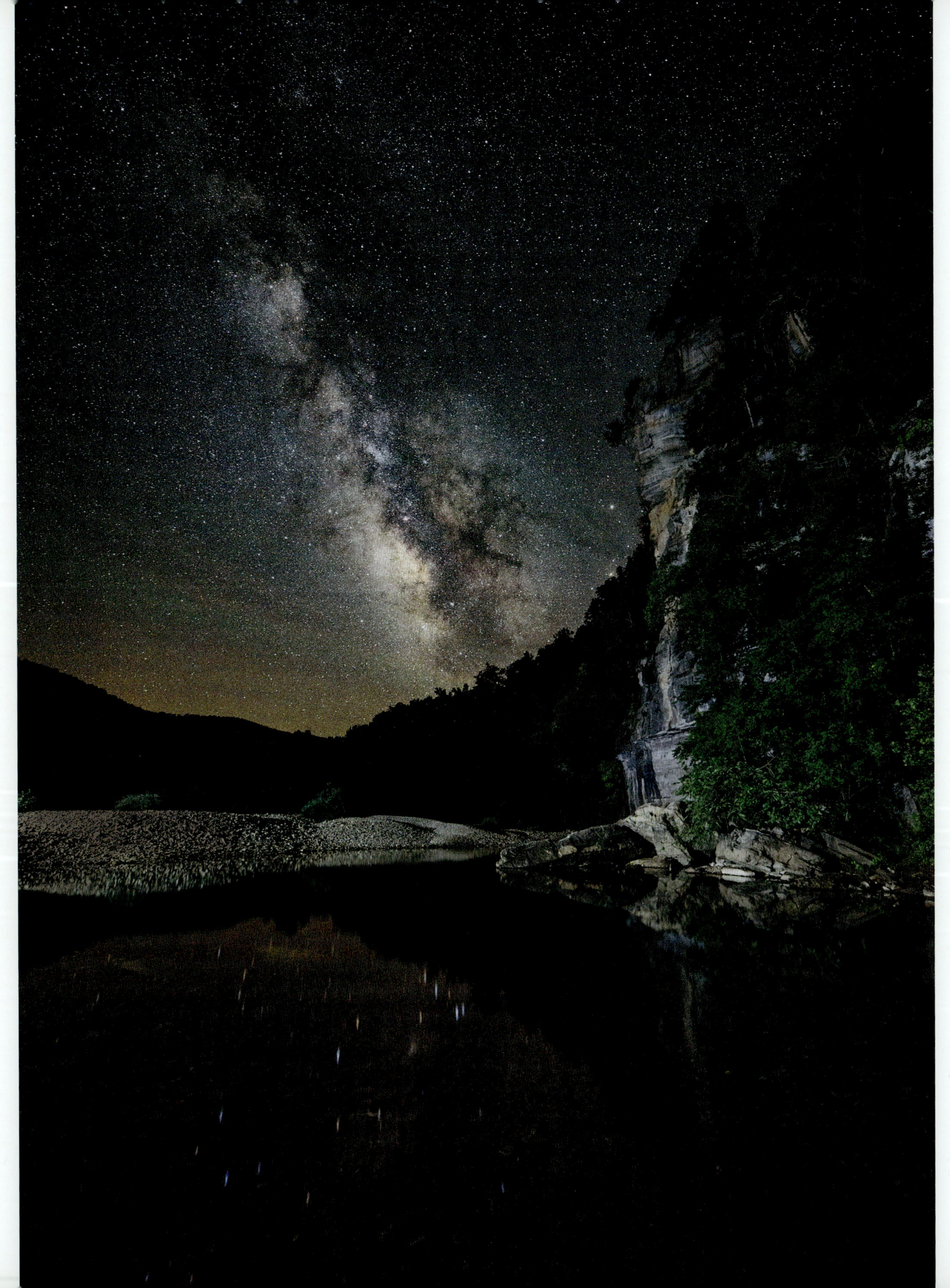

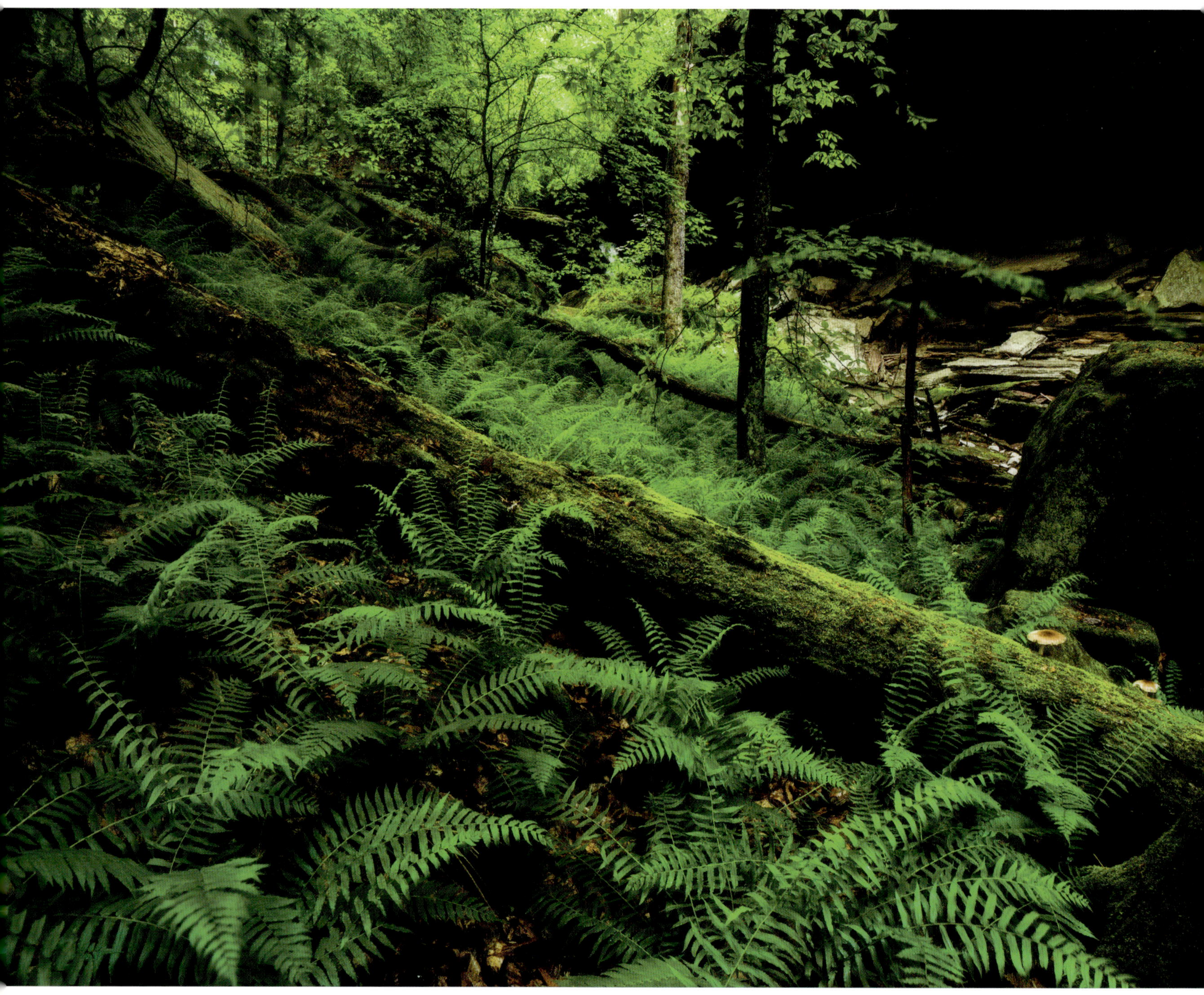

A lush forest of ferns and mosses along Leatherwood Creek, Buffalo National River

YIPPIE COYOTE - 14" of wet snow!

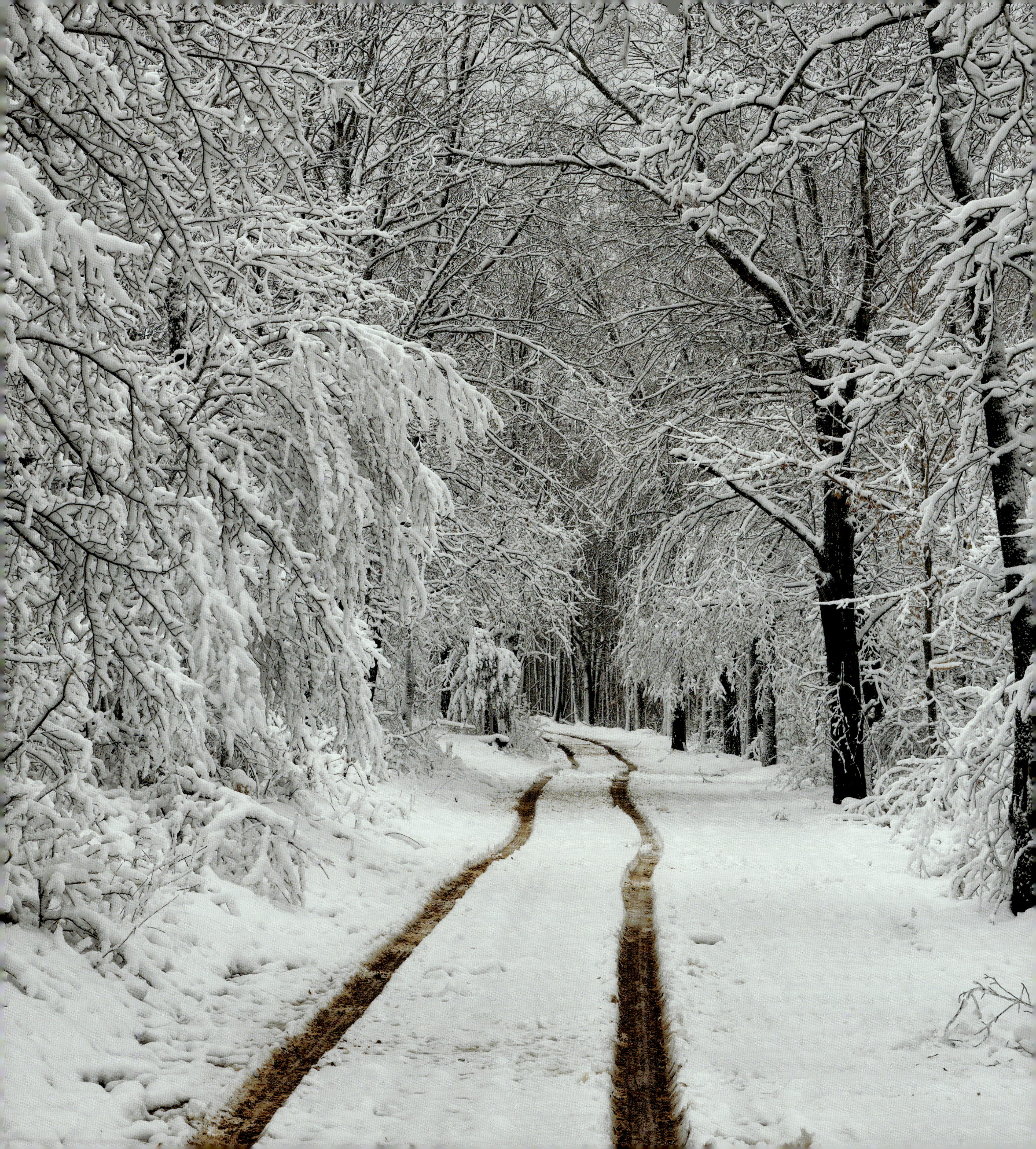

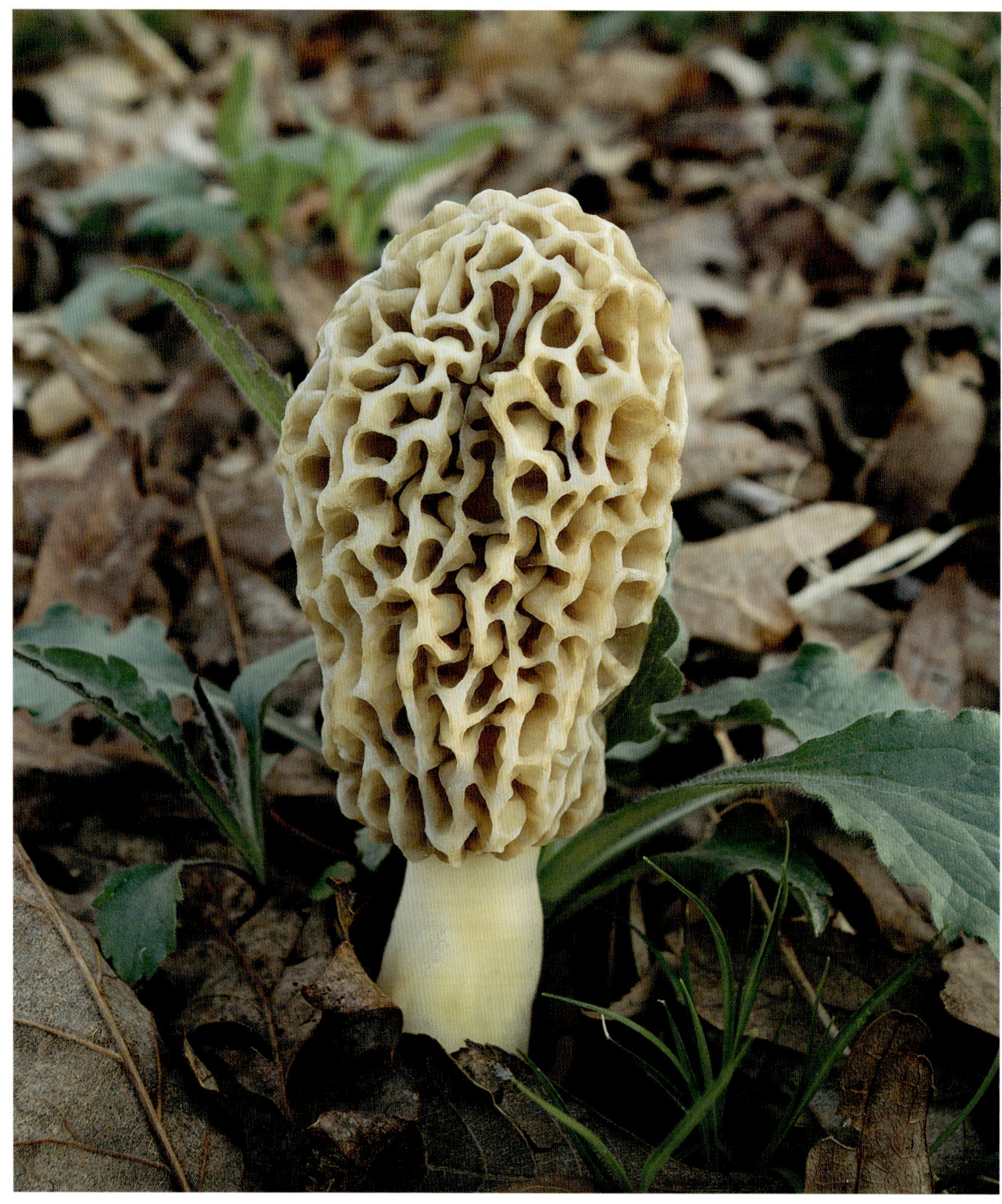

A morel mushroom makes a tasty treat, especially when it pops up in the front yard!

Sweden Creek Falls, Sweden Creek Natural Area

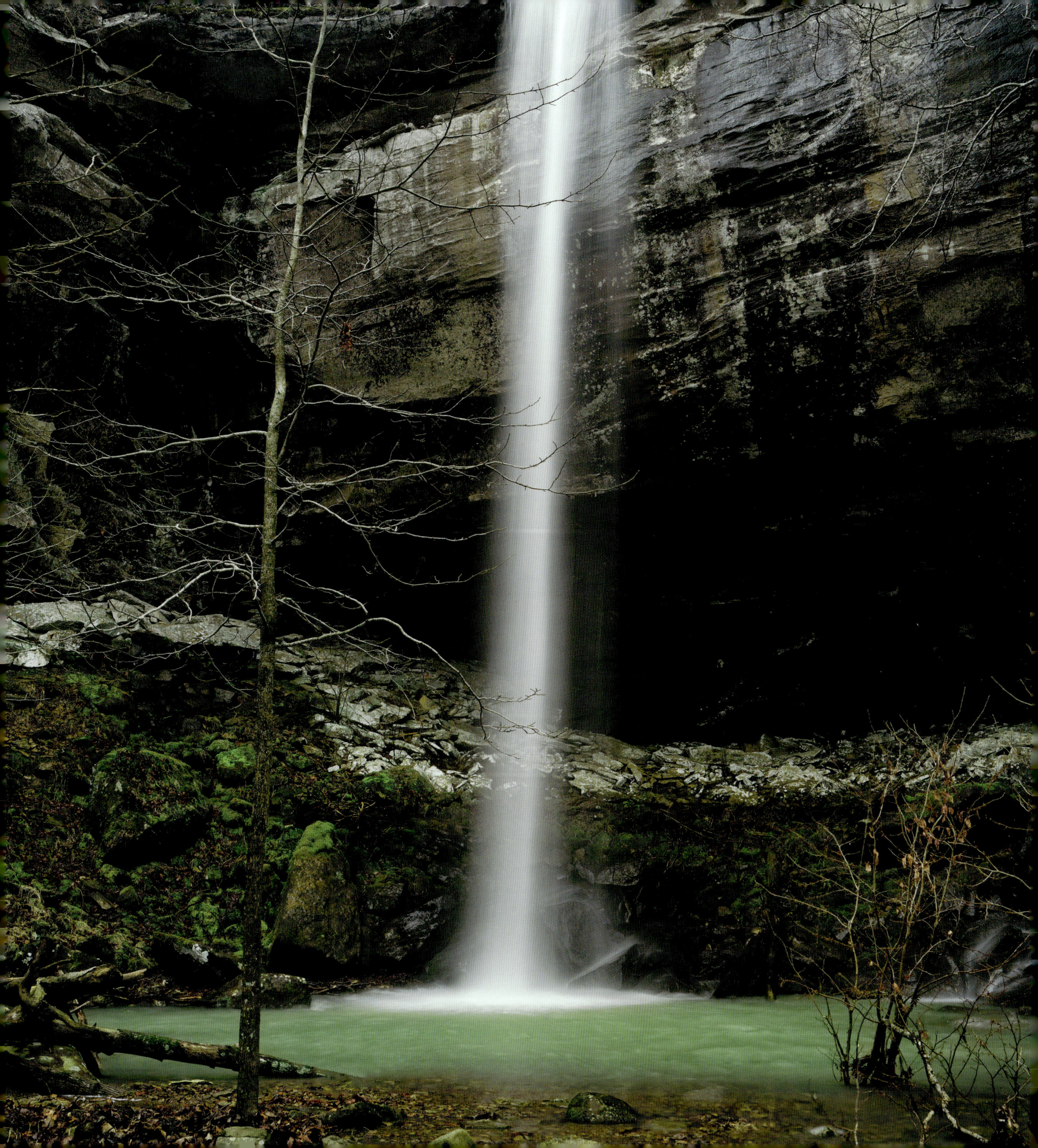

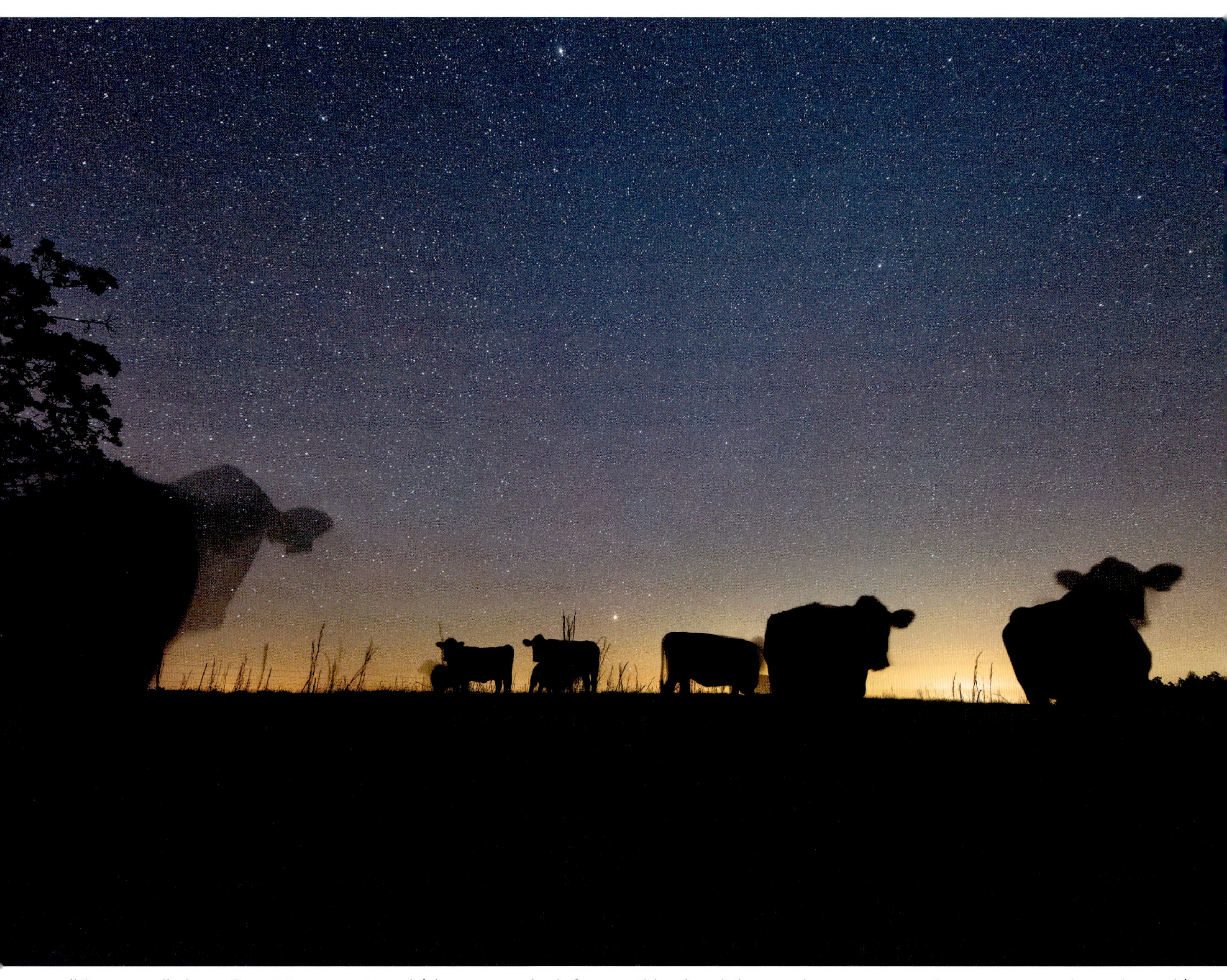

“Star cows” along Cave Mountain Road (the one on the left turned his head during the exposure to let some stars shine through)

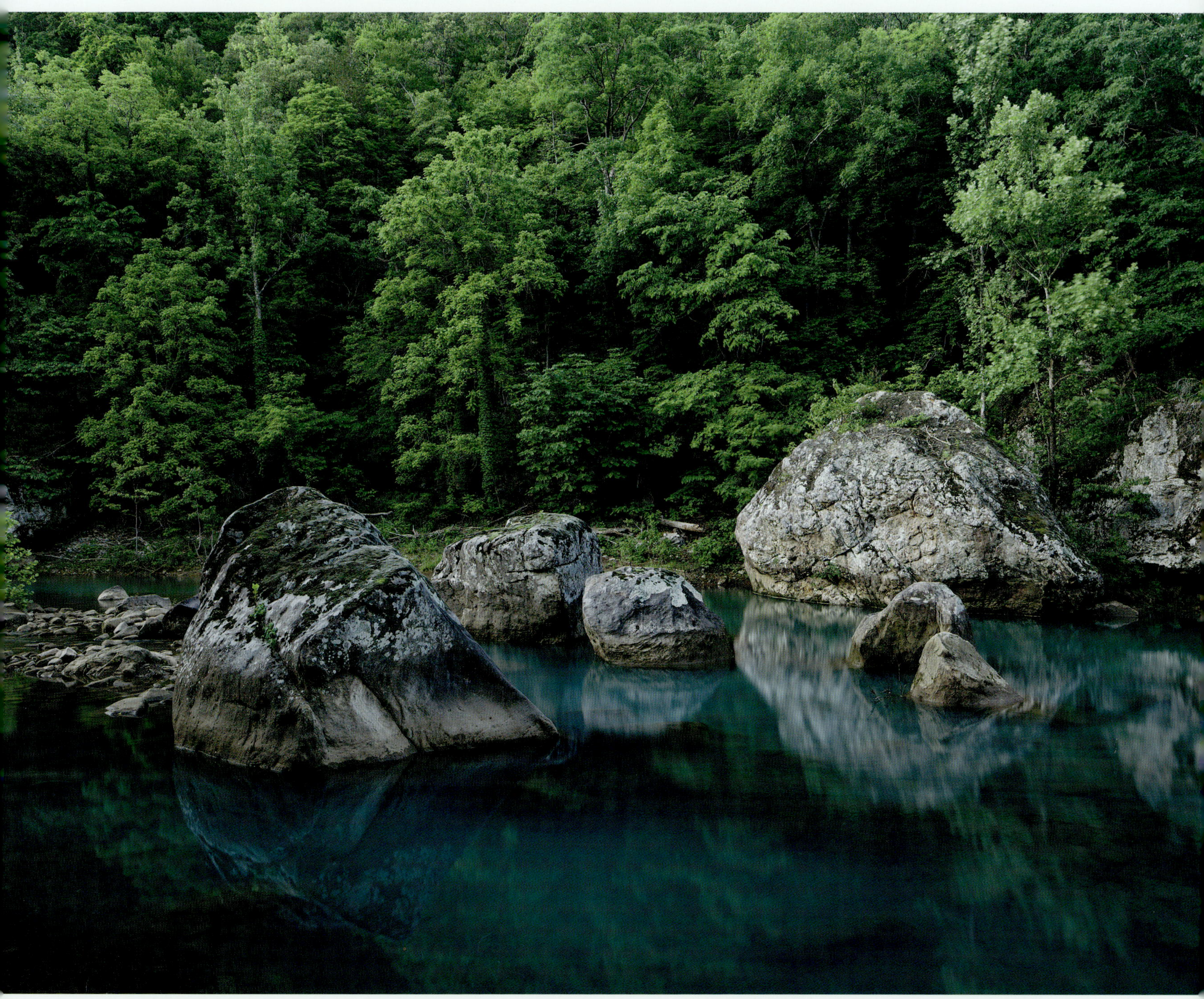

Minerals in the water create the amazing color of the Buffalo River; the sandstone boulders rolled down from bluffs far above

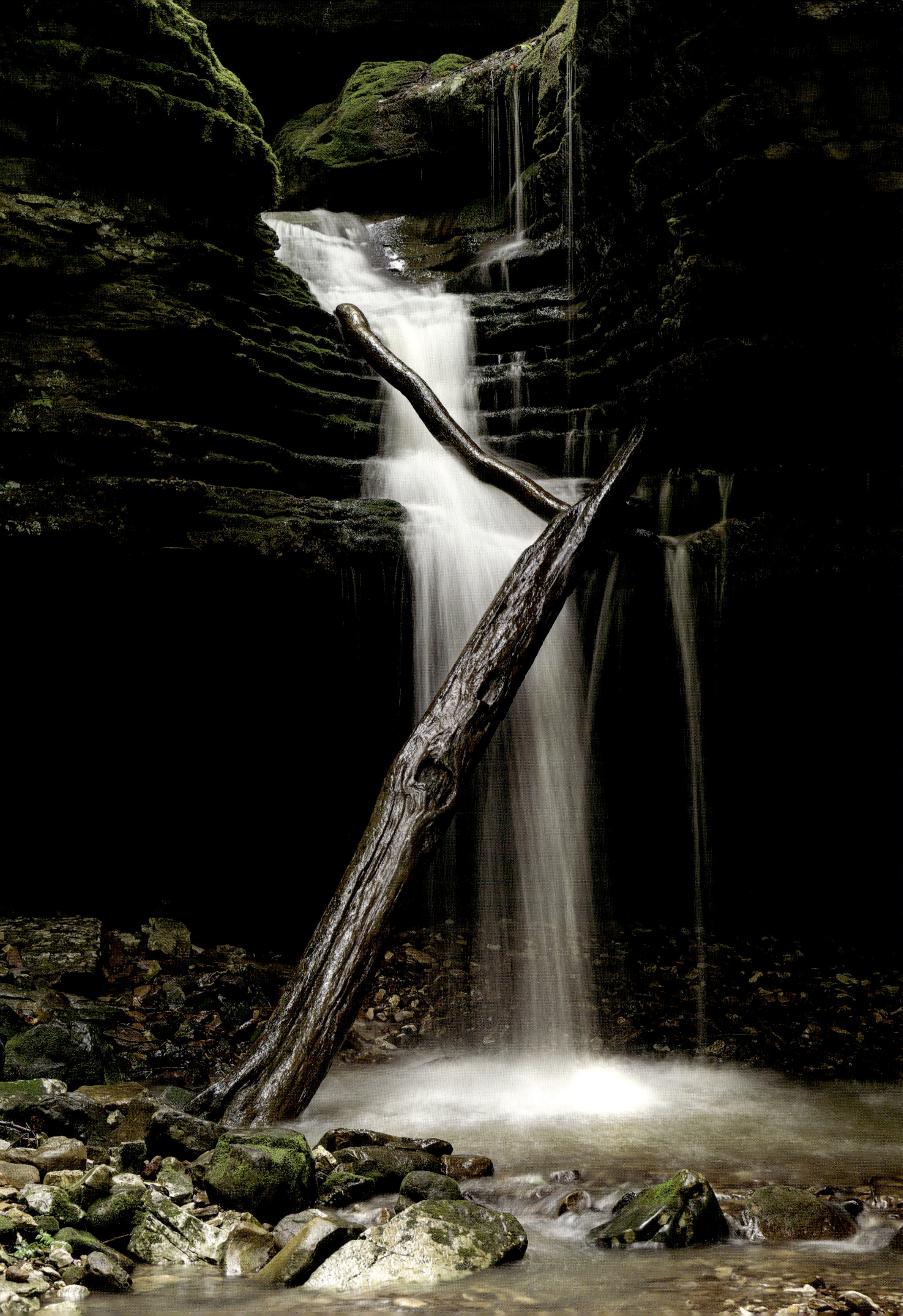

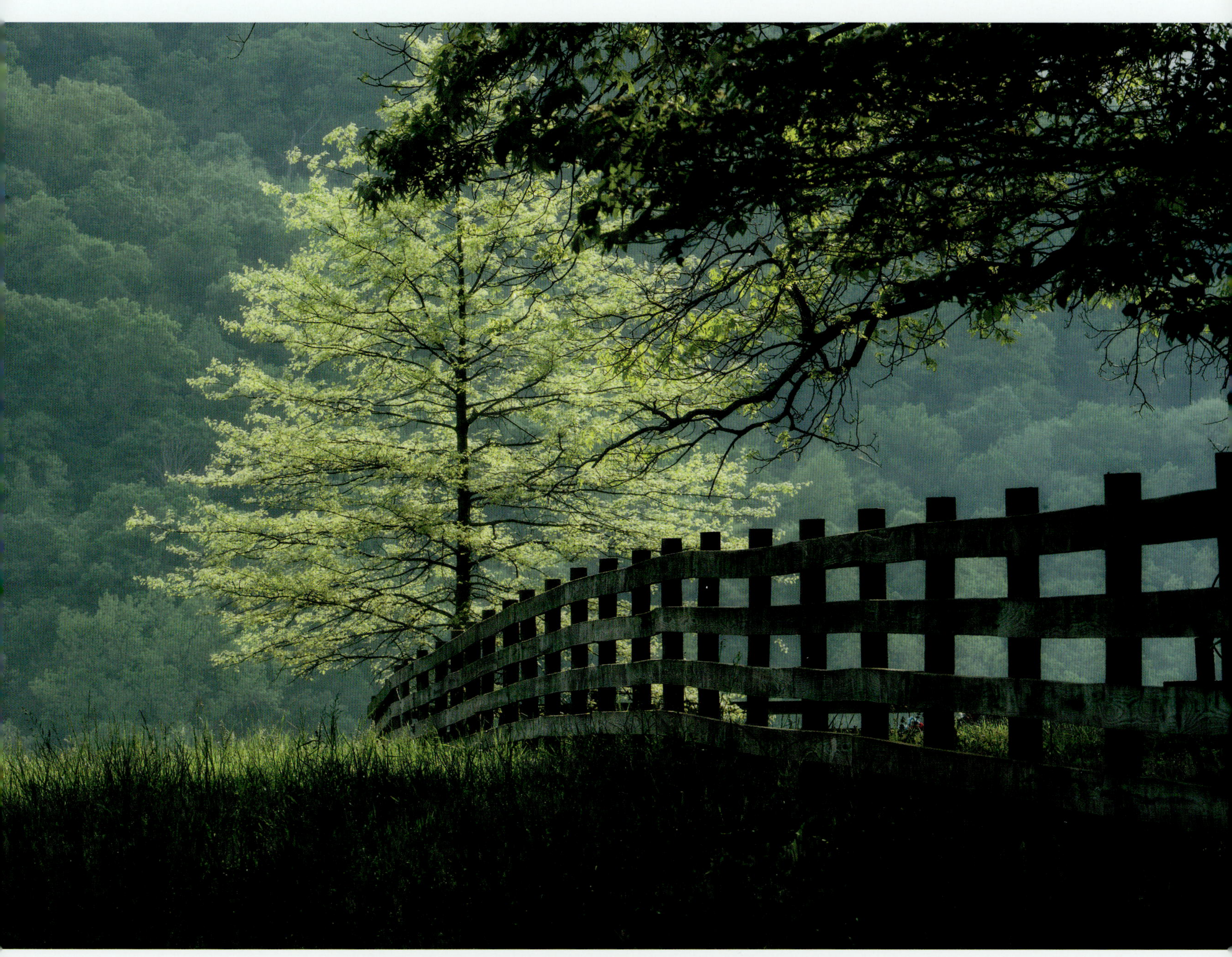

Early morning spring light, Boxley Valley Historic District

Waterfall on Leatherwood Creek, Buffalo National River

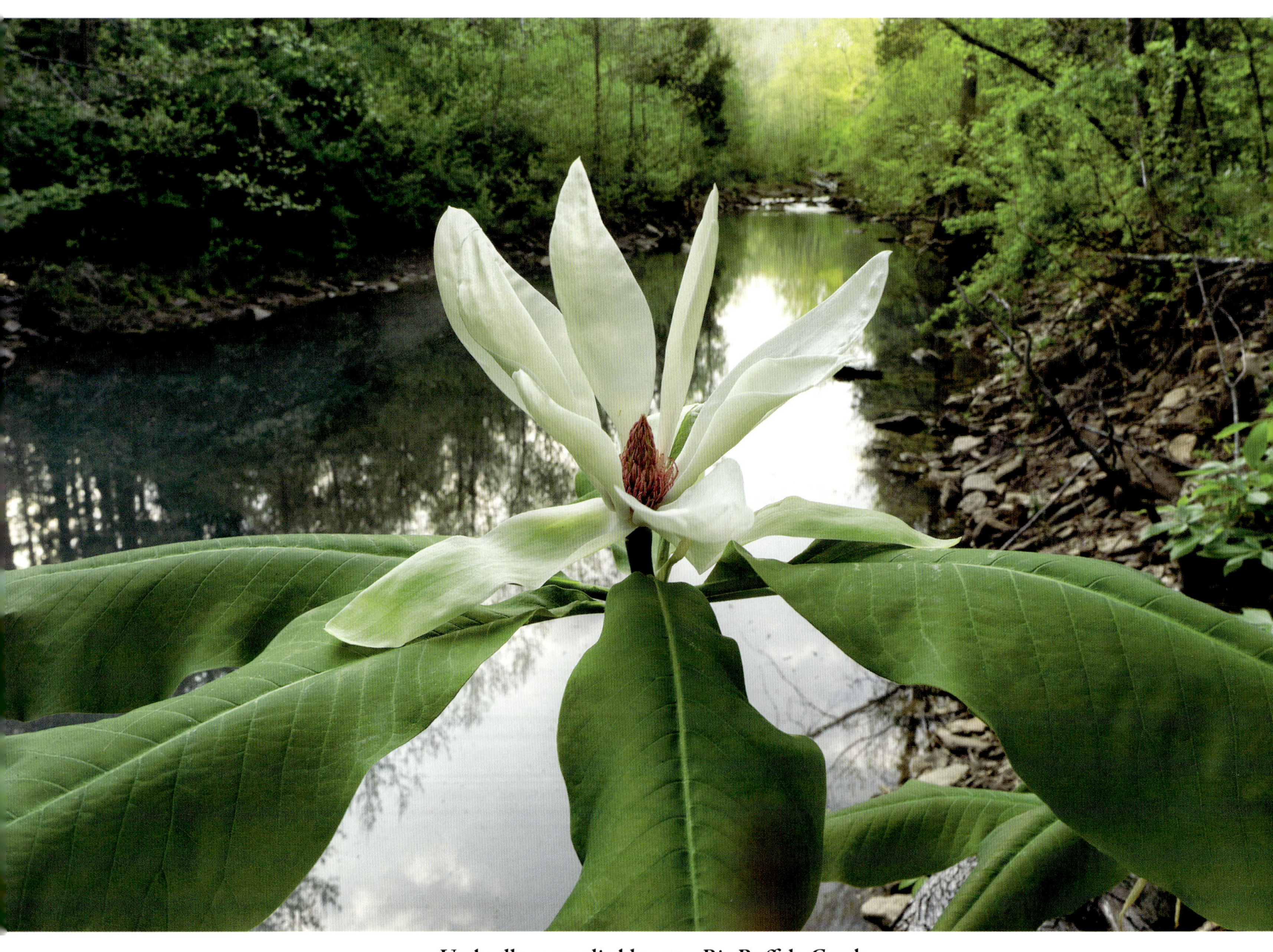

Umbrella magnolia blossom, Big Buffalo Creek

Looking down on the Buffalo River from high atop Roark Bluff near Steele Creek

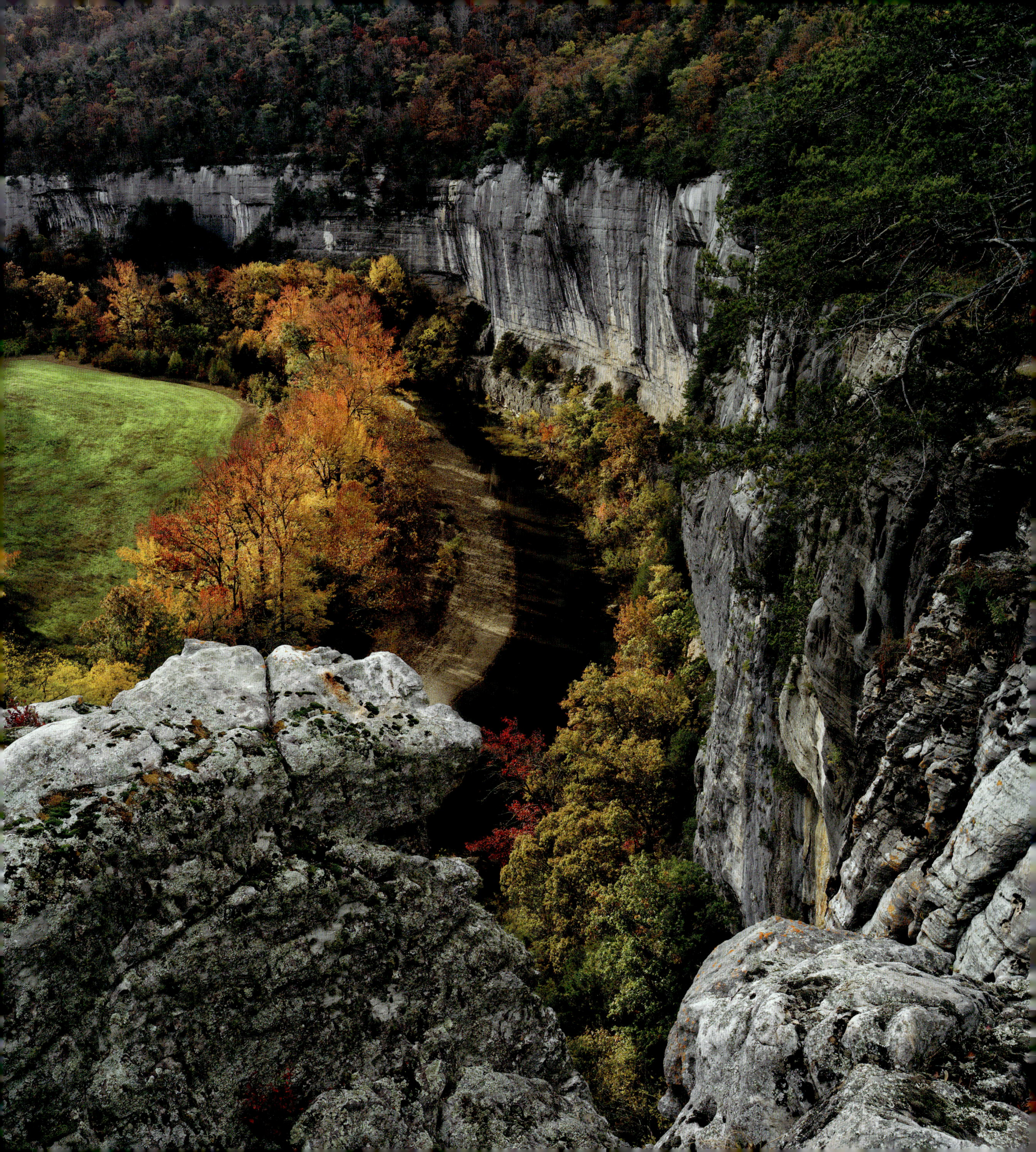

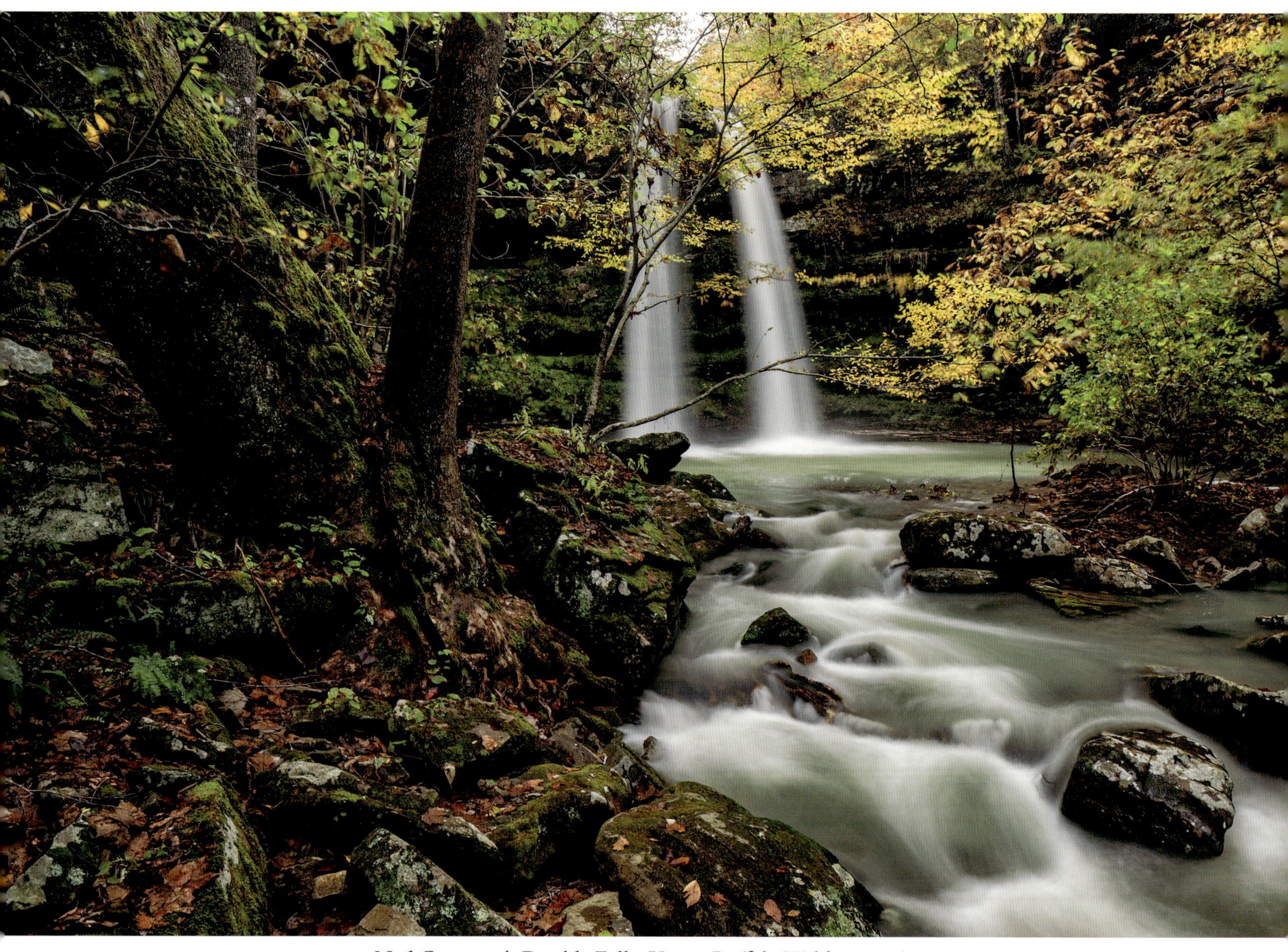

Neil Compton's Double Falls, Upper Buffalo Wilderness Area

Polished river rocks, Buffalo National River

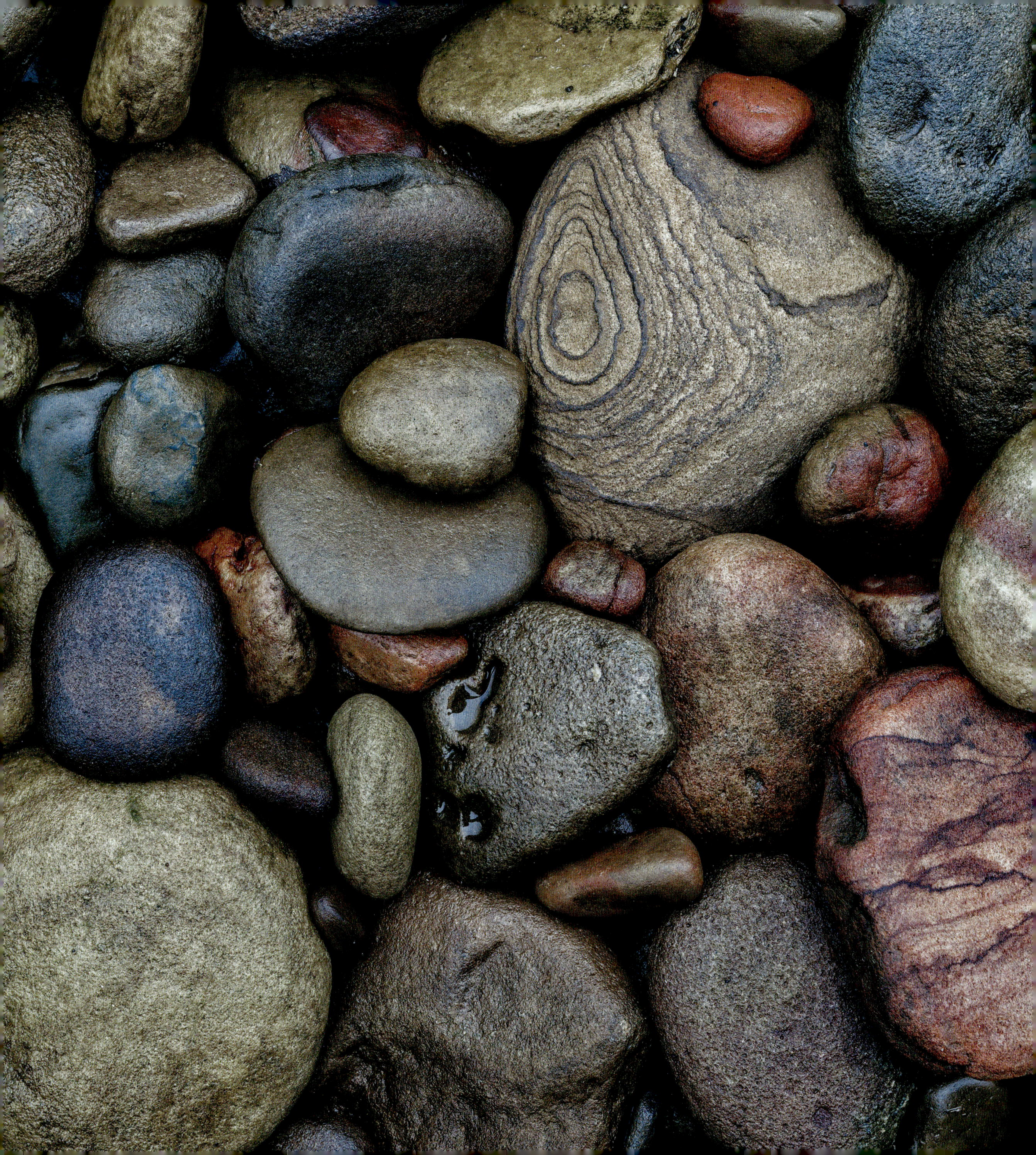

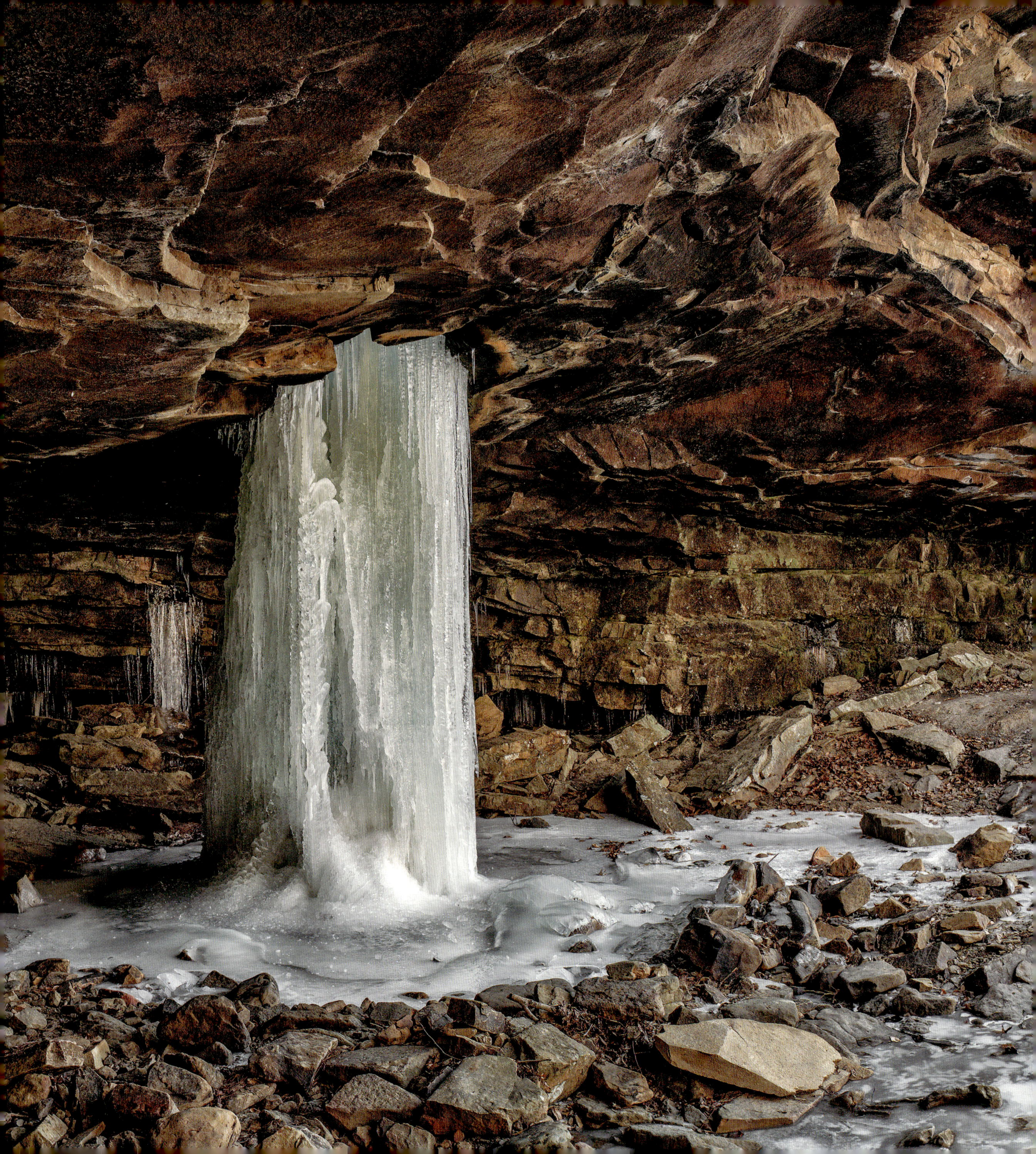

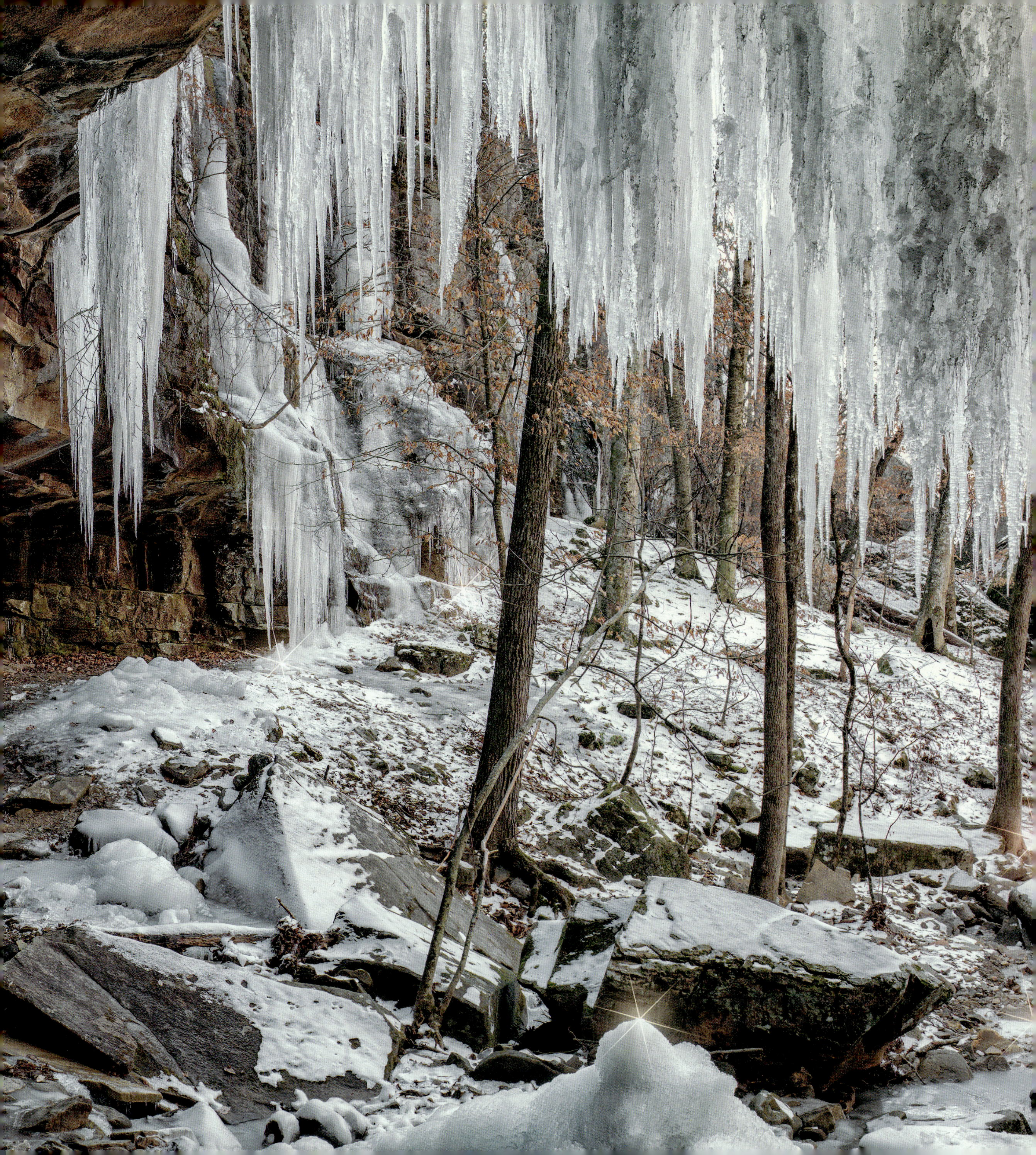

Daffodils at a rustic cabin along Cave Mountain Road

When Arkansas became a state in 1836 there were already settlers living in the circle around our cabin. The region is dotted with many homesteads and other structures from the early days. Those hearty folks had flower gardens, and often daffodils that are 100 years or more old continue to survive, bloom, and thrive. It is always a treat to be out bushwhacking through the wilderness in March and come across a patch of bright yellow flowers like these—all that is left from the old homesite.

This particular cabin is located right along Cave Mountain Road, and I've stopped to photograph the first blooms there for more than 20 years.

A very frozen Glory Hole Falls, Ozark National Forest (previous pages)

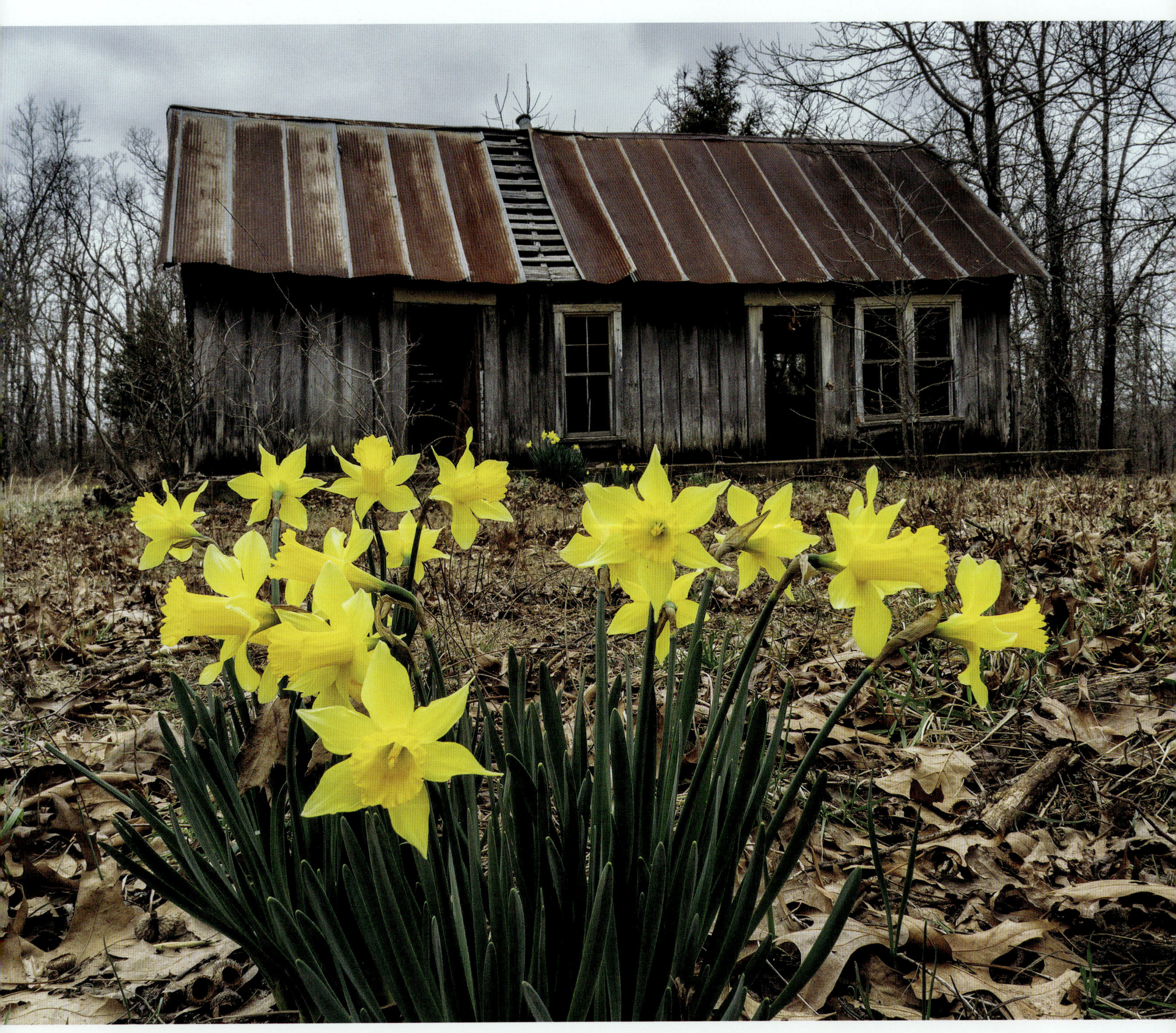

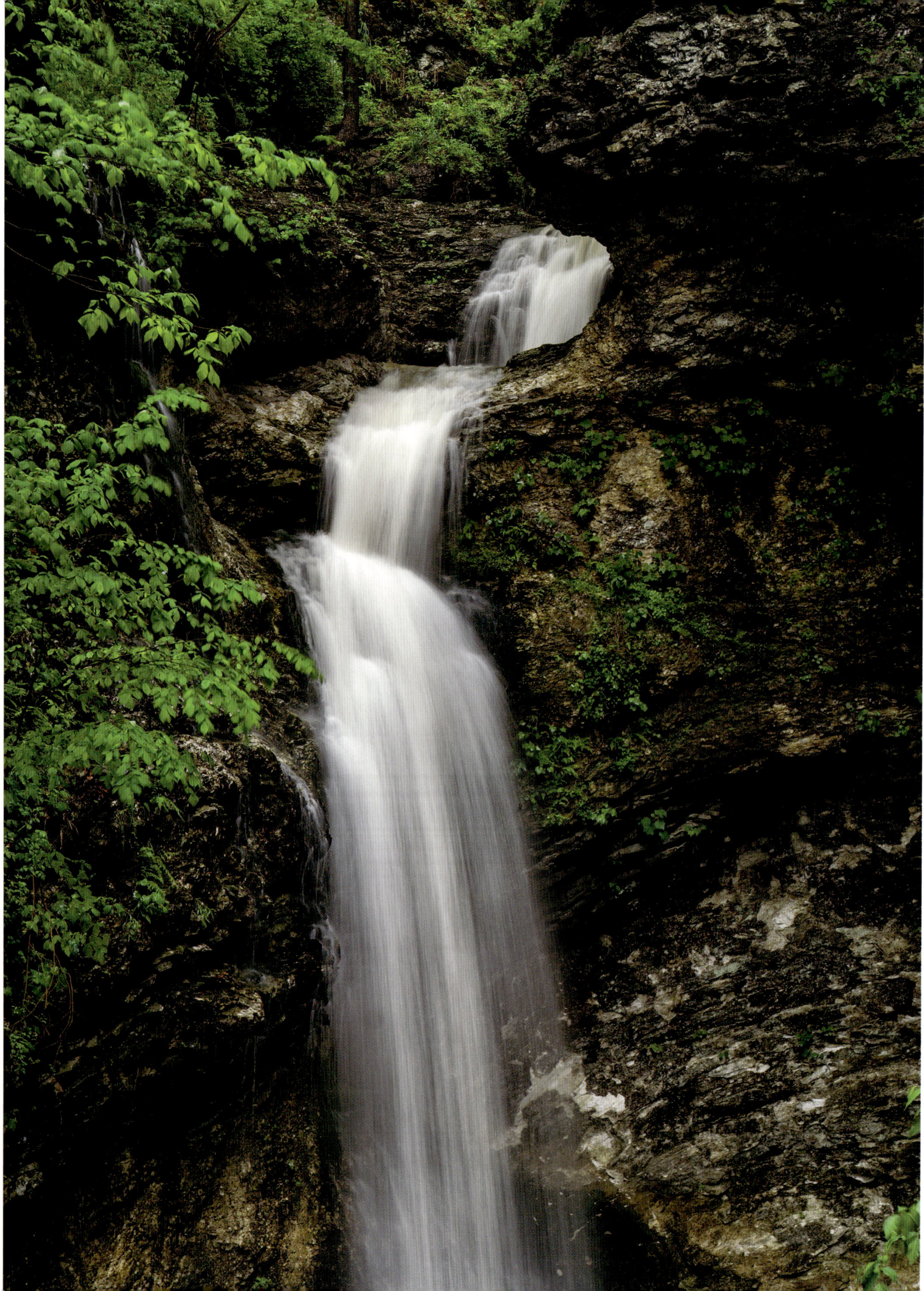

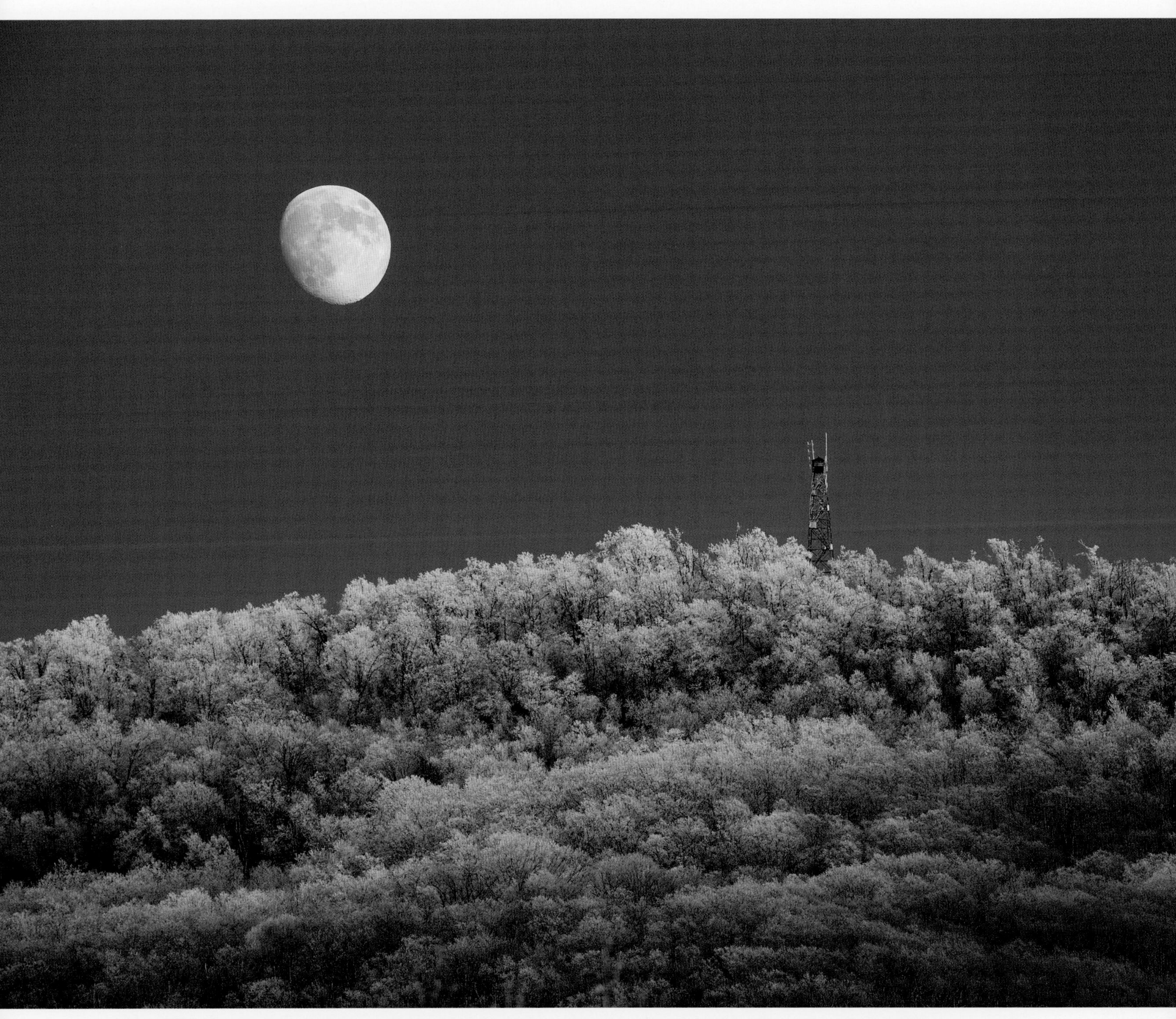

The rising moon is greeted by a landscape covered with frozen fog (aka "hoar frost") at the Buffalo Fire Tower
(This is the highest point in the Ozarks–2,561')

Eden Falls at the end of the Lost Valley Trail, Buffalo National River

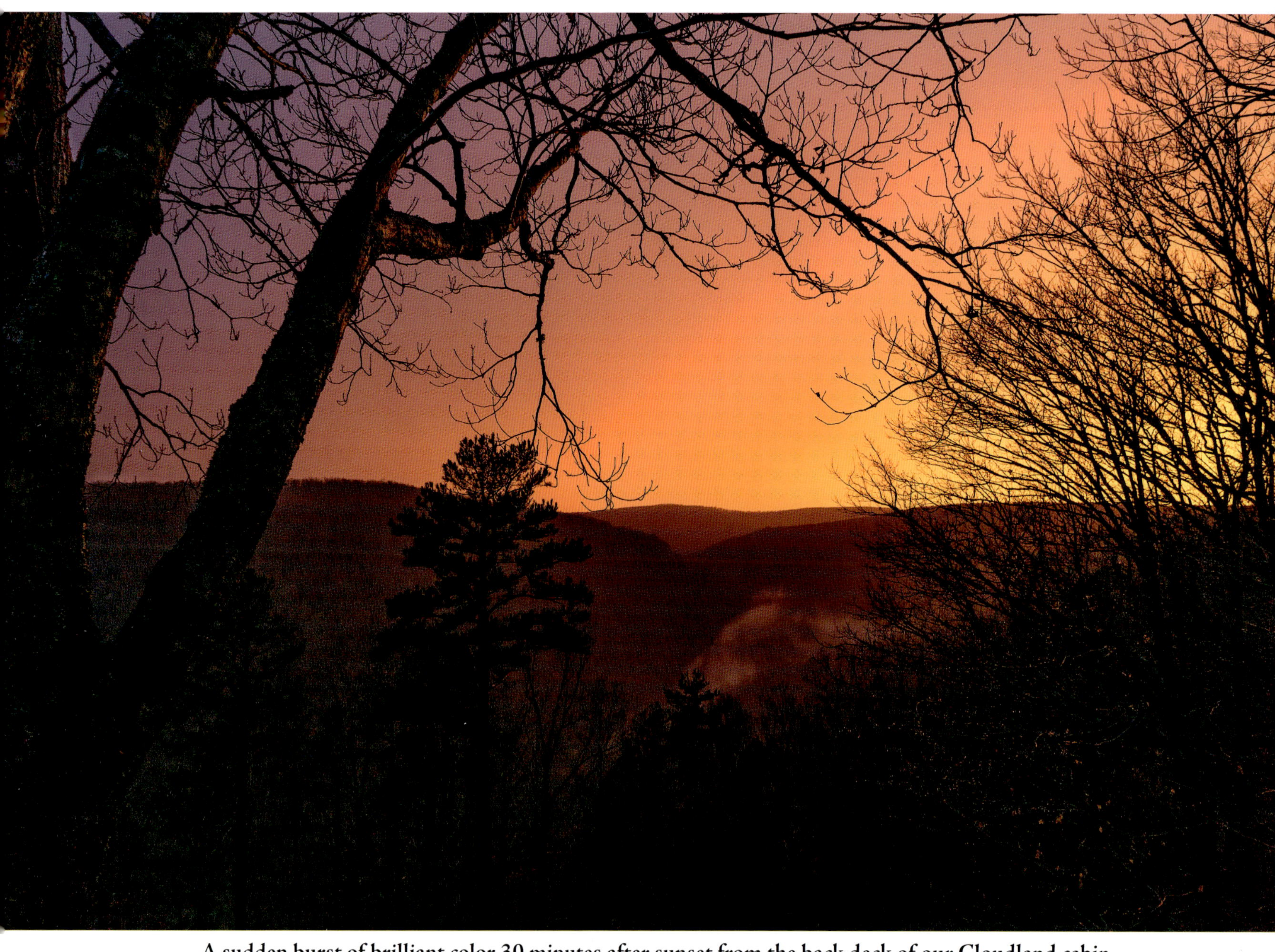

A sudden burst of brilliant color 30 minutes after sunset from the back deck of our Cloudland cabin

Hello—I'm one of many curious black bear cubs that roam the headwaters area looking for a treat!

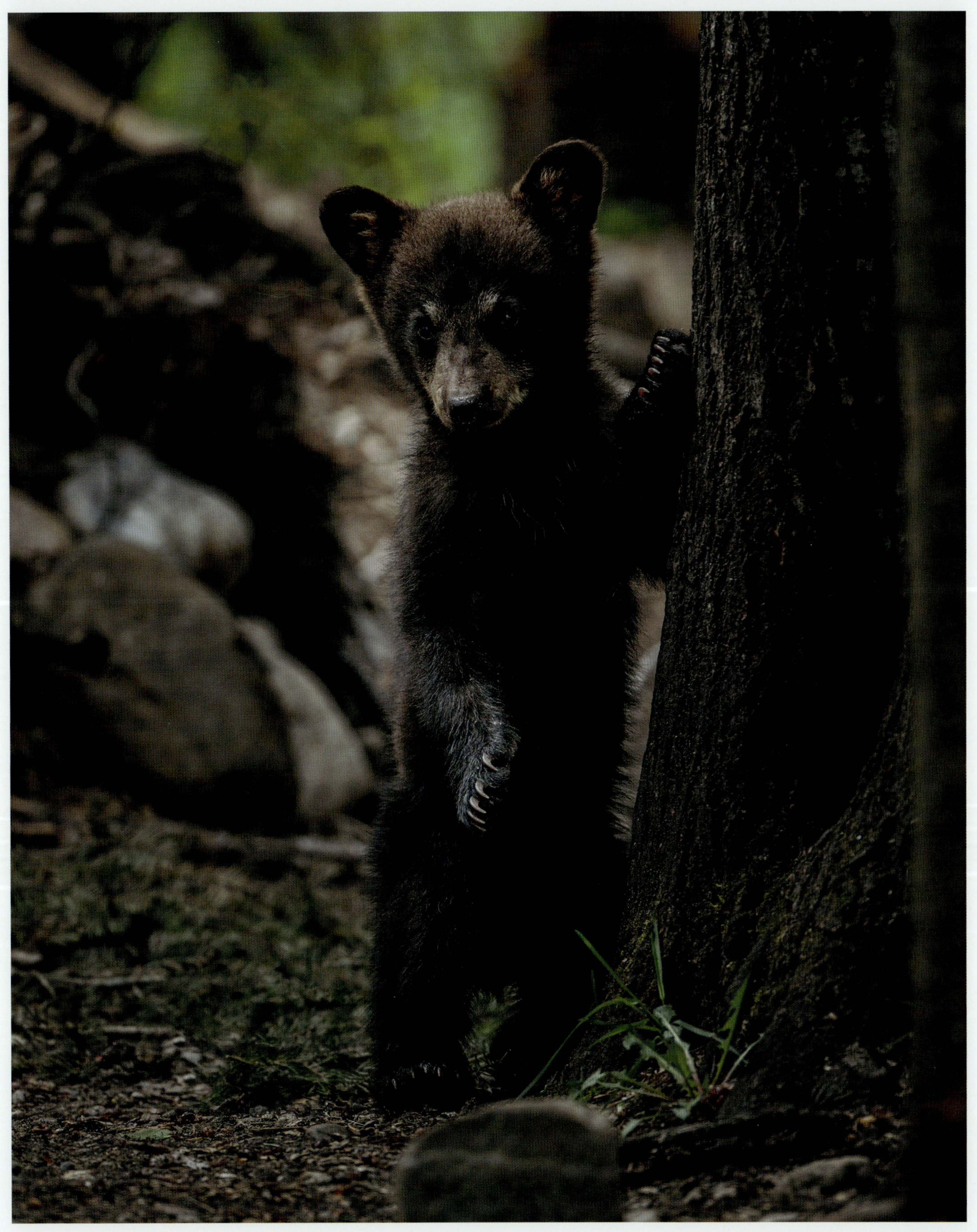

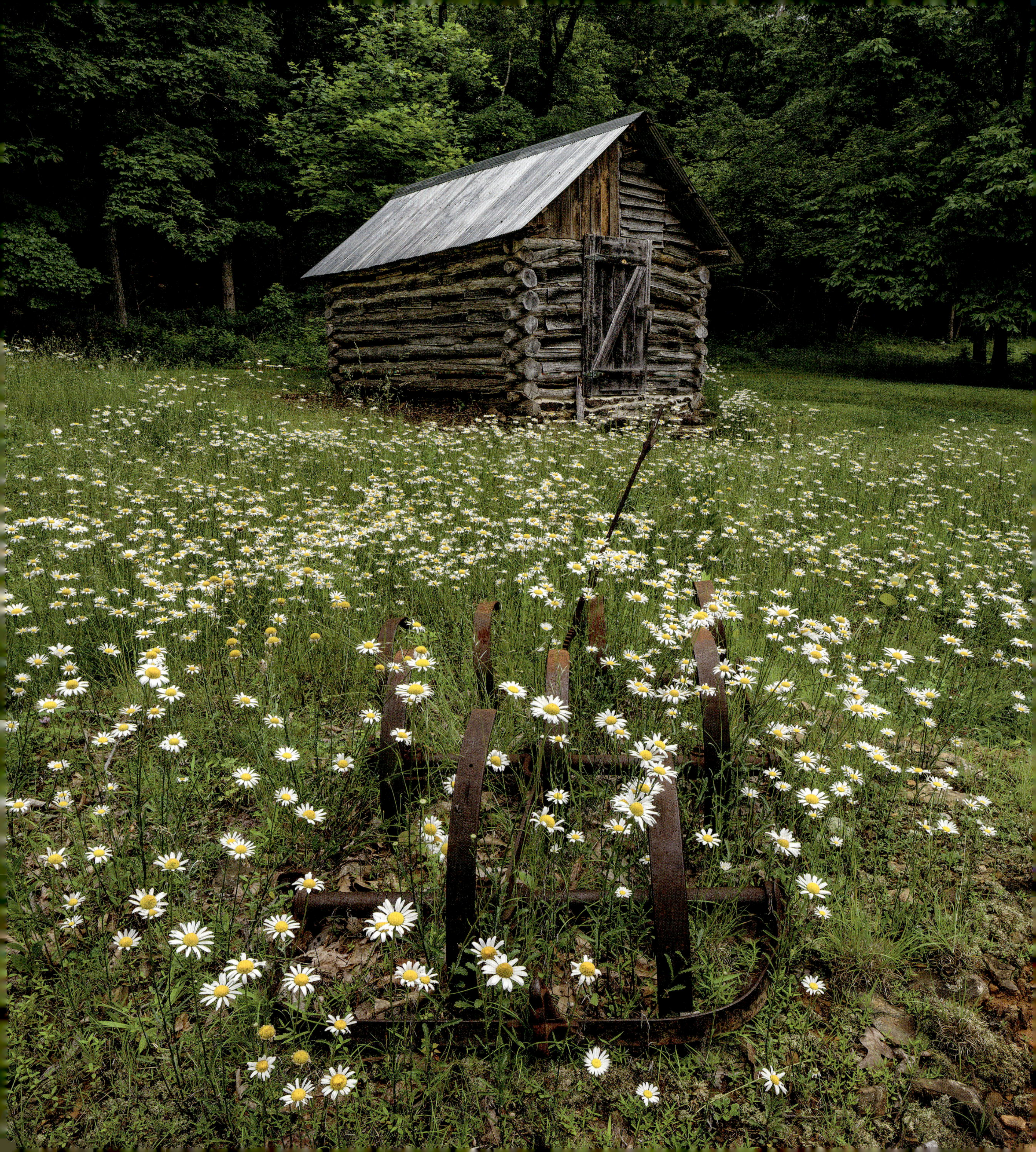

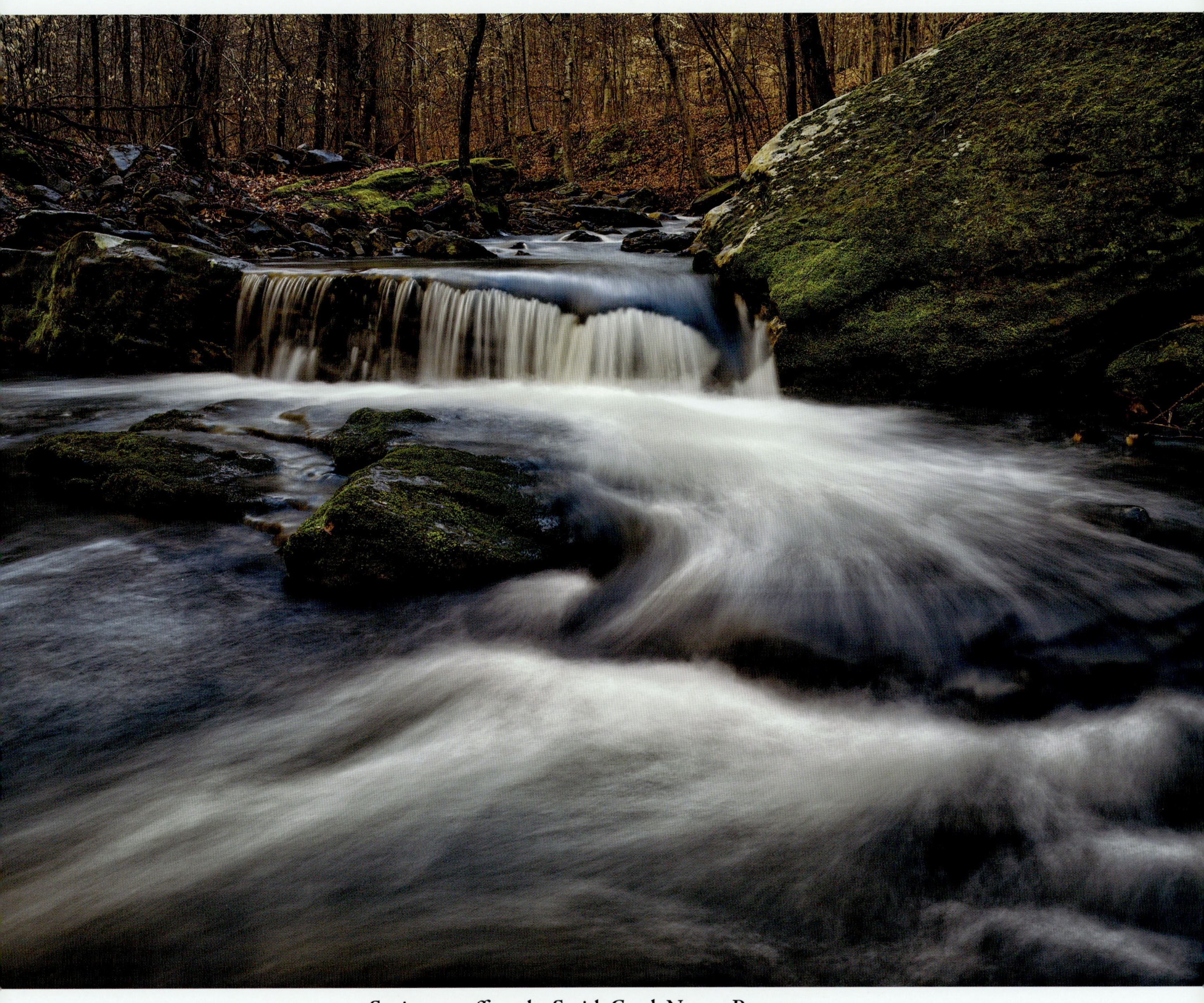

Spring runoff on the Smith Creek Nature Preserve

Horse-drawn harrow retired to the daisy meadow at our neighbor, Kennie's, smokehouse

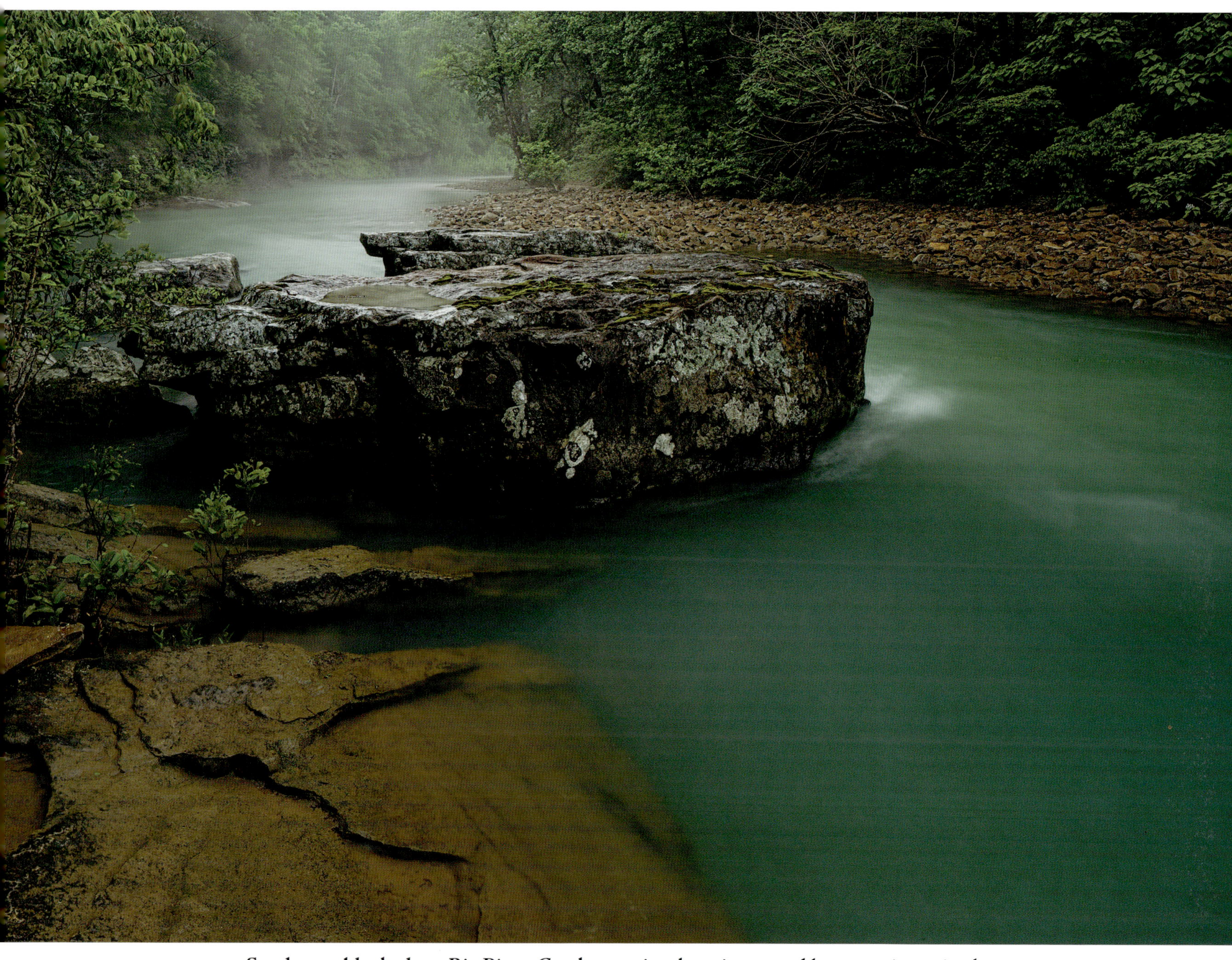

Sandstone block along Big Piney Creek—notice the mist caused by a passing rain shower

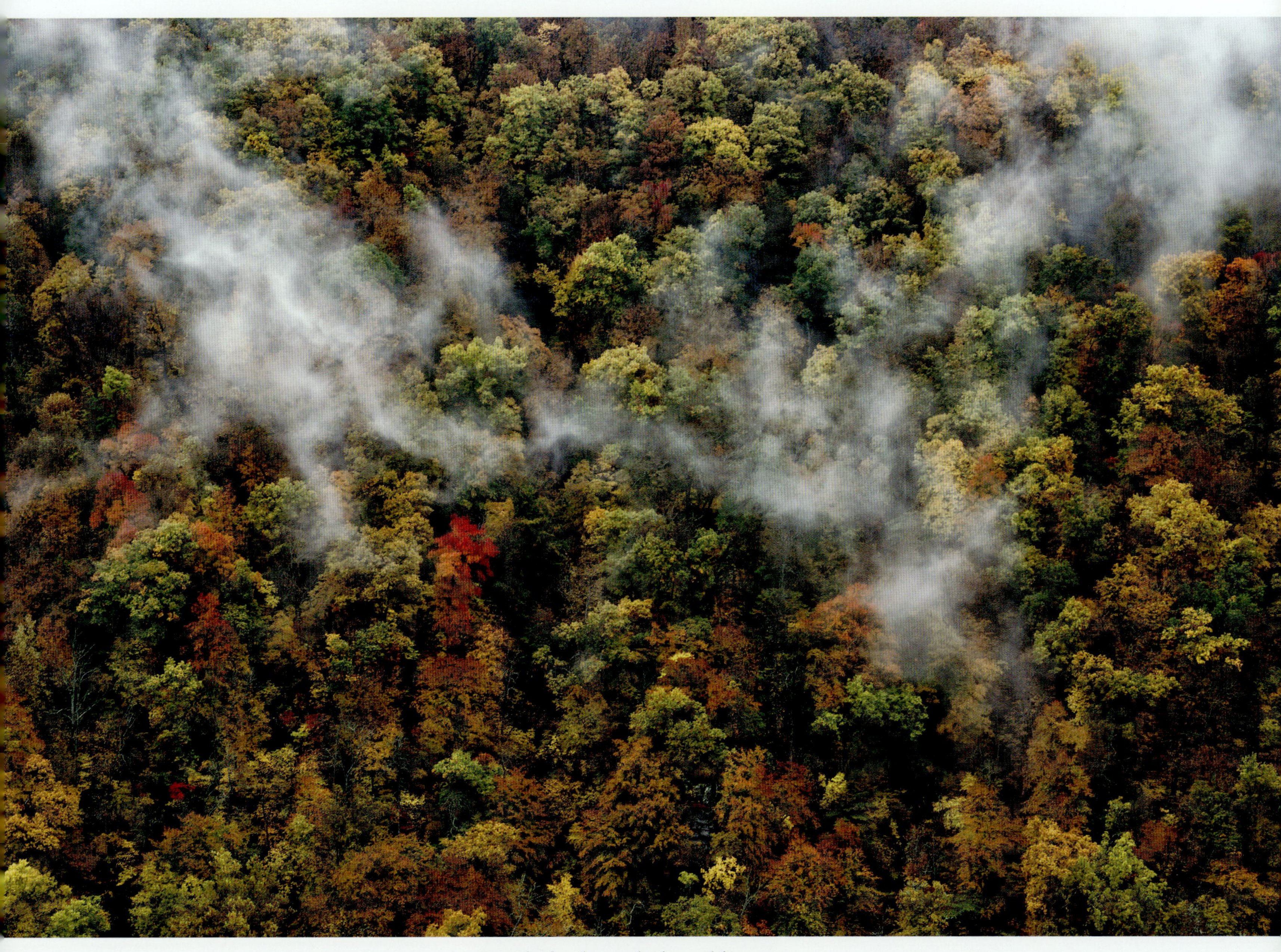

Fog drifts through the wilderness

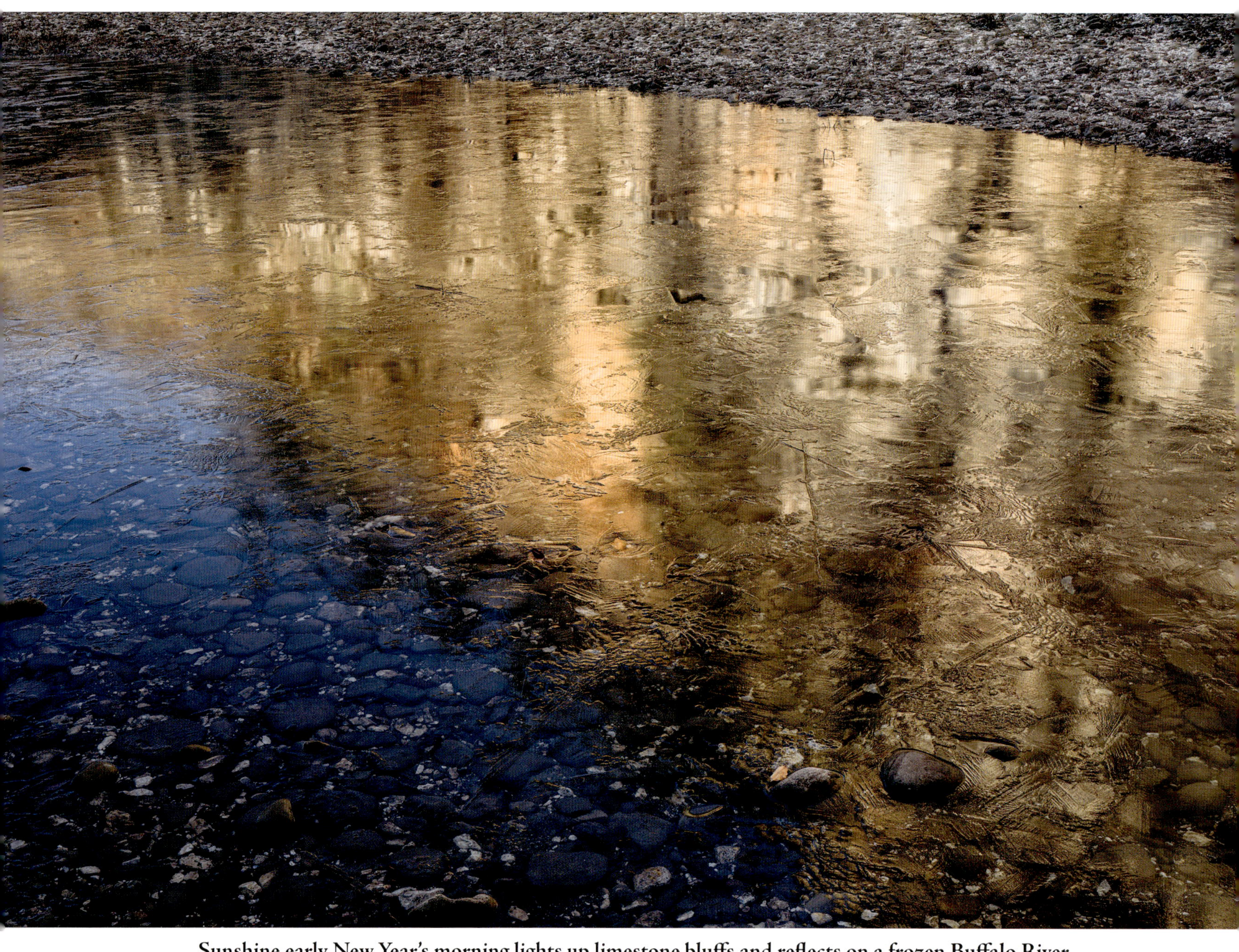

Sunshine early New Year's morning lights up limestone bluffs and reflects on a frozen Buffalo River

Winter camping is great under the stars

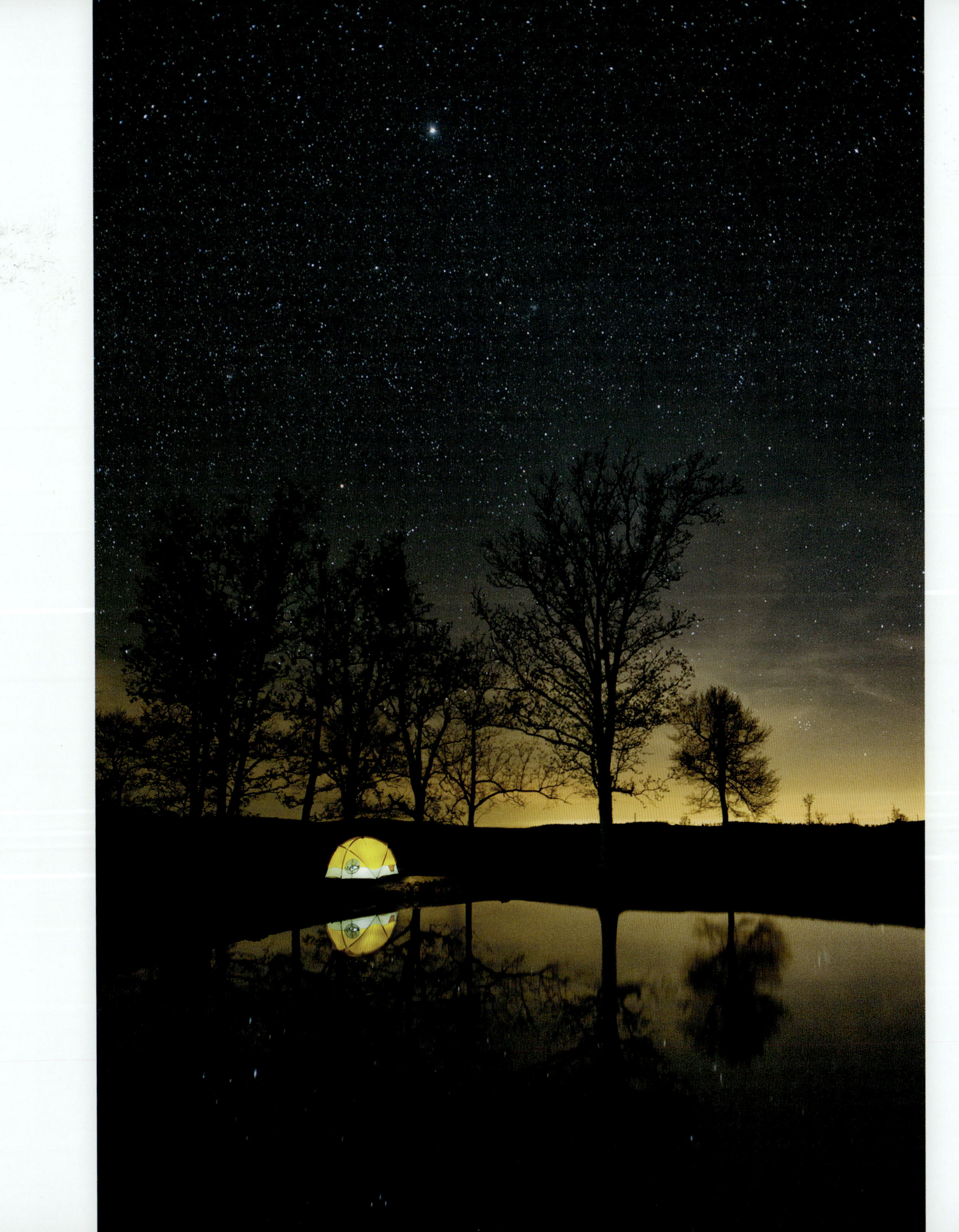

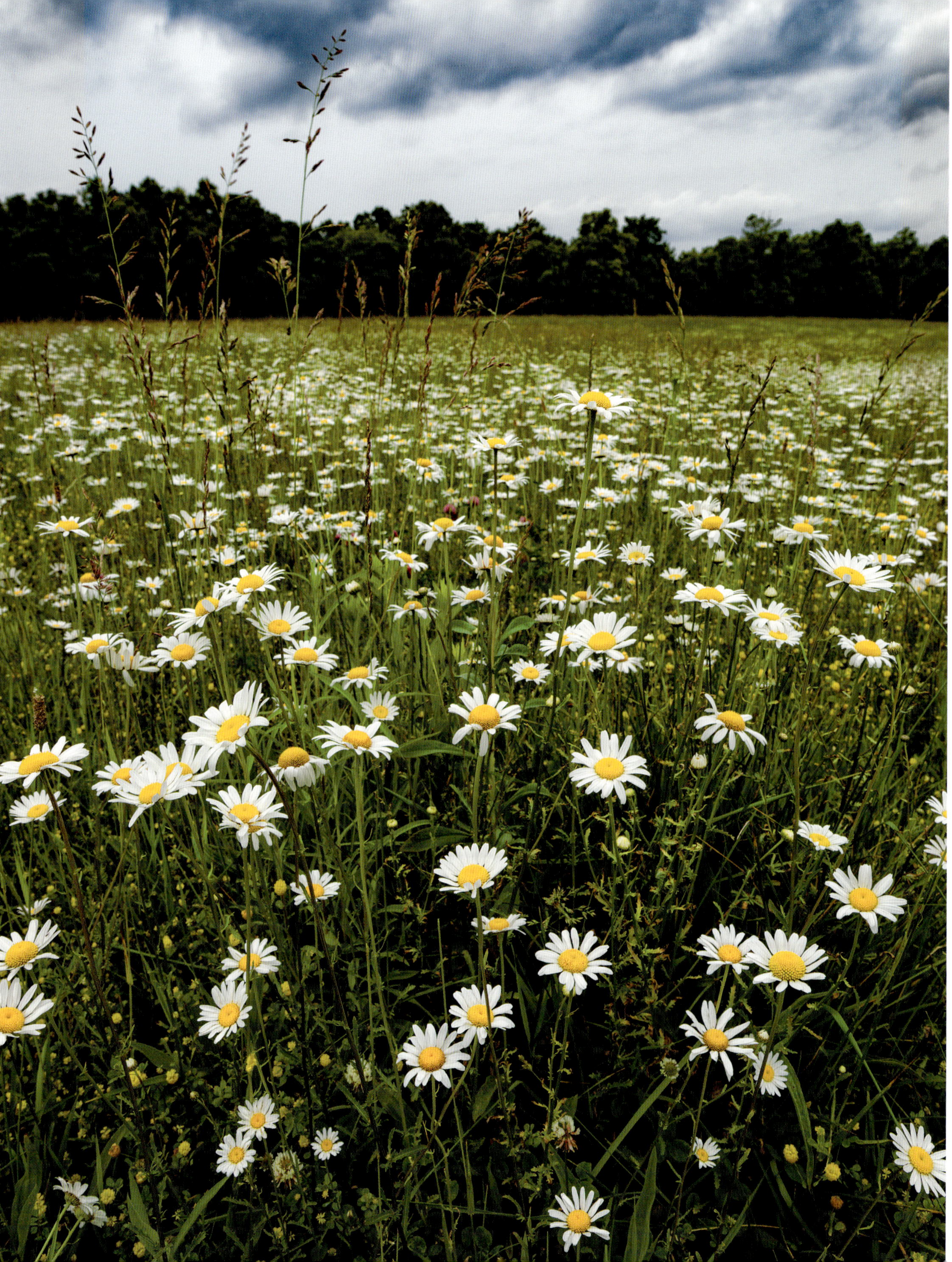

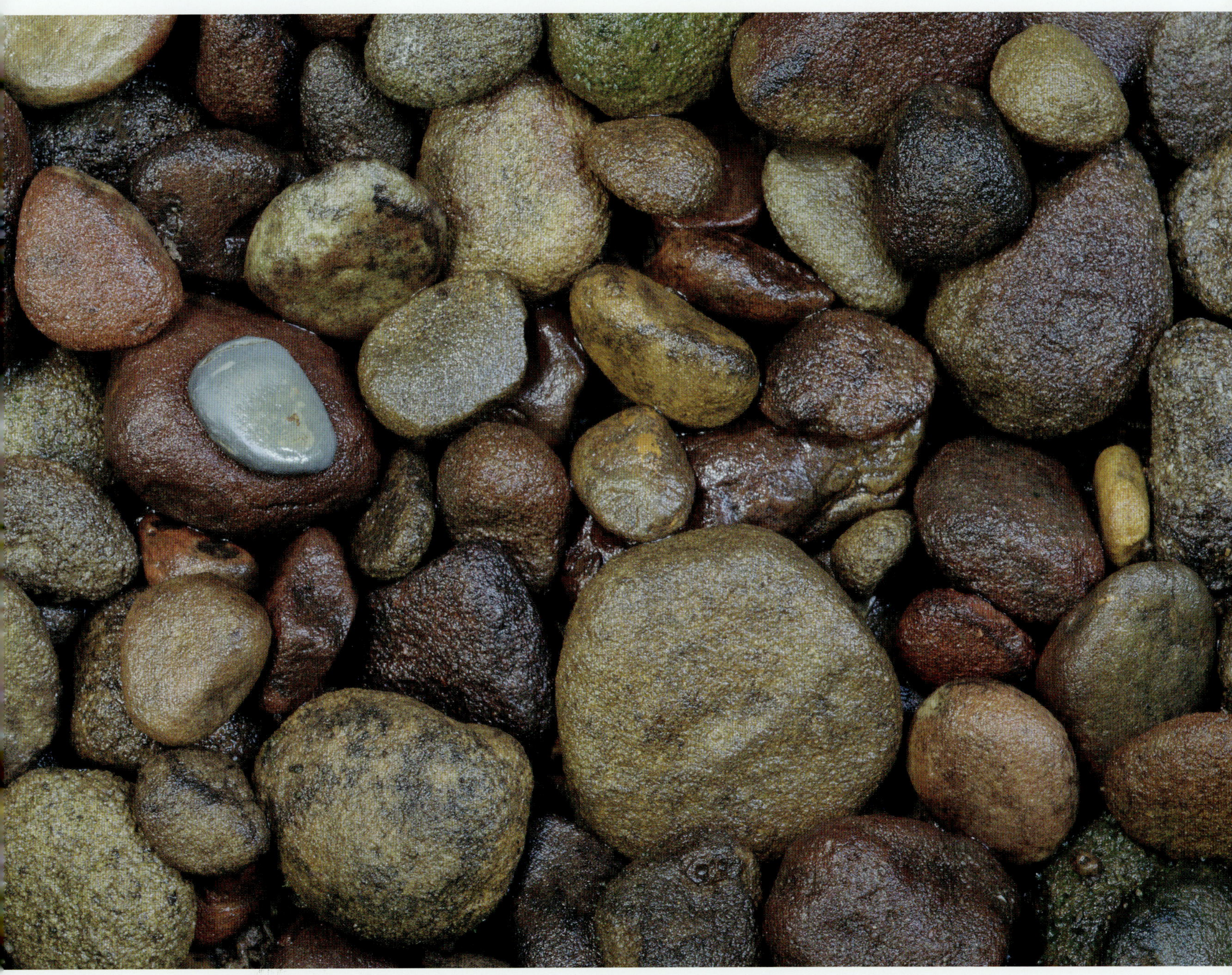

Polished river rocks, East Fork of the White River (the largest stone is only 2" across)

Wildflower meadows filled with happy daisies are everywhere in early summer

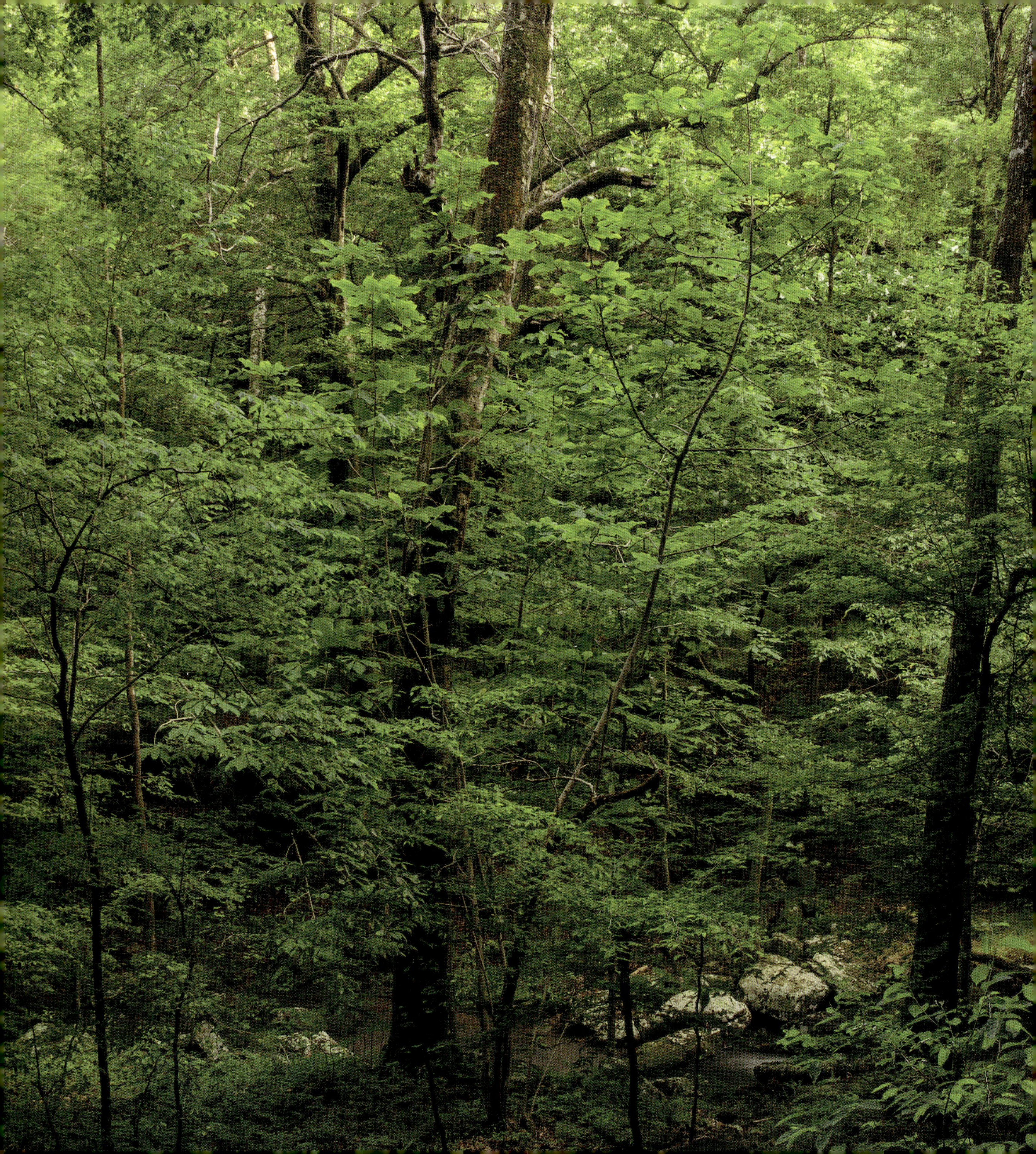

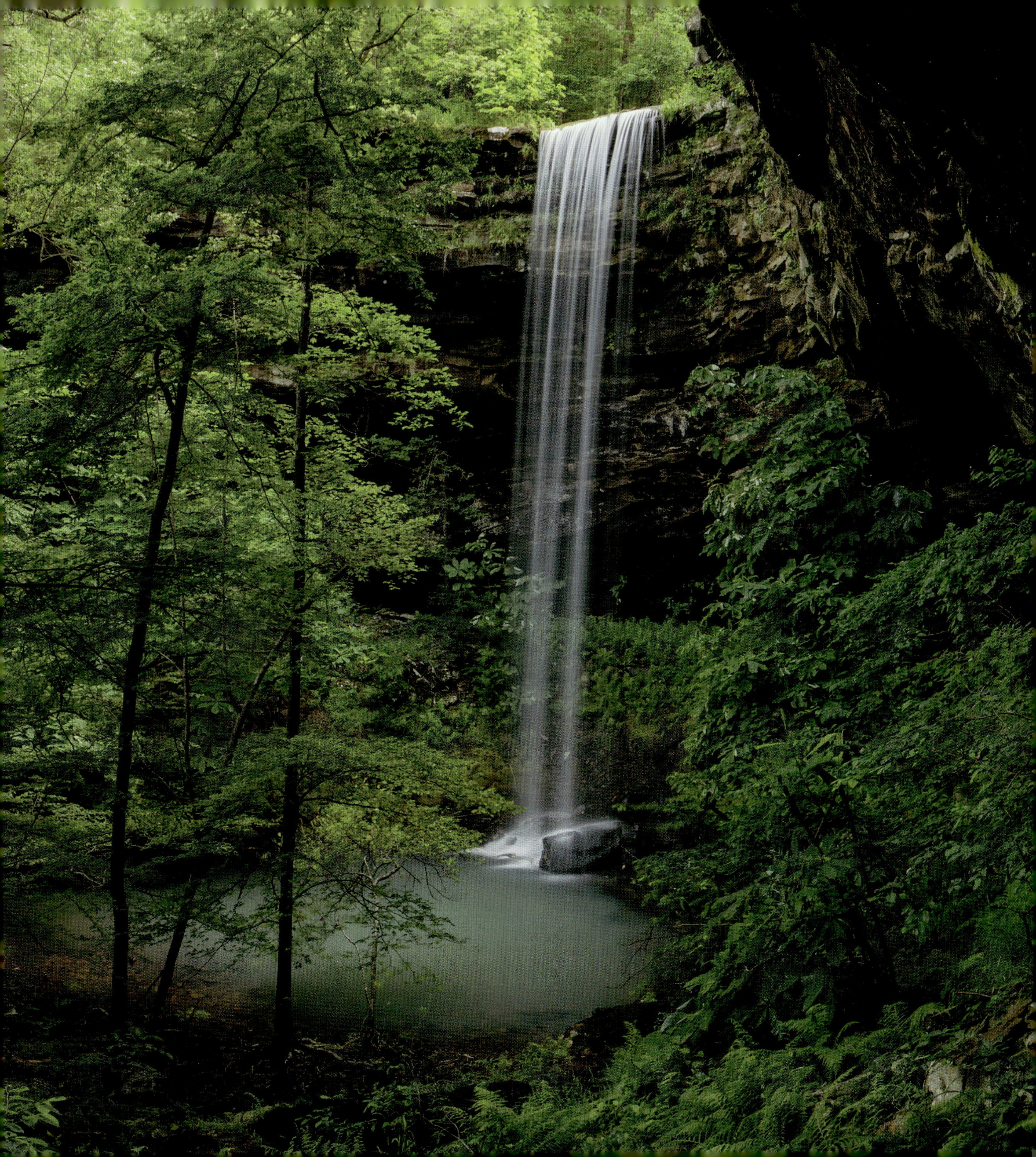

Winter sunrise at Hawksbill Crag, Upper Buffalo Wilderness Area

Hawksbill Crag is considered to be the most photographed natural feature in Arkansas. I've been there hundreds of times and never tire of it—nor have I captured the best photo yet, so I plan to return. I love being there before sunrise, when the air is quiet and sweet.

This photo was taken at sunrise on December 21st when the sun was all the way to the right (south). After that date the sun moves to the left a little bit each day until September when it moves out of sight until spring.

Bowers Hollow Falls, Upper Buffalo Wilderness Area (previous pages)

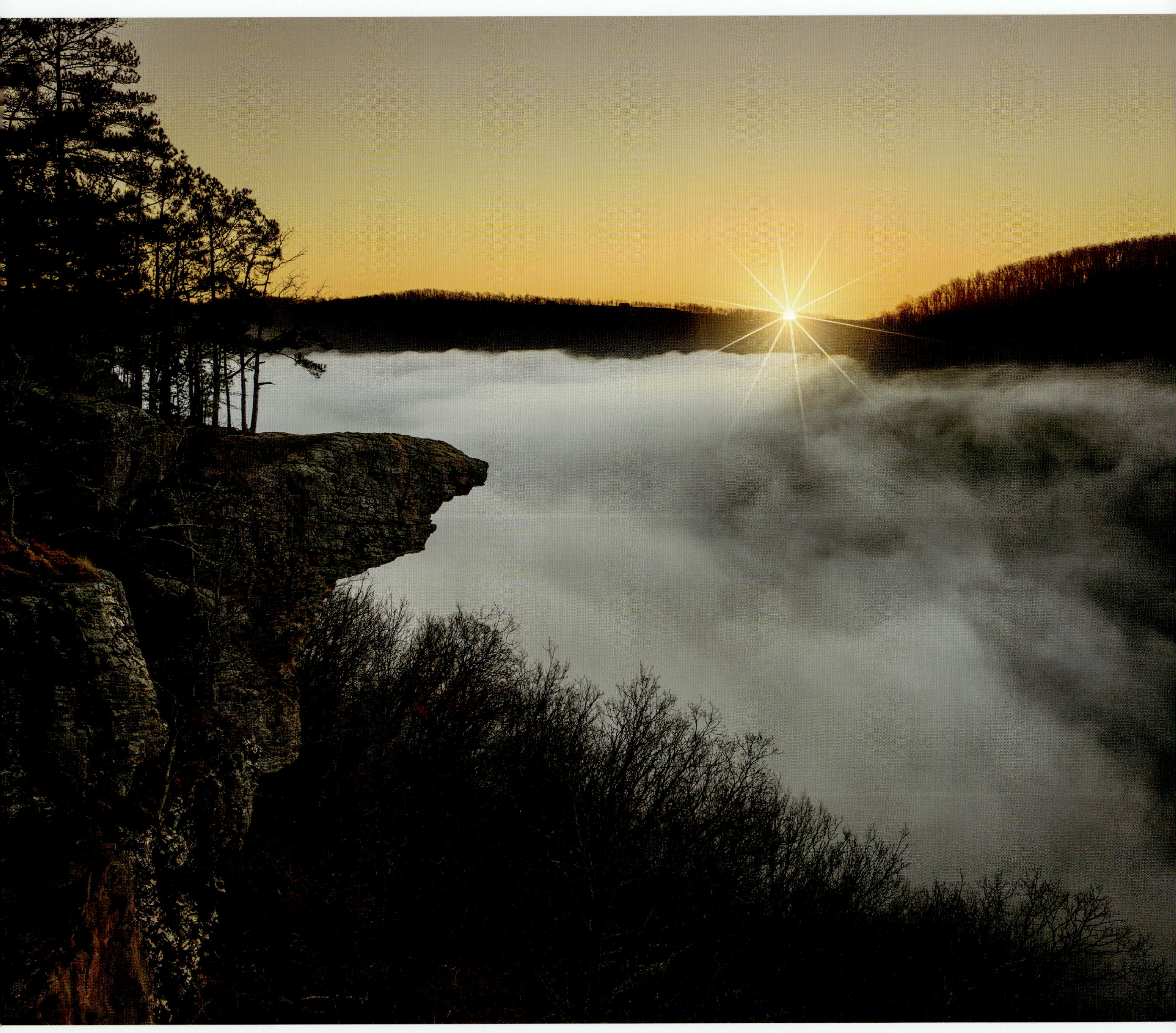

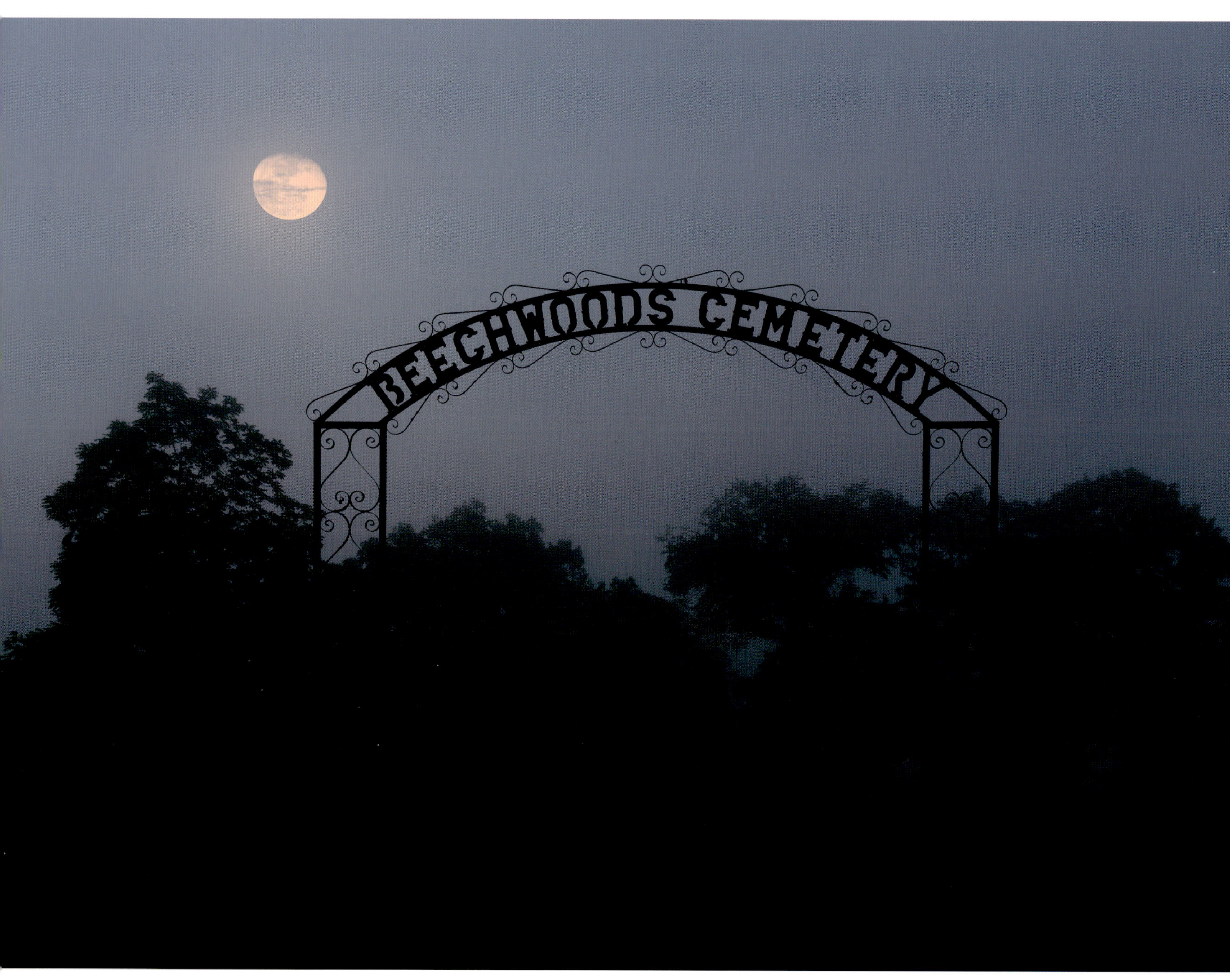

I just *love* a foggy moonrise in a cemetery, Boxley Valley Historic District

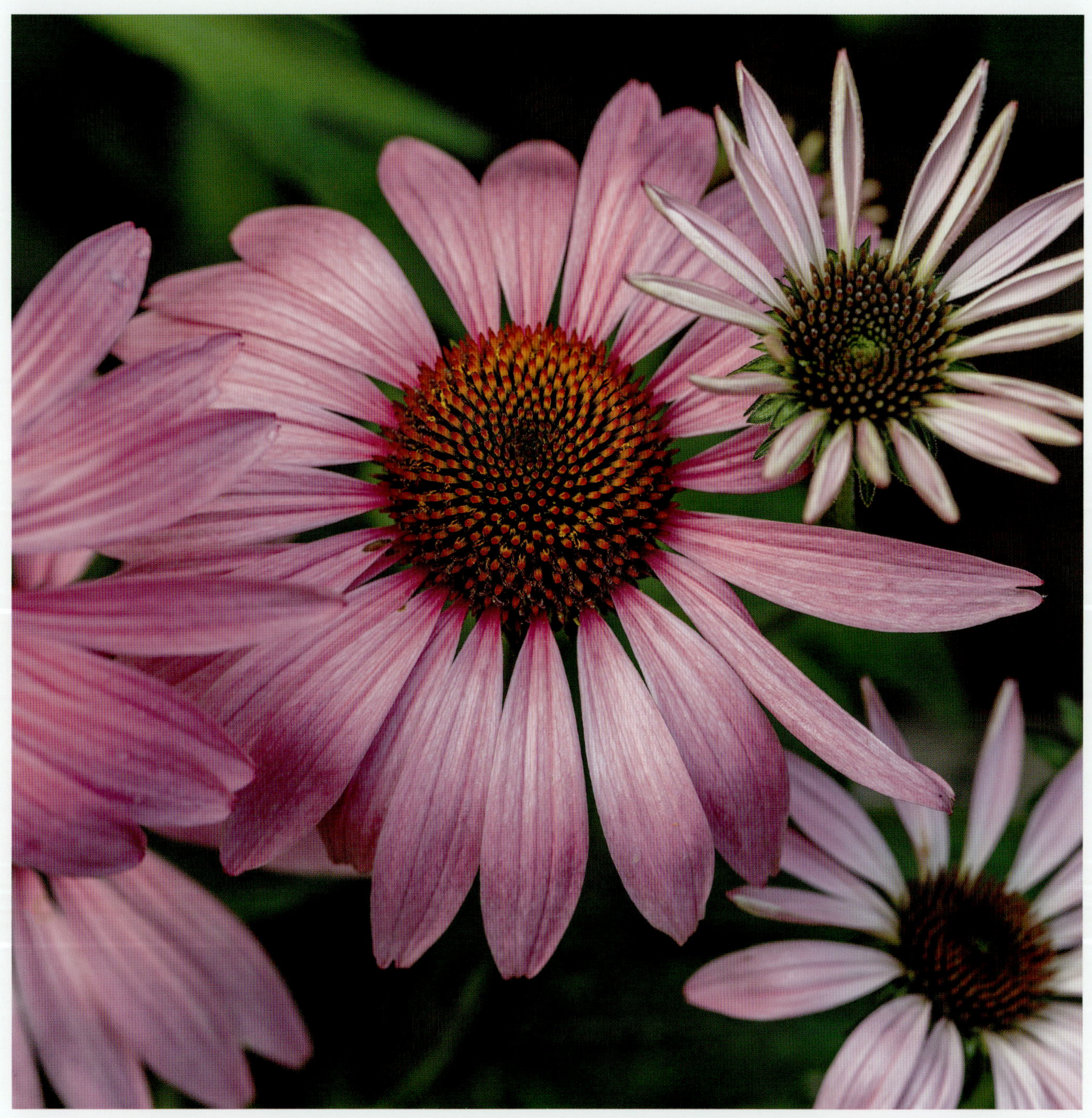

Purple coneflowers—one of our largest and most colorful summer wildflowers

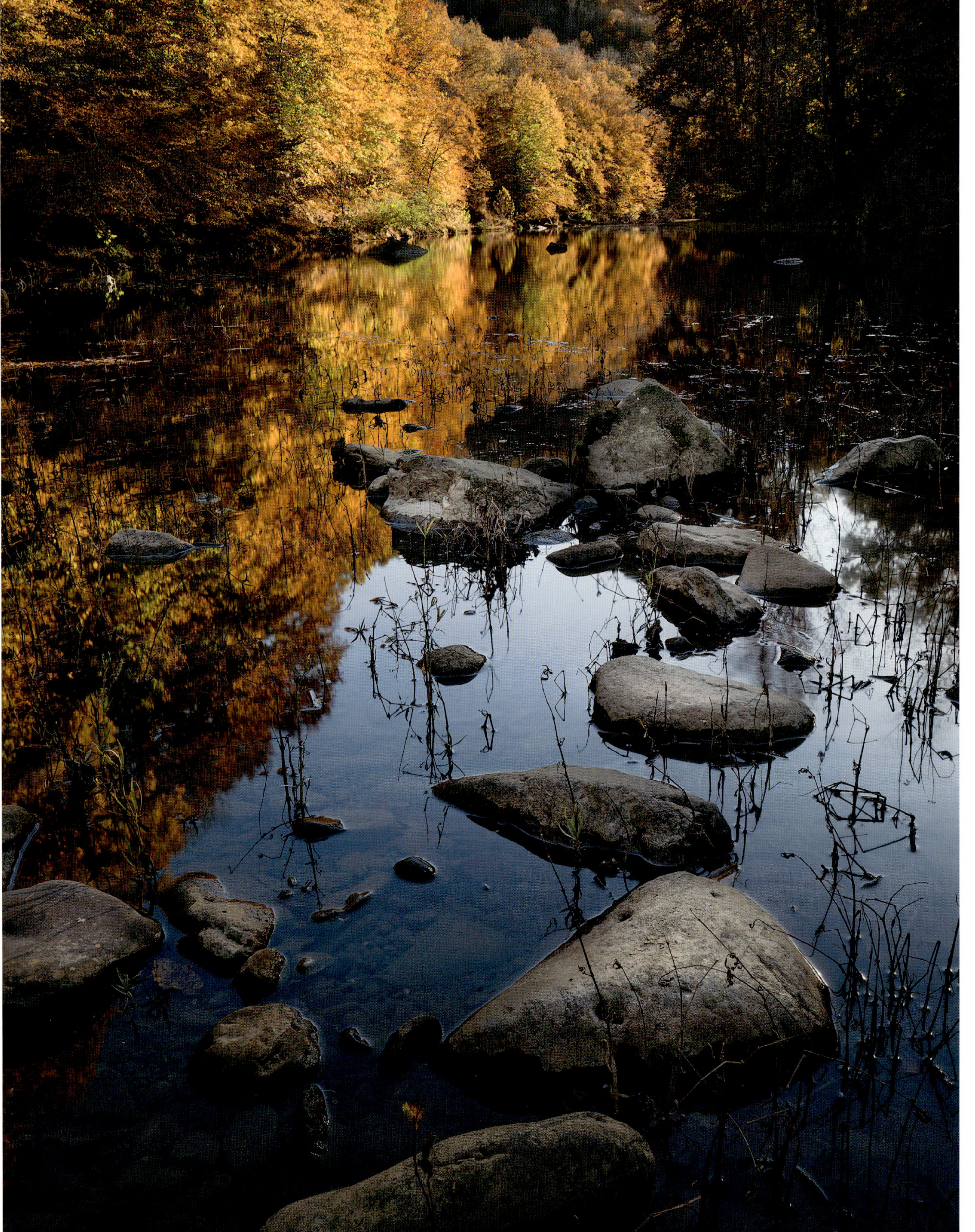

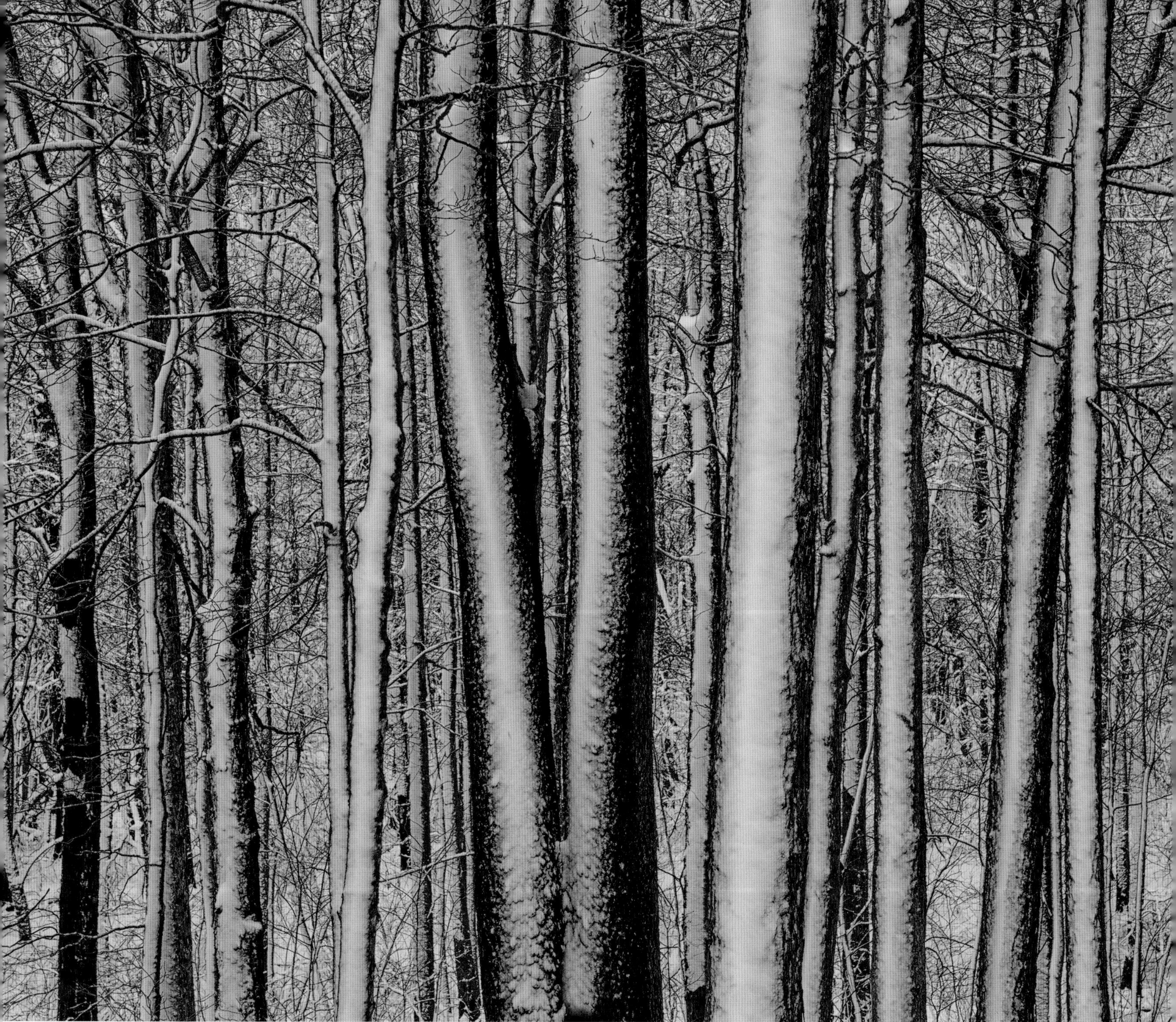

Wind-driven snow coats the forest

Boulders and fall color, Buffalo National River

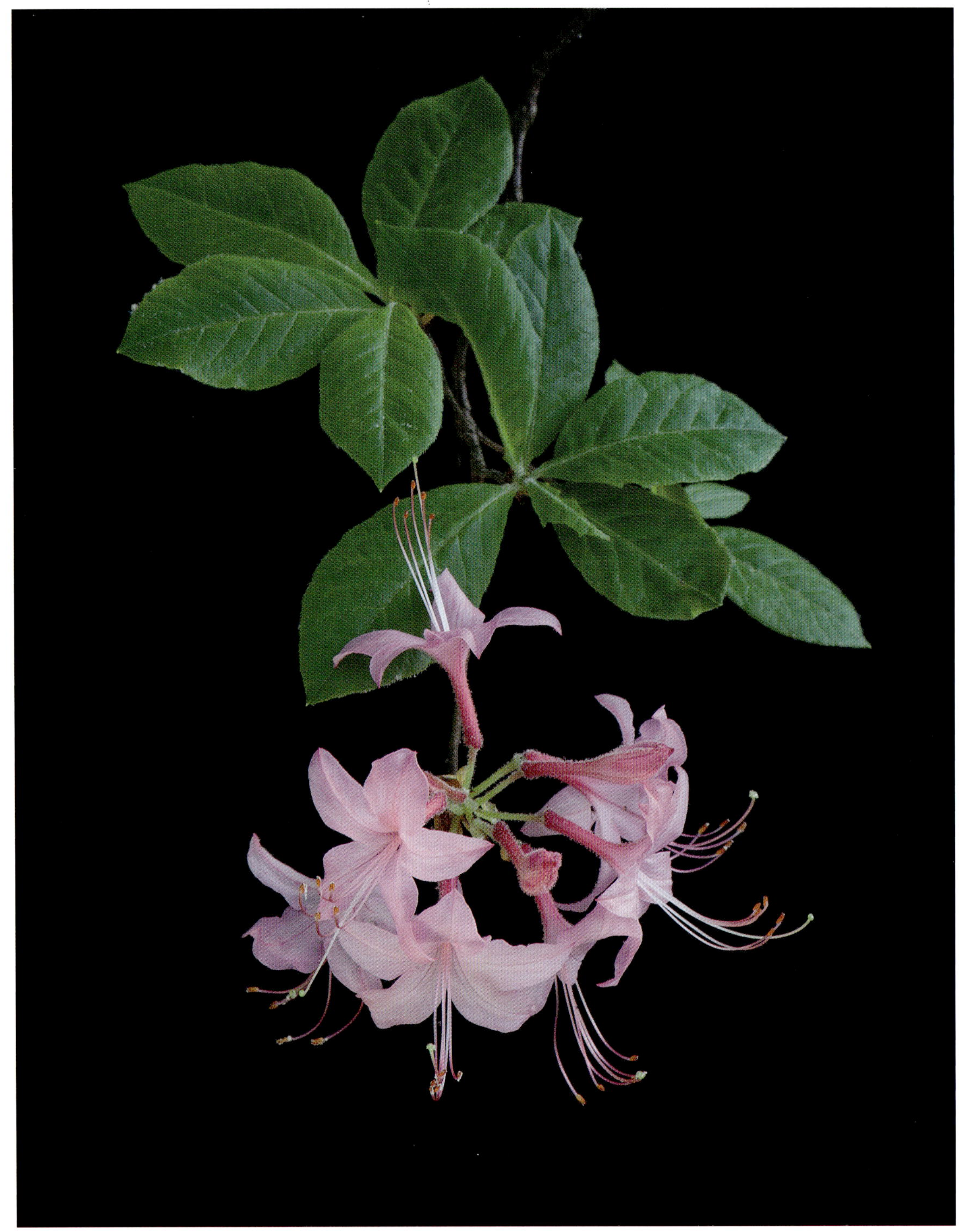

Wild mountain azaleas = wilderness perfume

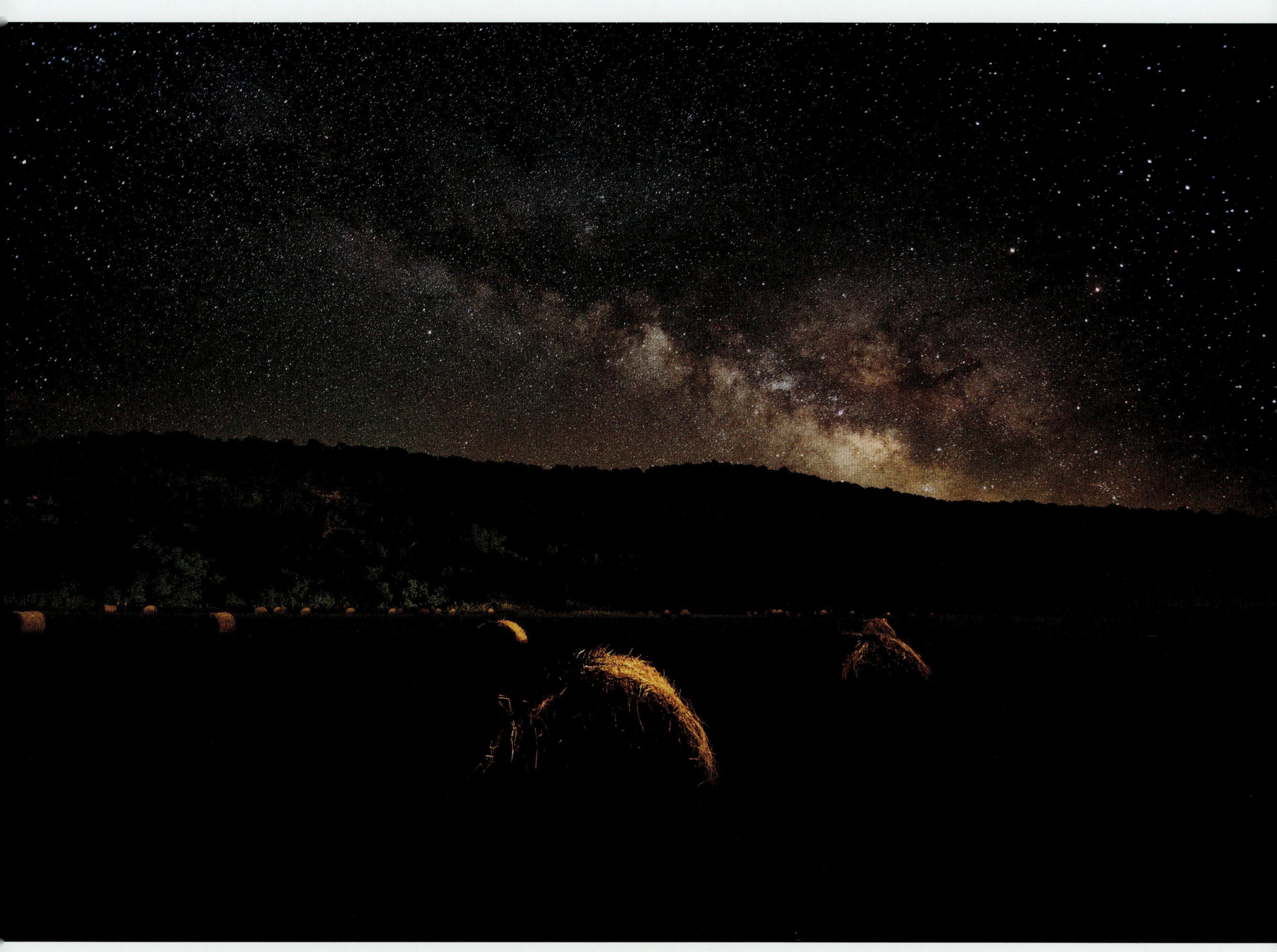

Fading moonlight lights up hay bales while the Milky Way rises, Boxley Valley

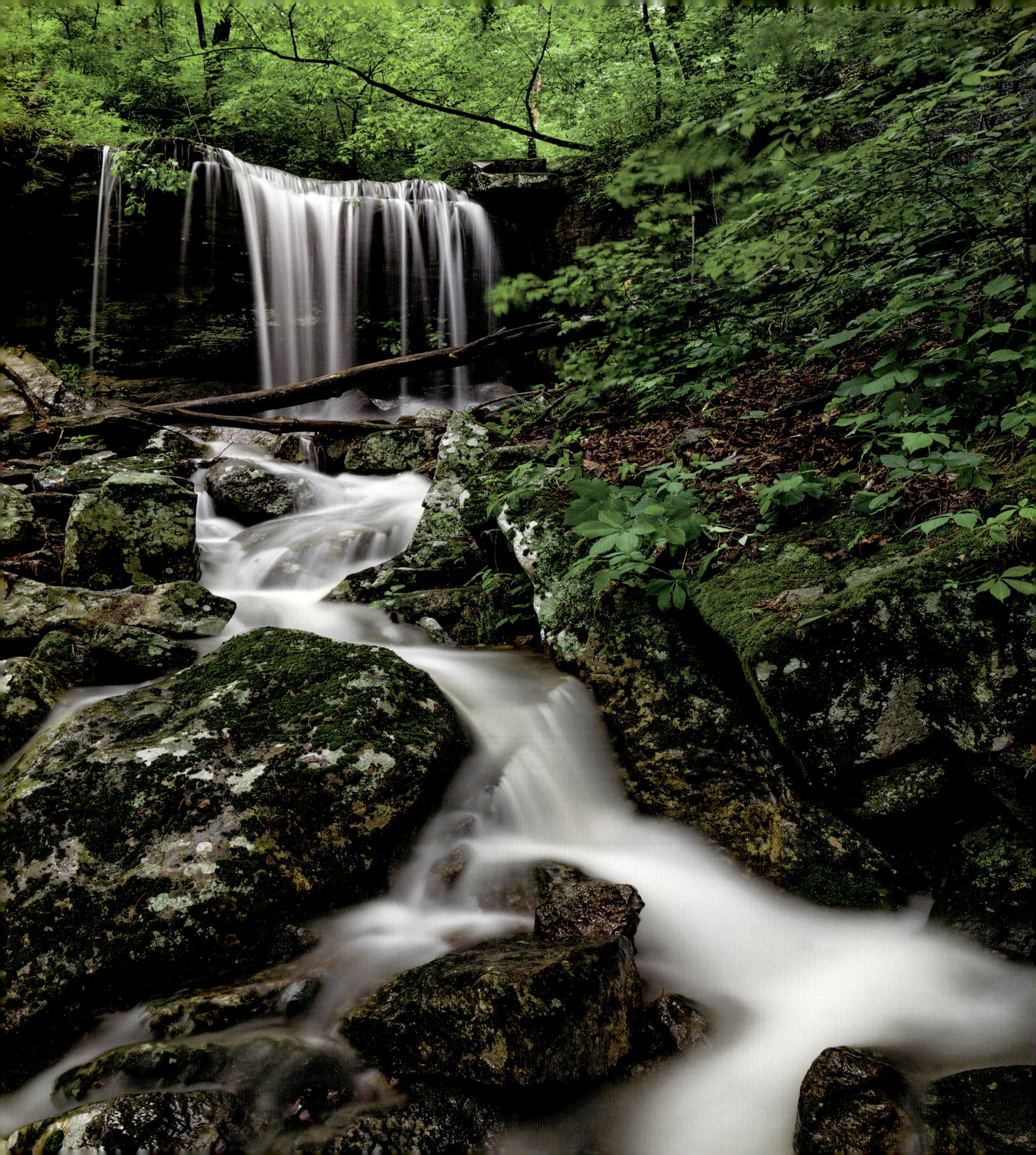

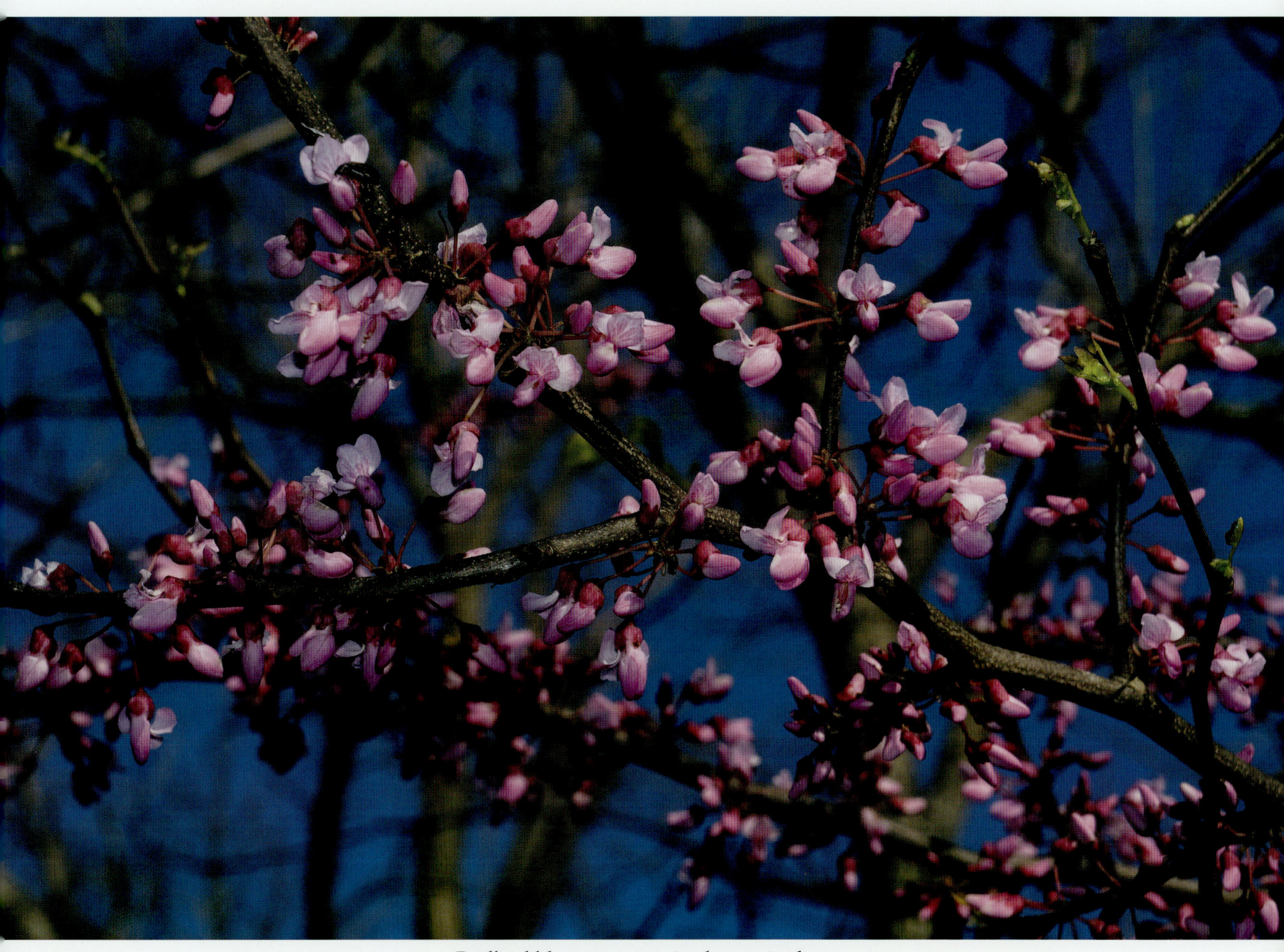

Redbud blossoms—*spring has arrived!*

Waterfall #2 in Waterfall Hollow along the Ozark Highlands Trail, Ozark National Forest

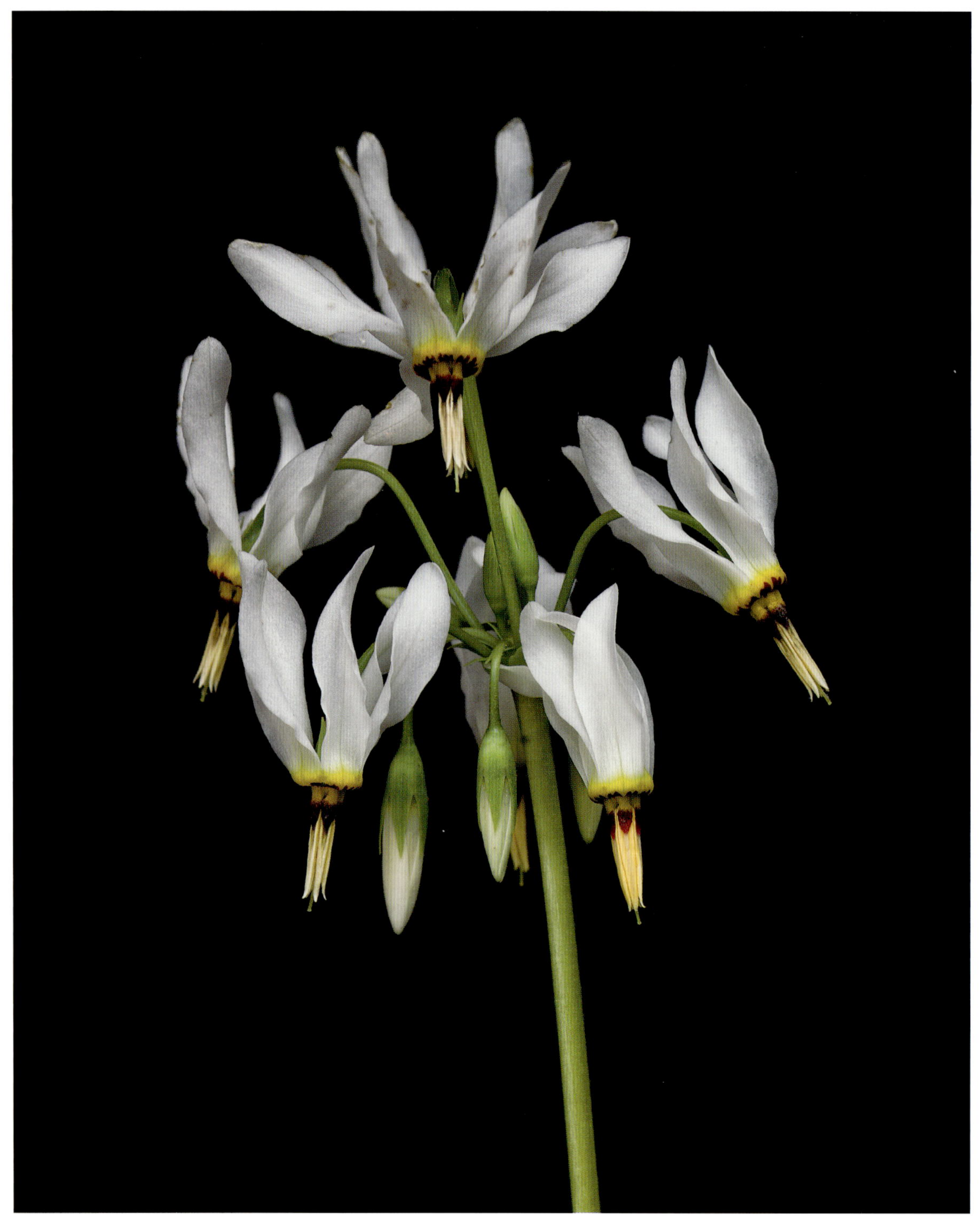

Shooting star wildflowers will shake with the slightest breeze

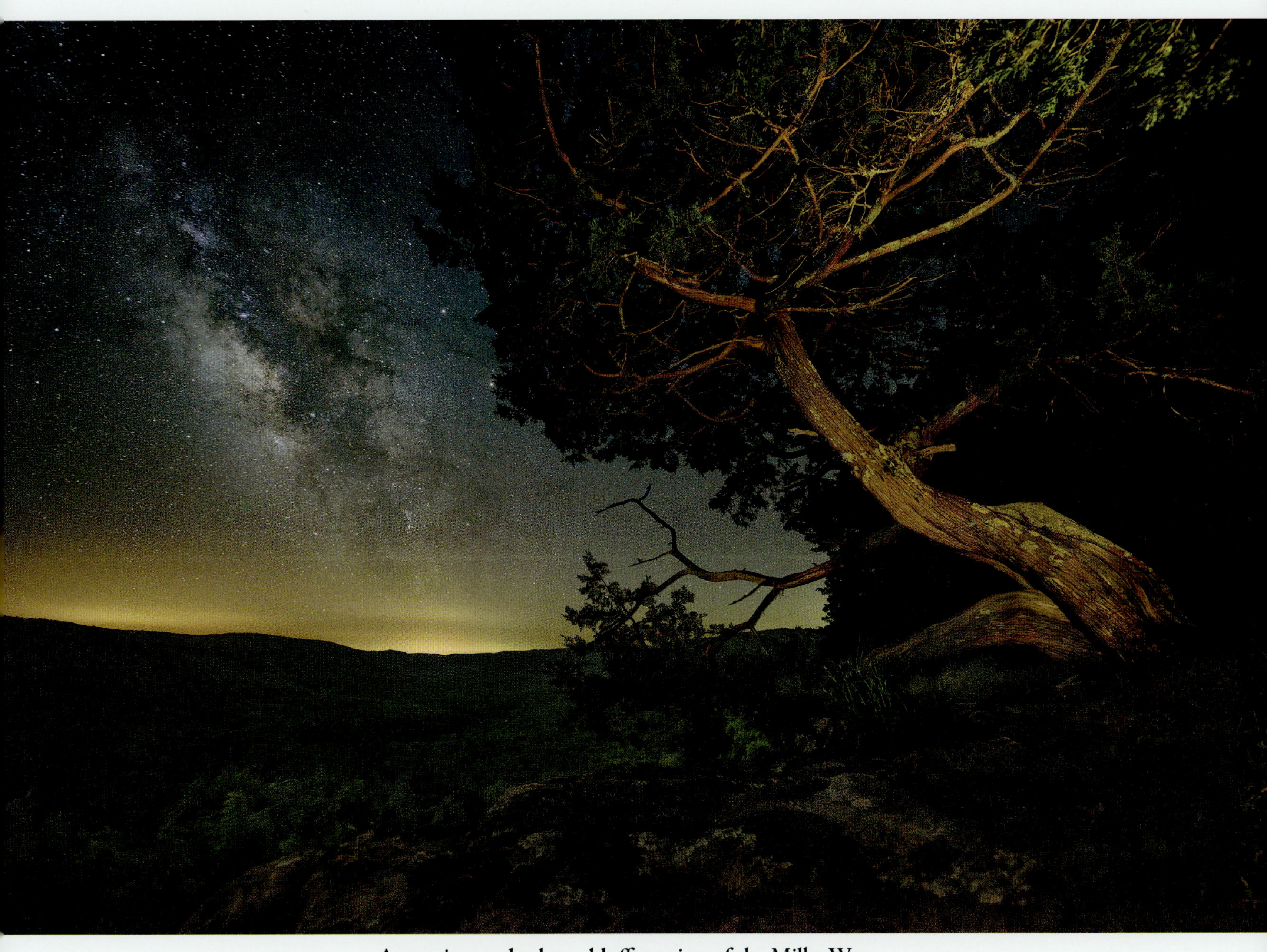

An ancient cedar has a blufftop view of the Milky Way

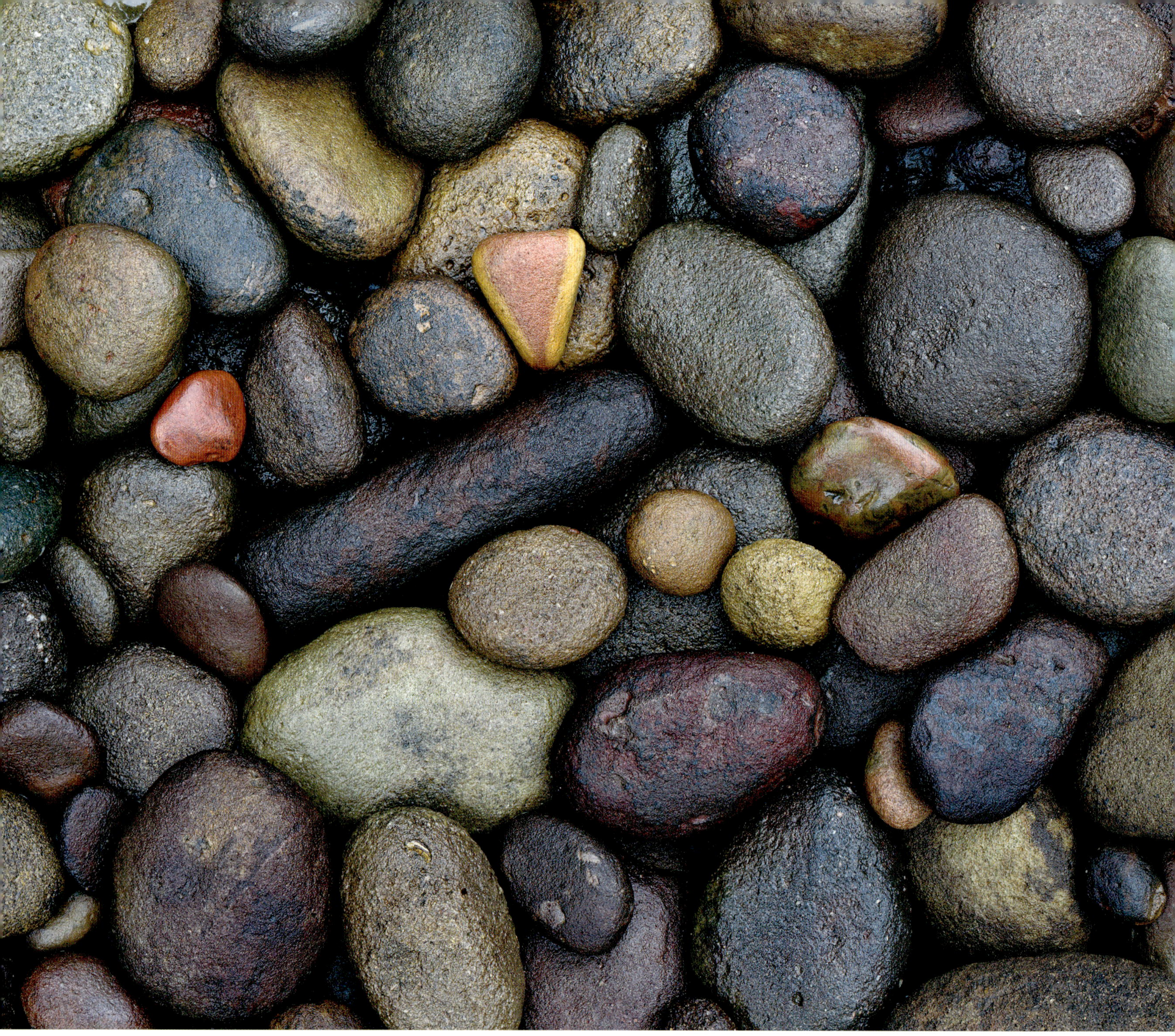

Polished river rocks, Big Piney Creek

Sometimes I will wait until after sunset to catch maple trees glowing in the fading light

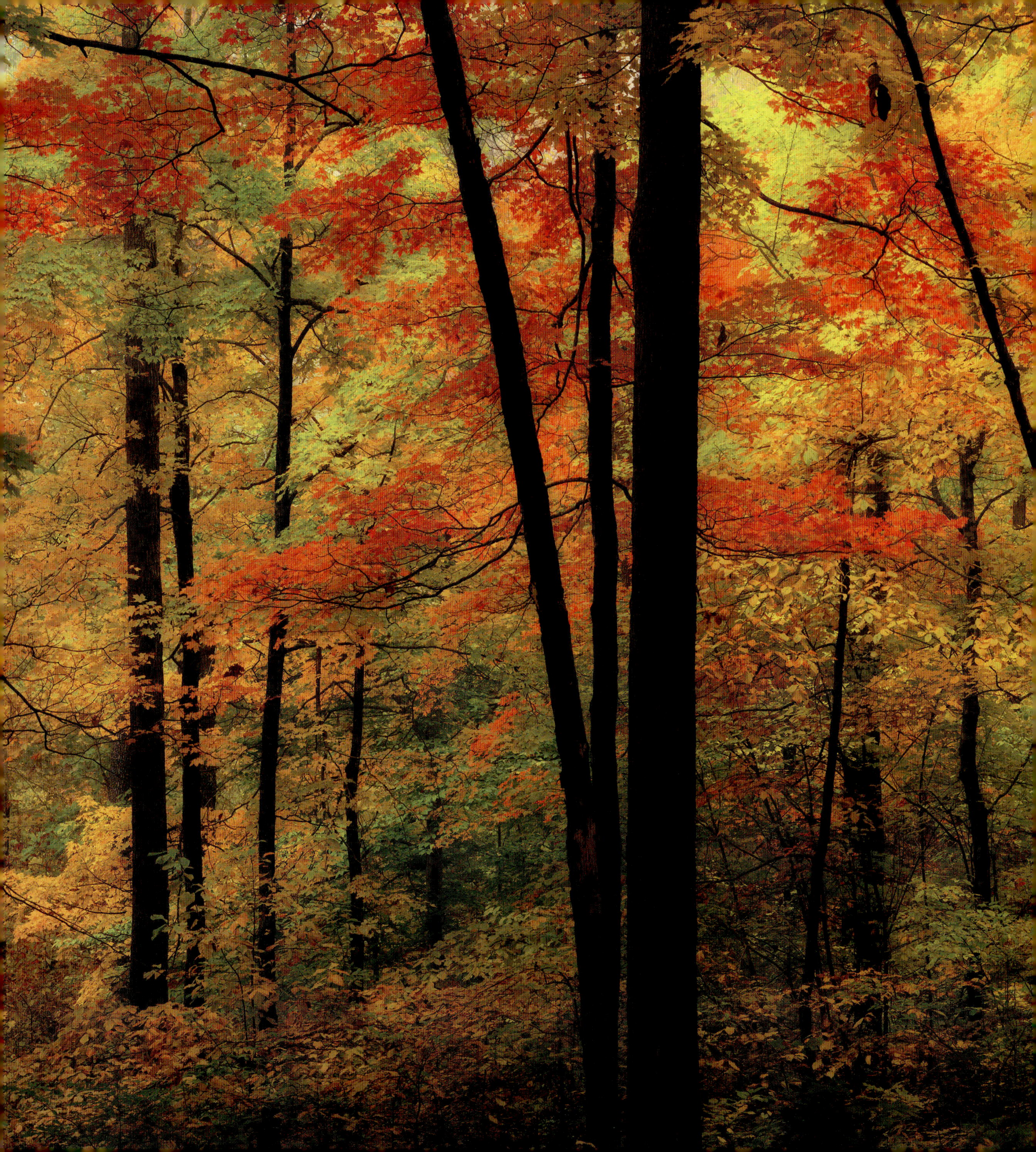

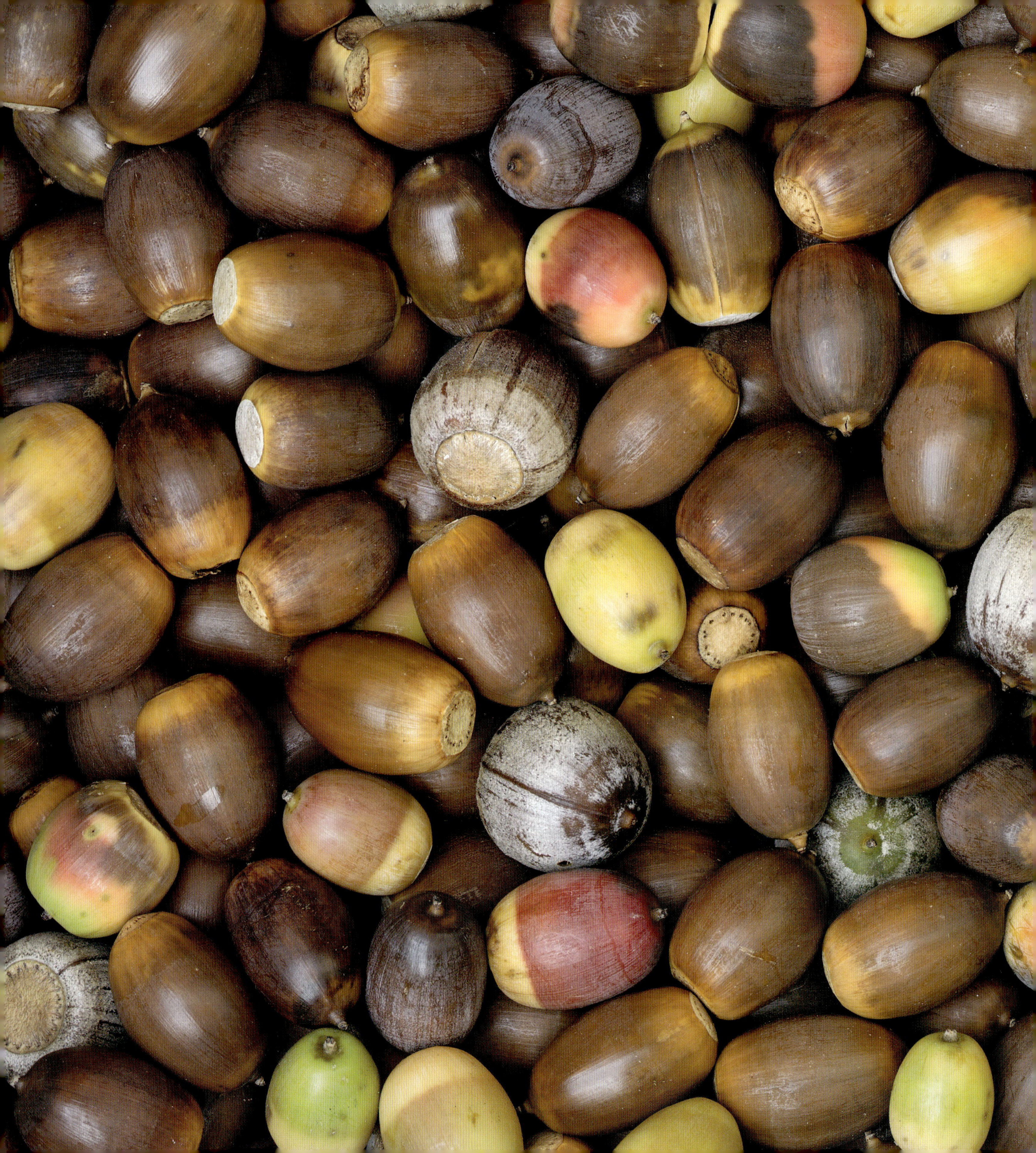

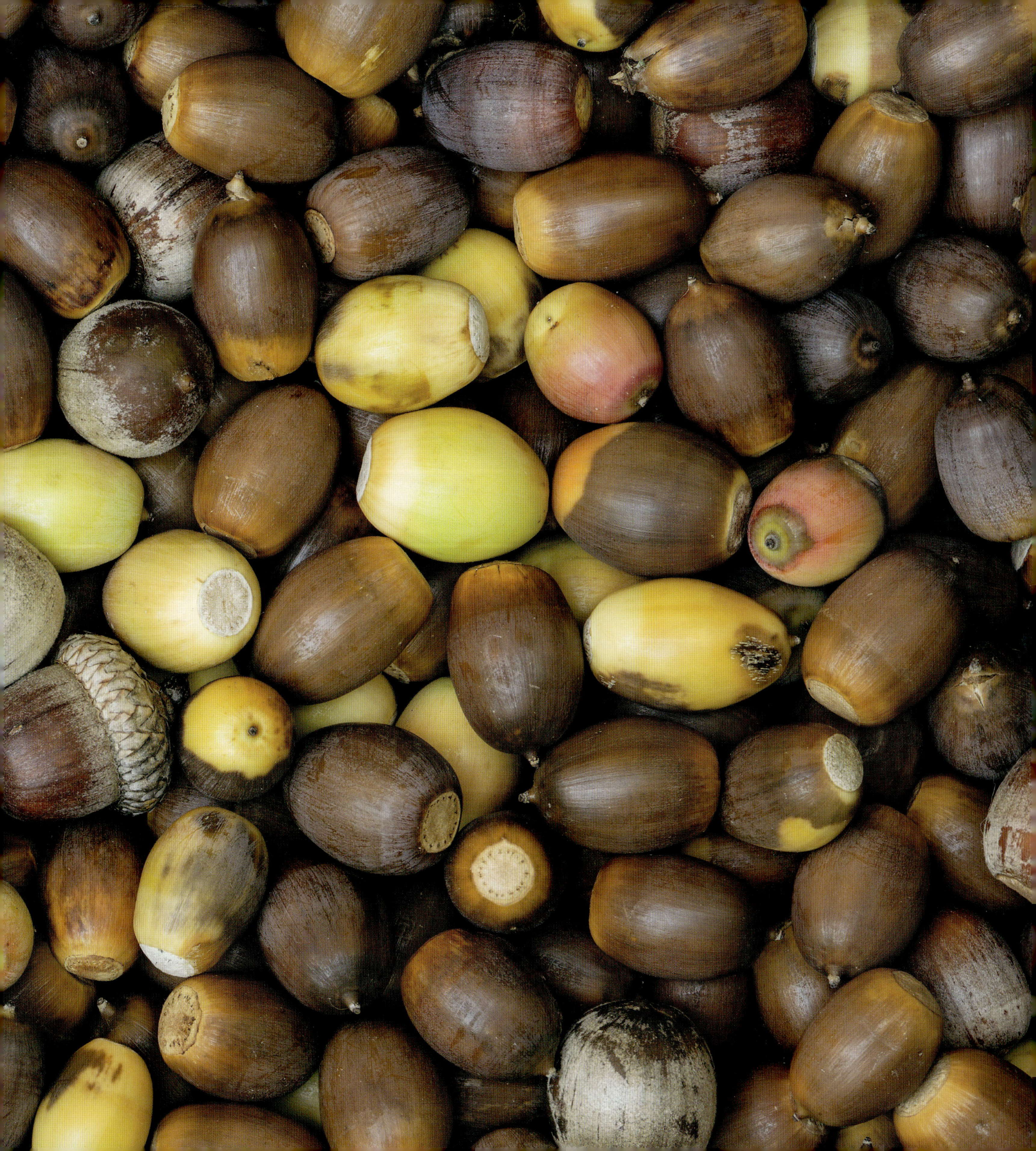

The original, wild trumpeter swans at the Mill Pond in Boxley Valley

An amazing event happened on Christmas day in 2005—a pair of wild trumpeter swans arrived in Boxley Valley (this photo of them was taken that first day). They aren't native to Arkansas, and at the time had only been seen in one other location (Magness Lake near Heber Springs). Swans mate for life, typically spend winters much farther south, then fly north to summer and have babies in Canada.

Large, graceful, and quite animated, the swans immediately drew the attention of anyone passing through Boxley—I spent hours photographing them and just watching. A couple of months later they left us for Canada. The following December they returned to the Mill Pond in Boxley, along with a brand new baby cygnet, so we had three swans that winter!

The next winter the trio brought back another adult pair of swans with them and we had five wild trumpeter swans for the winter—WOW! They liked the Mill Pond because it is spring fed and doesn't freeze in the winter, plus there is a smorgasbord of treats for them growing at the bottom of the pond.

The five wild swans left to fly north later that winter and have never returned. That same year wildlife officials released a group of captive swans at the Mill Pond. These swans wore tall green bands on their necks with ID numbers so they could be identified and tracked if someone reported them at another location. The idea was that they too would fly north for the summer and later return with friends to winter in Arkansas and increase the local population. That pattern never developed and all the swans but one eventually disappeared—he maintains a solitary life in Boxley.

Each year around Christmas I make special trips to the Mill Pond in hopes of finding new wild swans there—keep your eyes out, they may come back this winter...

A heavy acorn crop made it a great year for squirrels! (previous pages)

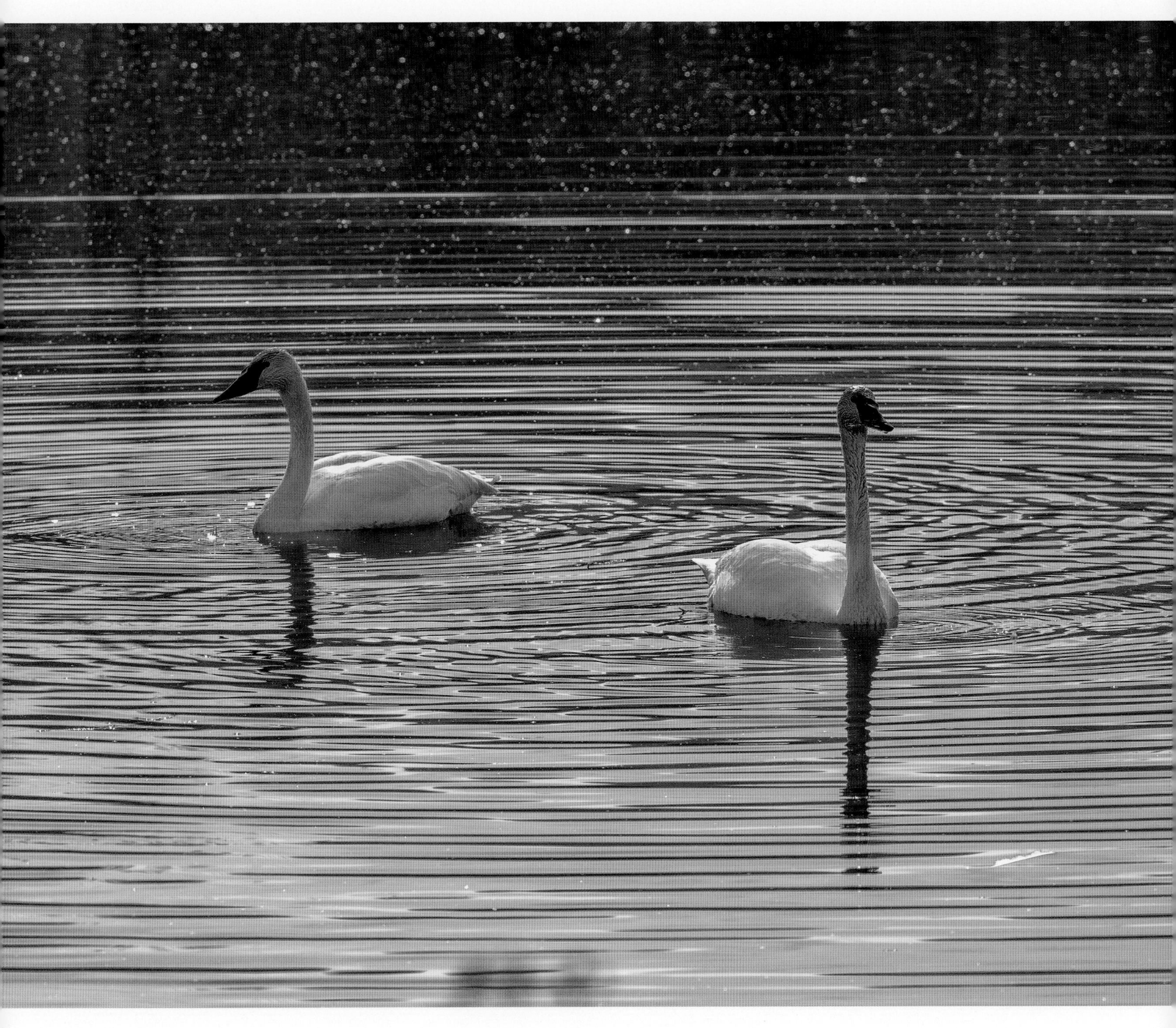

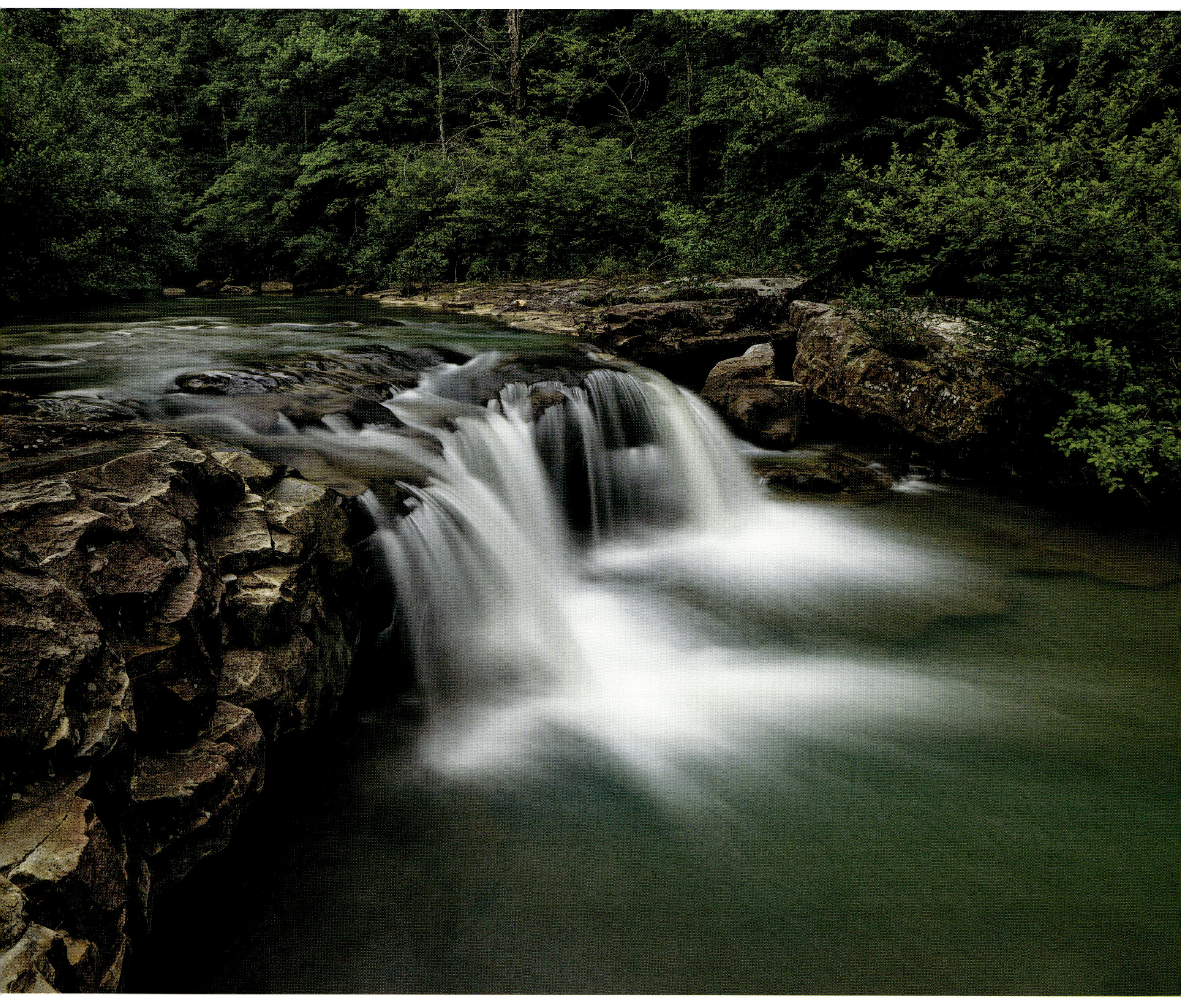

Blue Hole Falls on the Little Mulberry River

Limestone bluffs and evening water, Buffalo National River

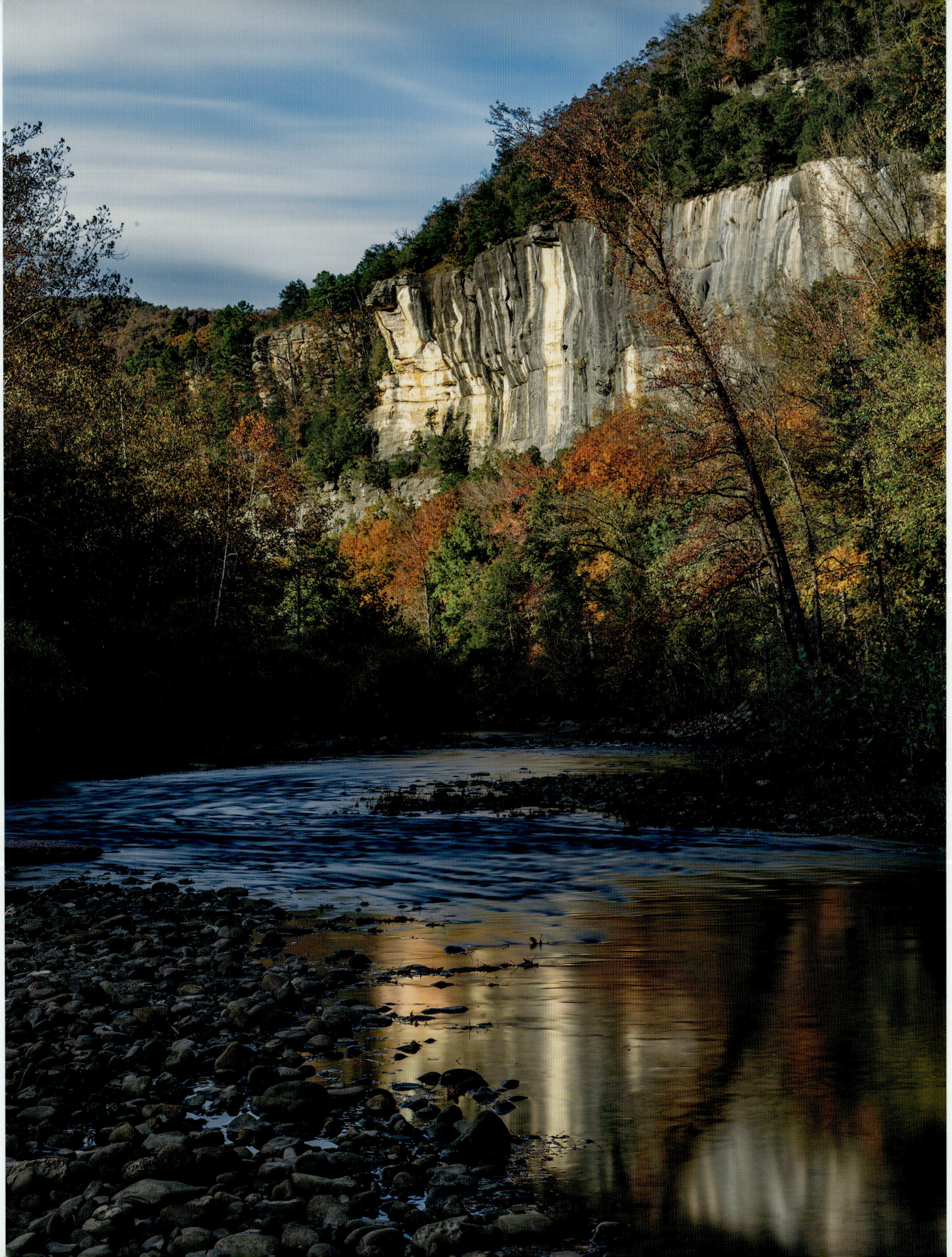

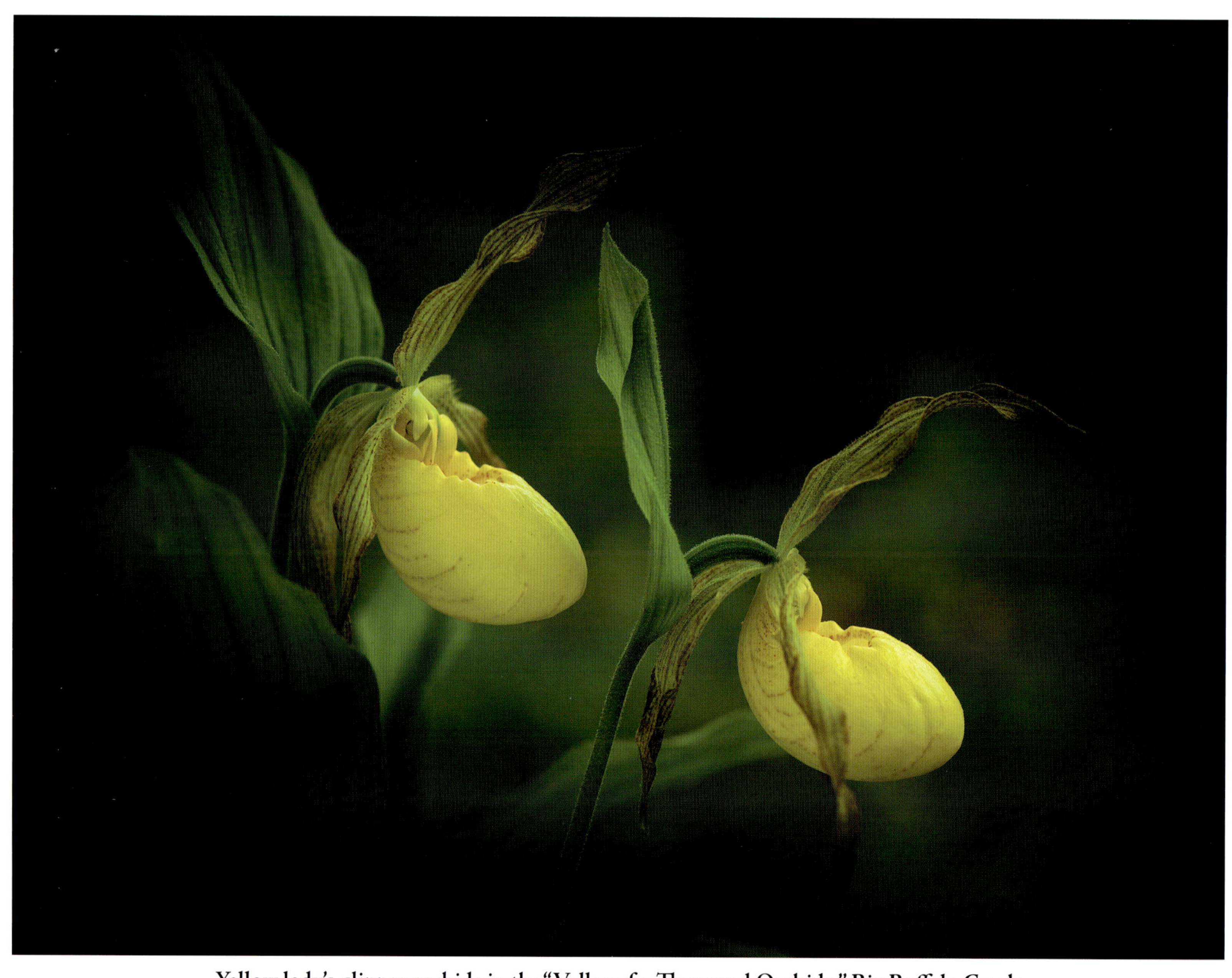

Yellow lady's-slipper orchids in the "Valley of a Thousand Orchids," Big Buffalo Creek

Oops—someone forgot to haul in the hay and it all got snowed on!

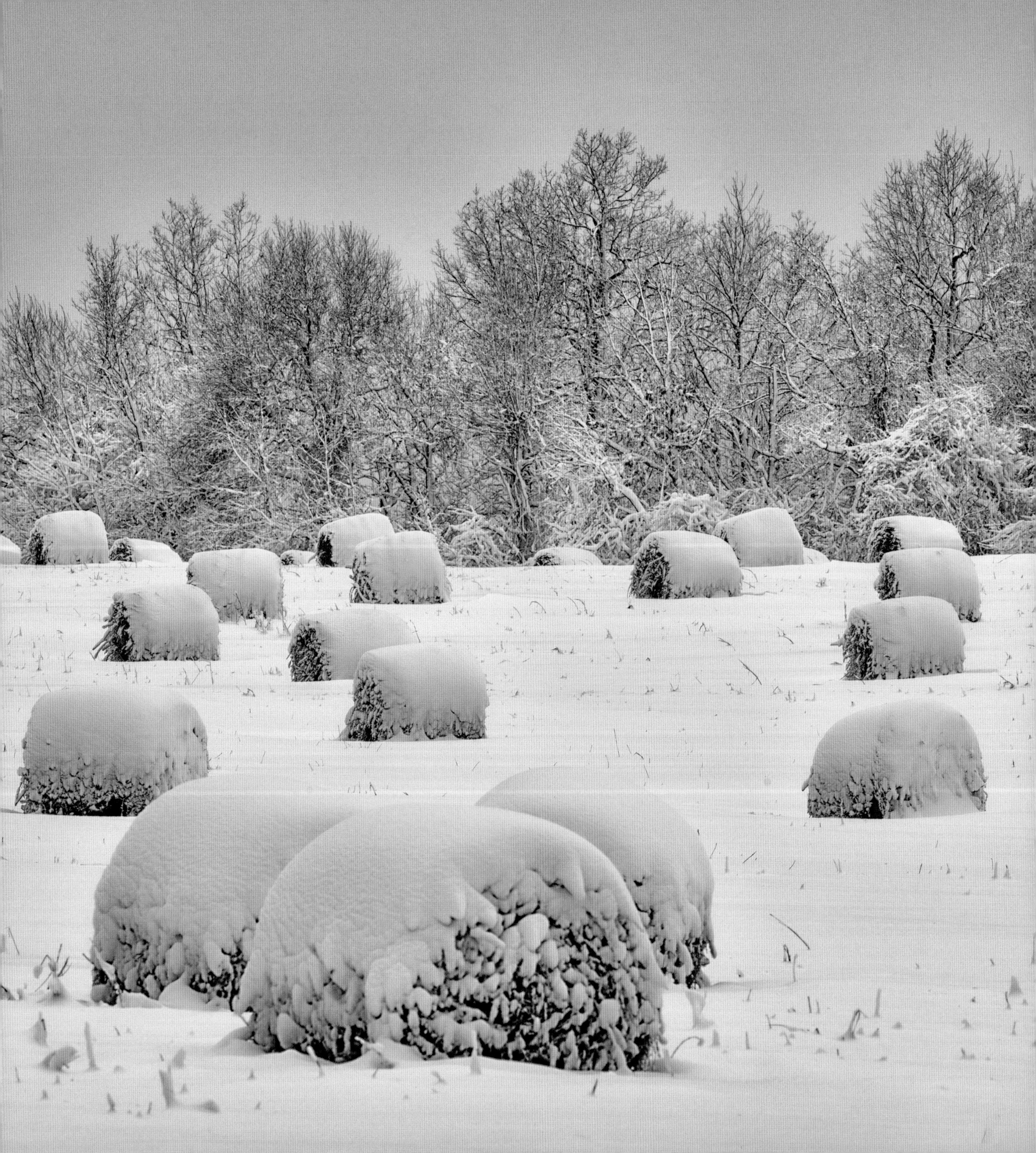

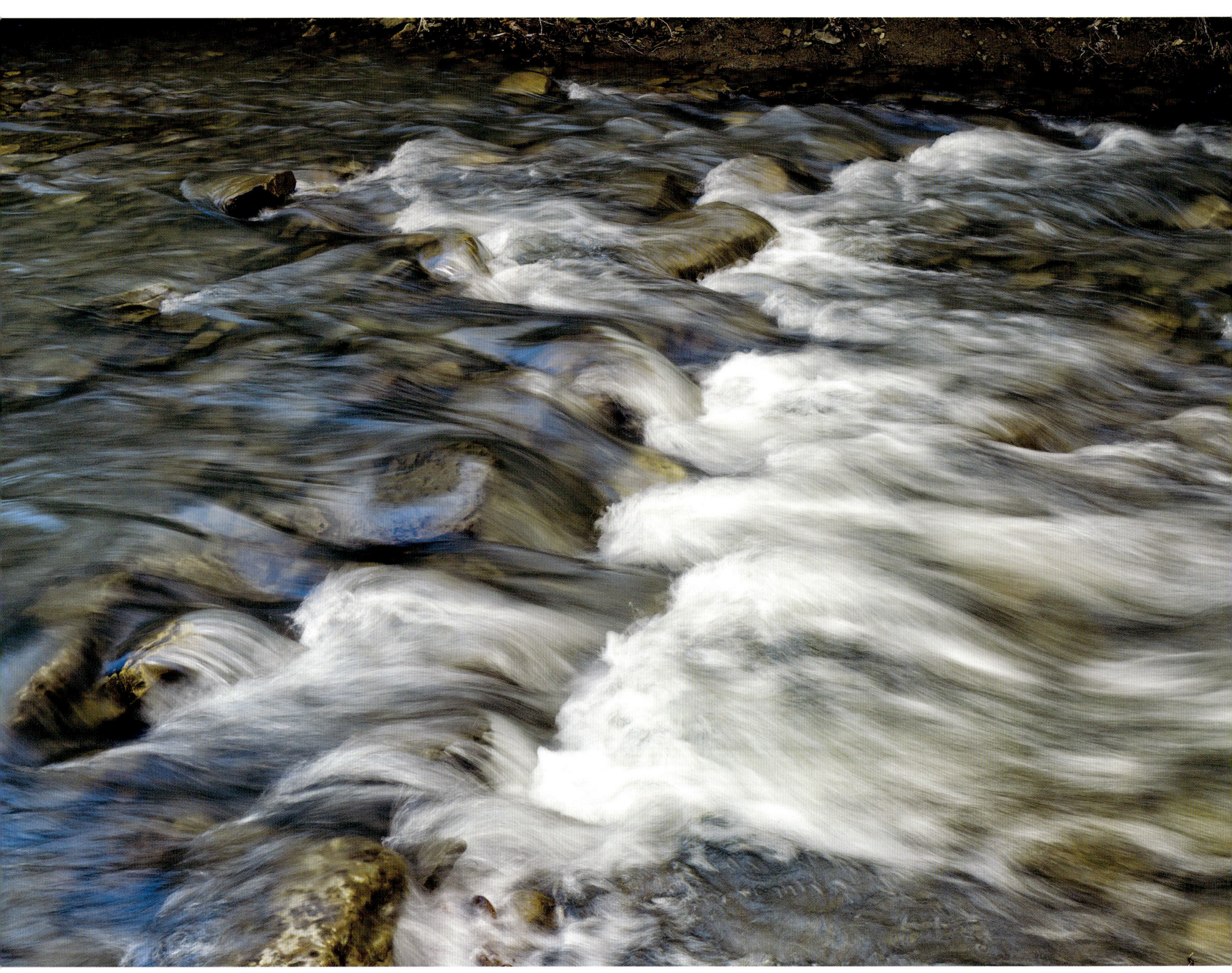

In the headwaters area of the Buffalo River, the old maps call this Big Buffalo Creek

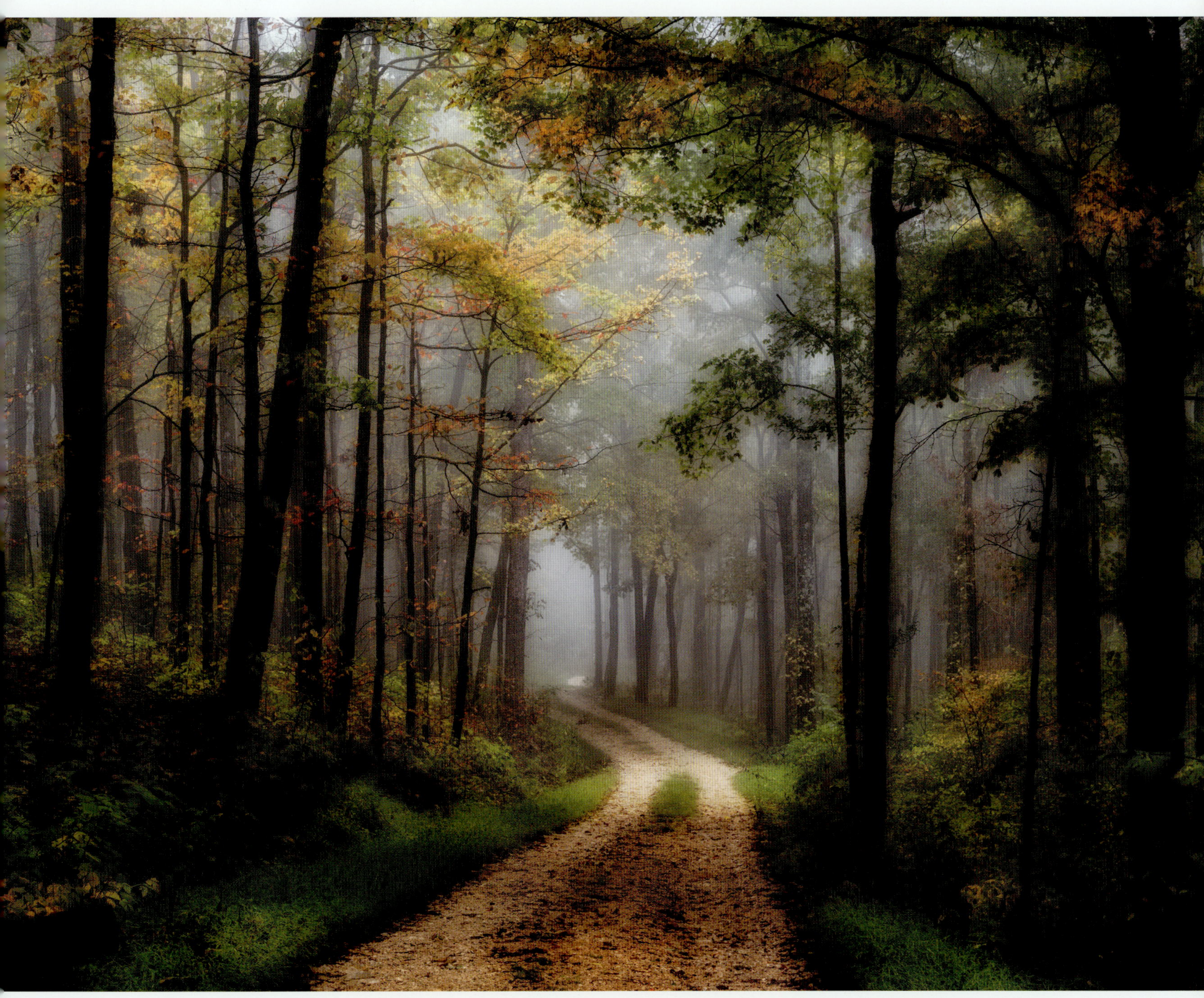

A foggy fall morning along the driveway—our log cabin is just around the corner through those trees

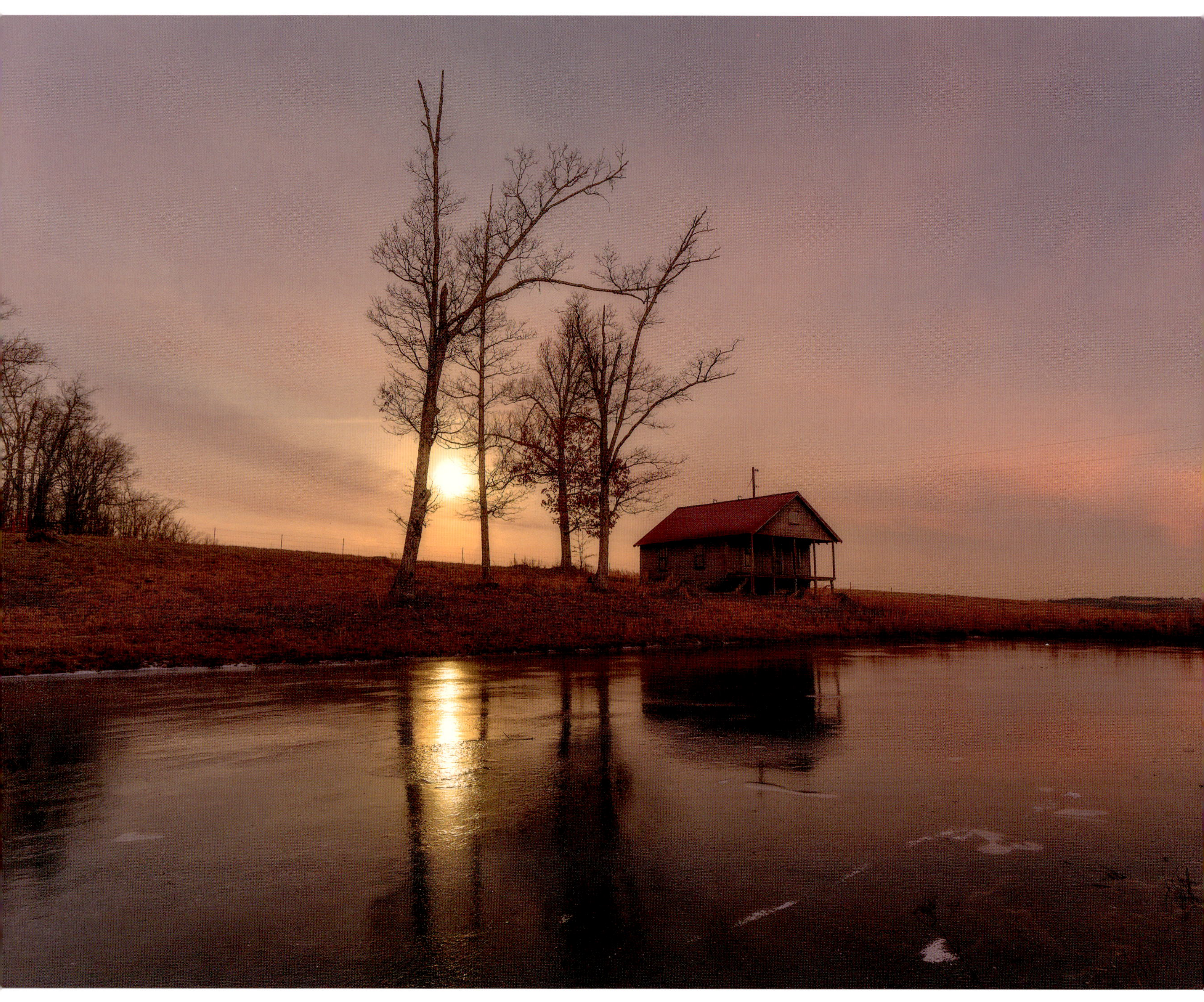

And icy moonset along Cave Mountain Road (ice on the frozen pond was not thick enough to walk on—I tried)

Summer moonset, Tea Table Rocks, Ozark National Forest

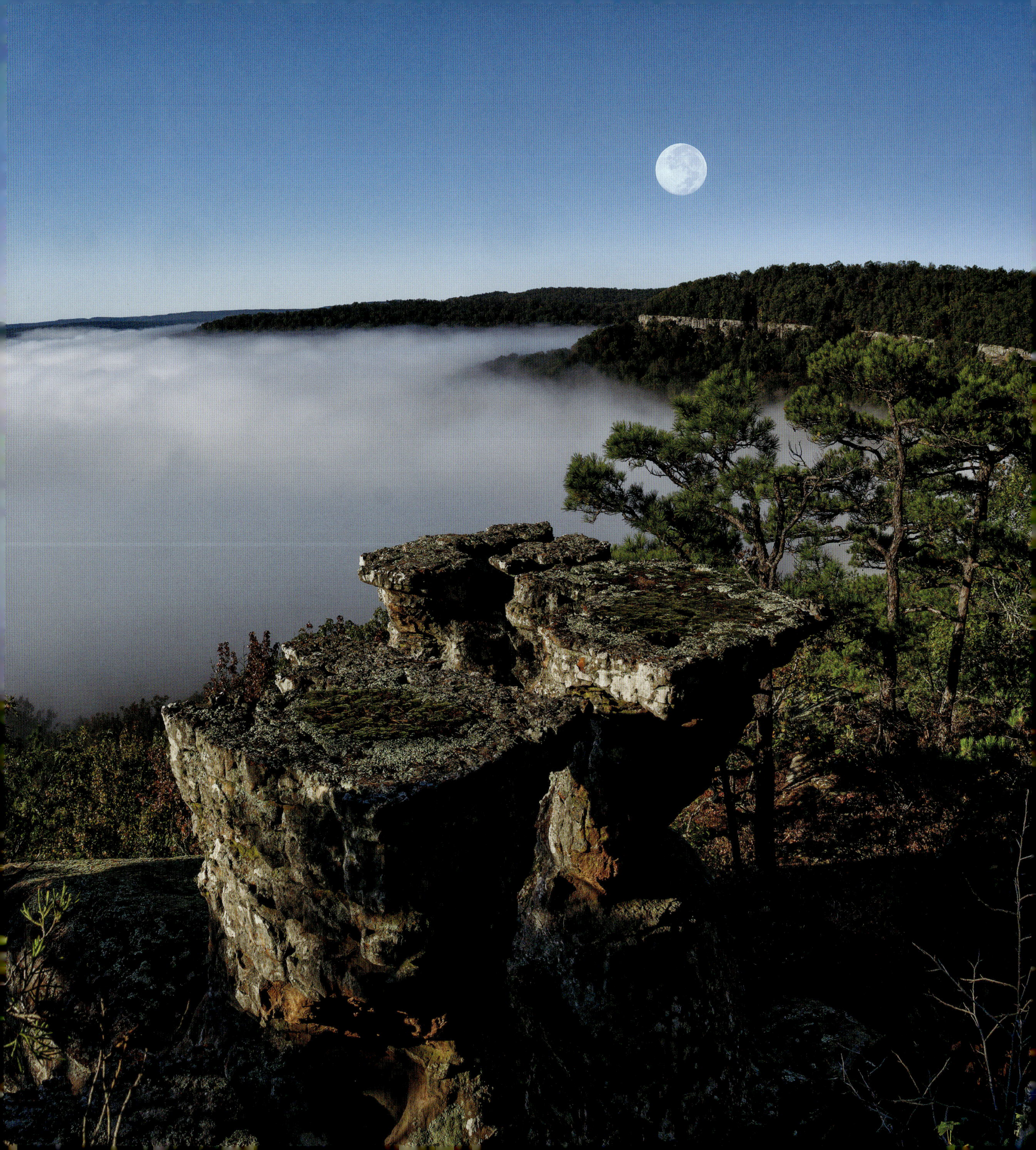

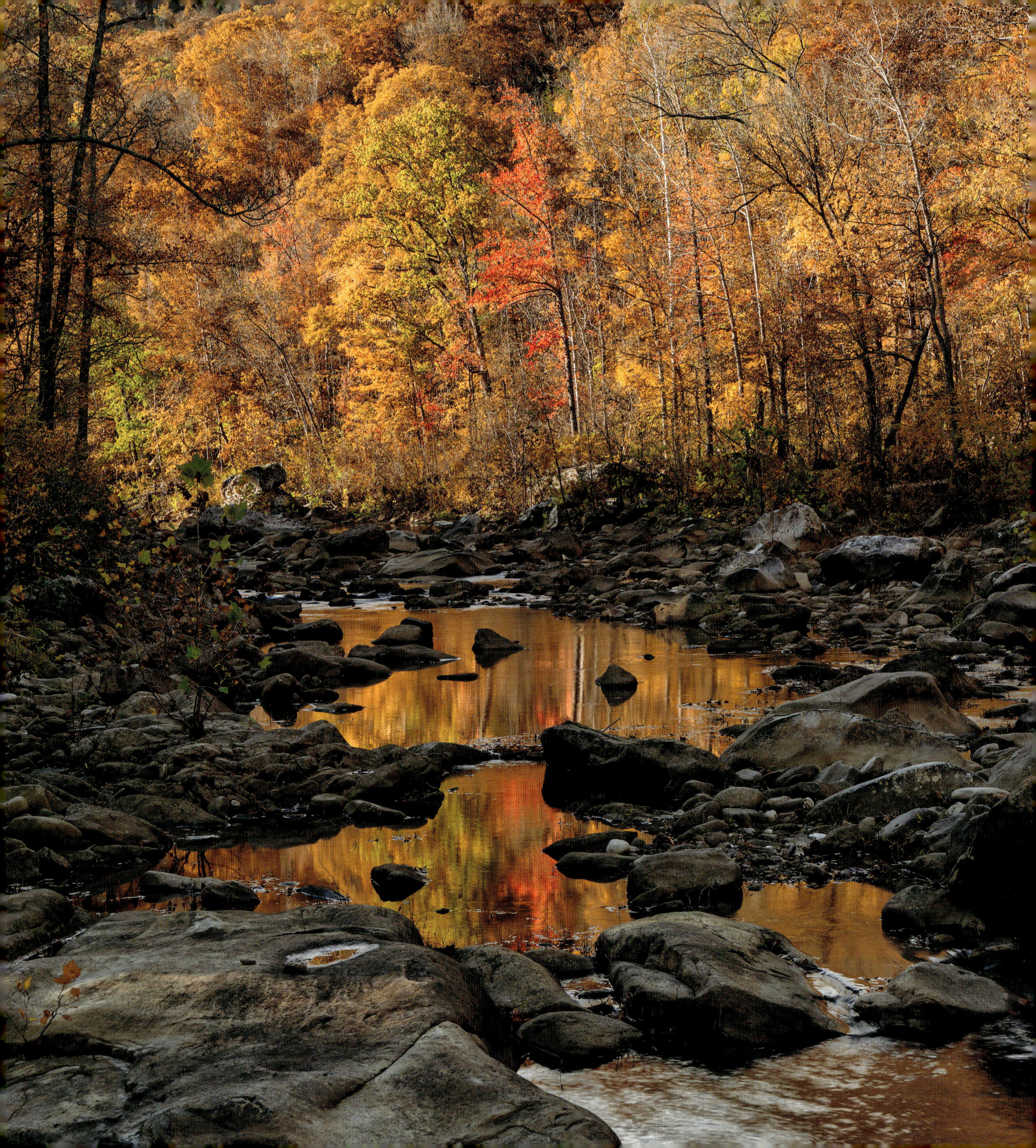

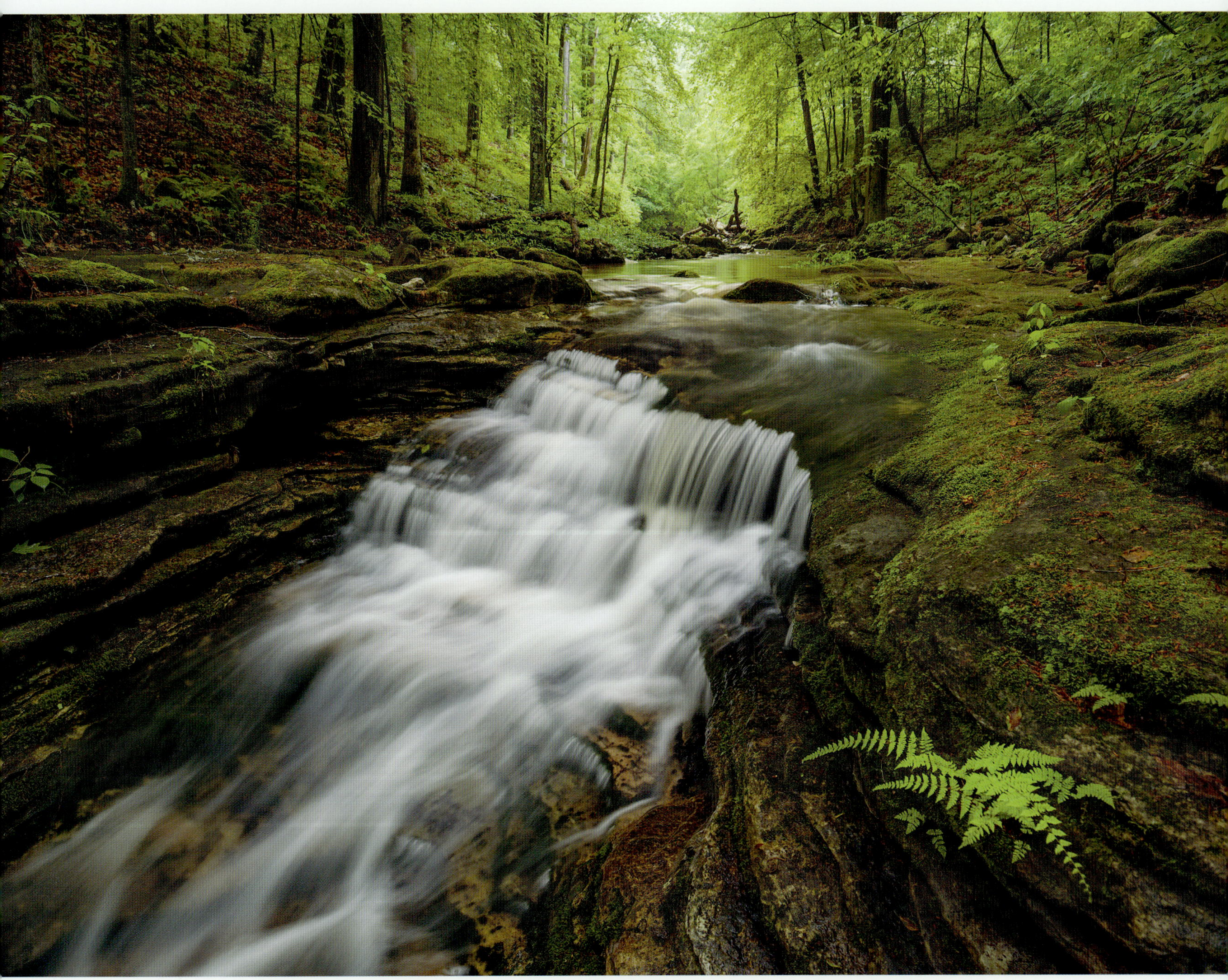

There's a little fern talking to the waterfall, Leatherwood Creek, Buffalo National River

Fall color along the Buffalo National River

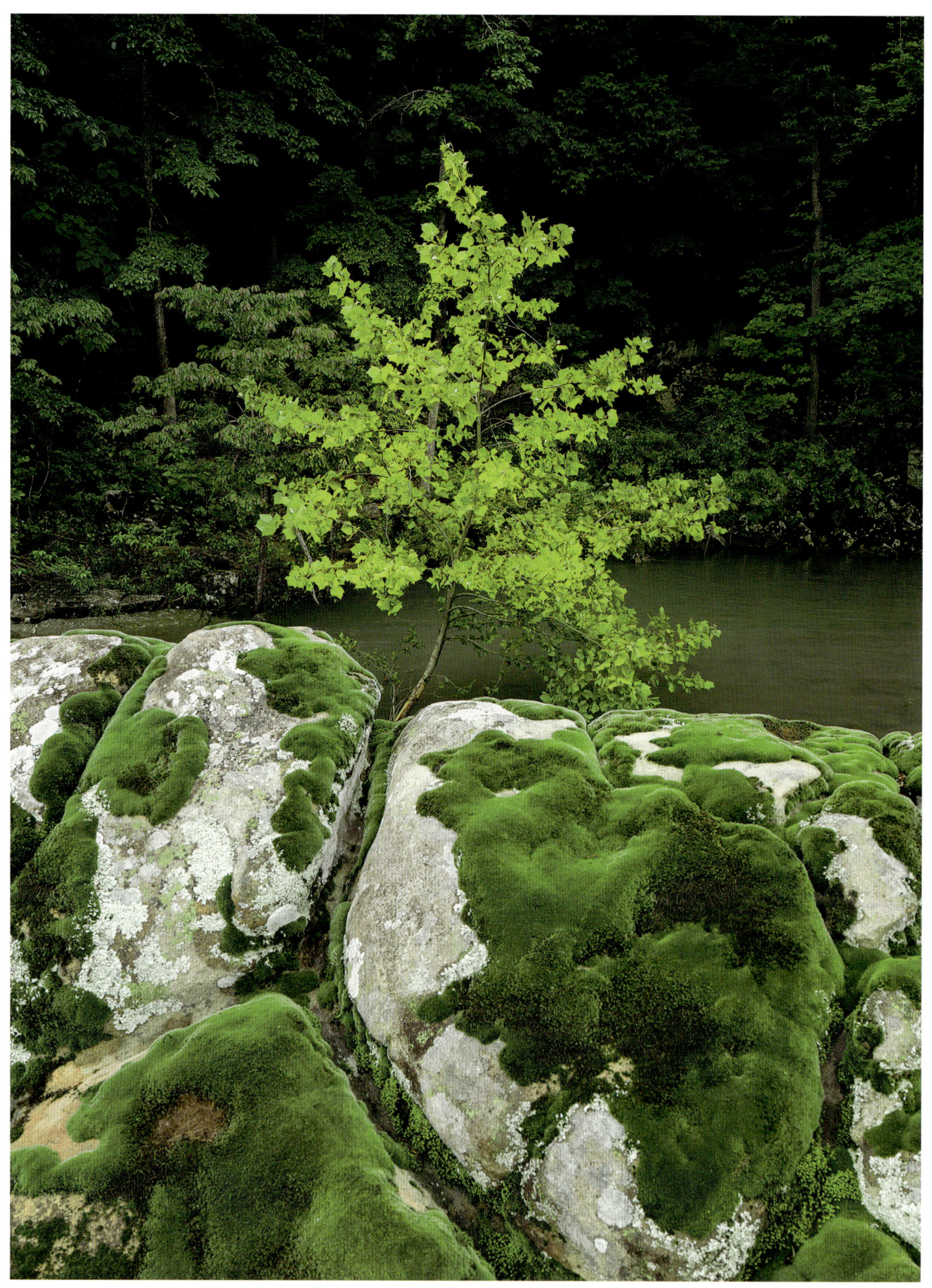

Young sycamore tree and sandstone boulder, Big Piney Creek

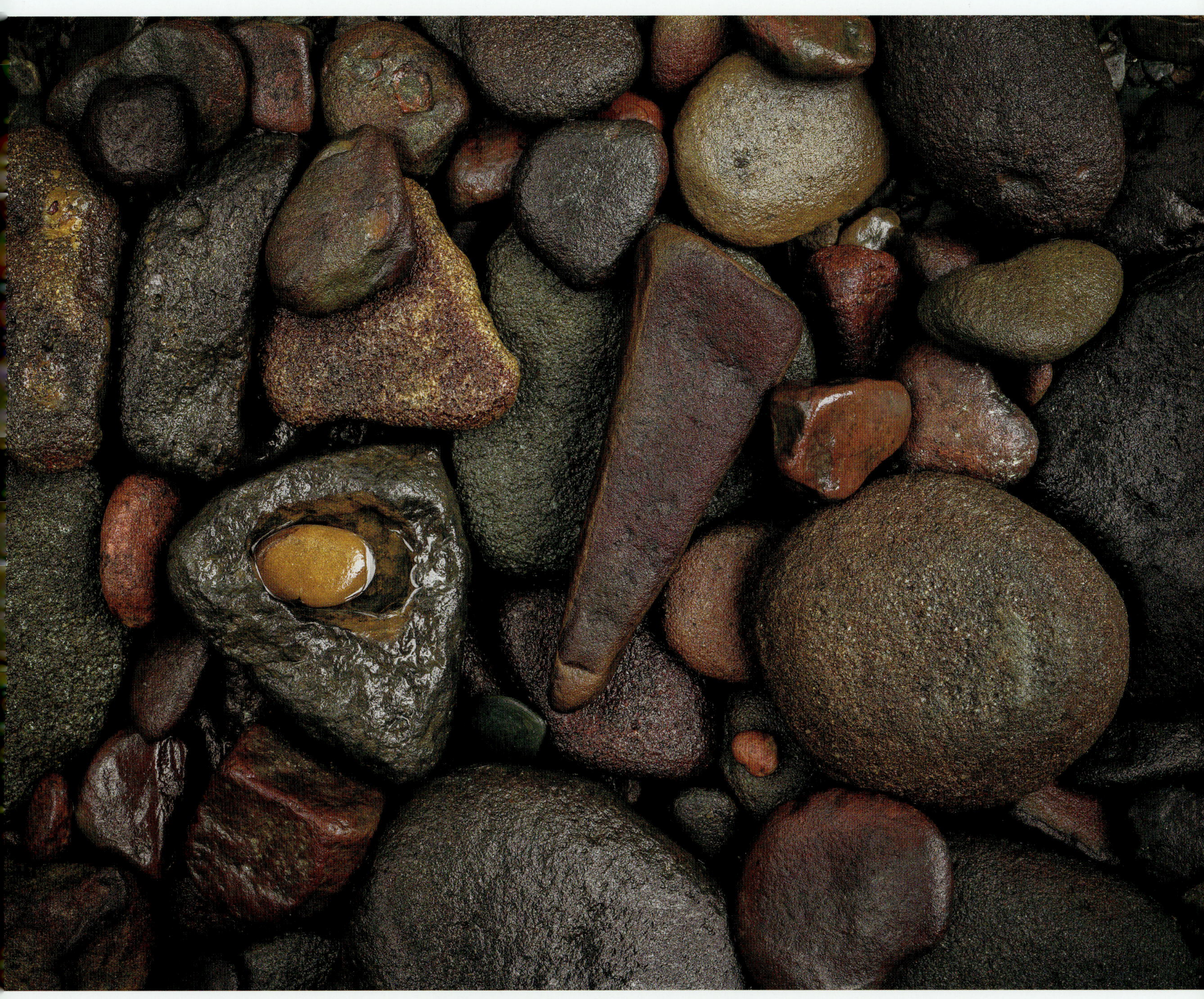

Polished river rocks, Mulberry River

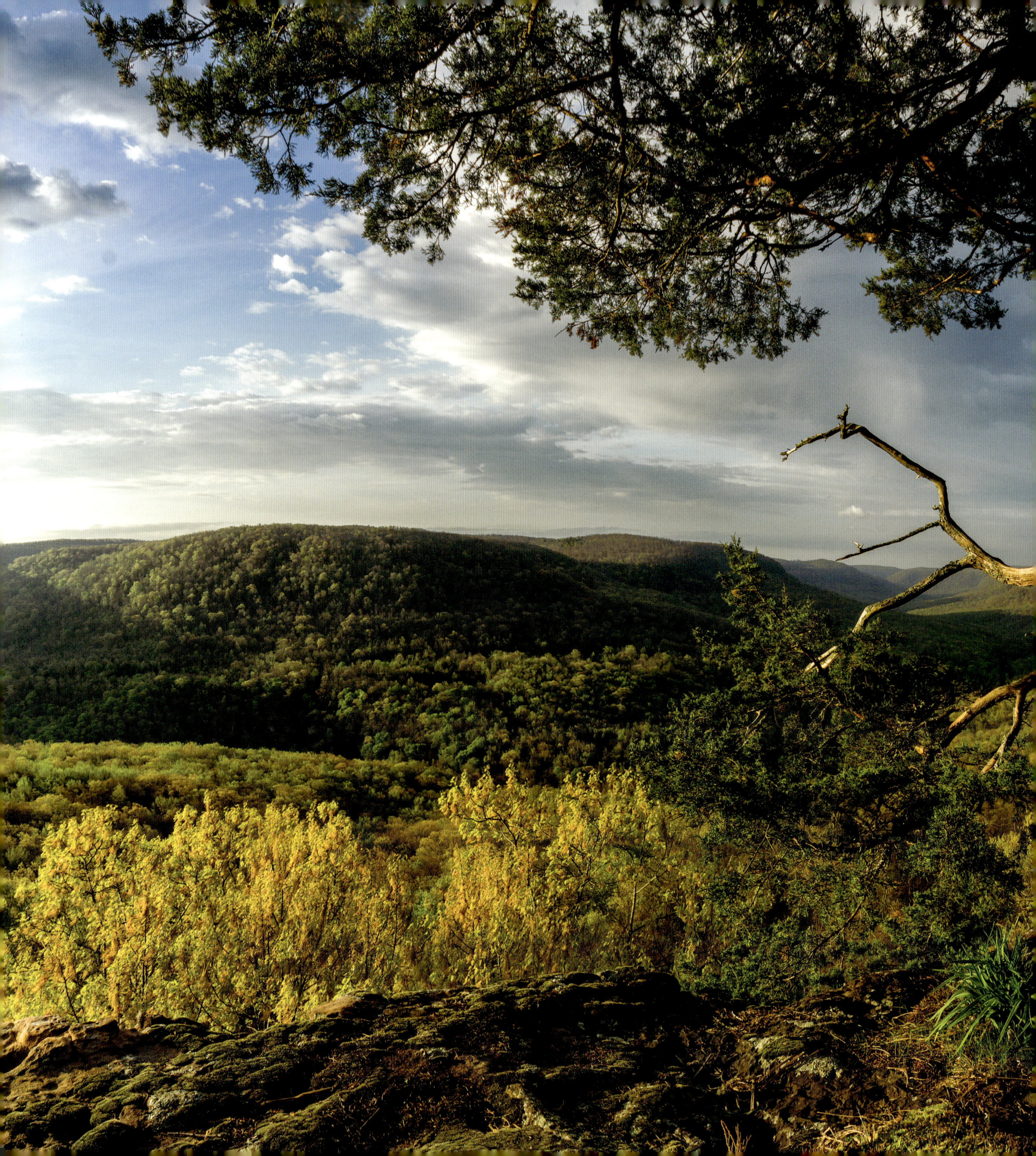

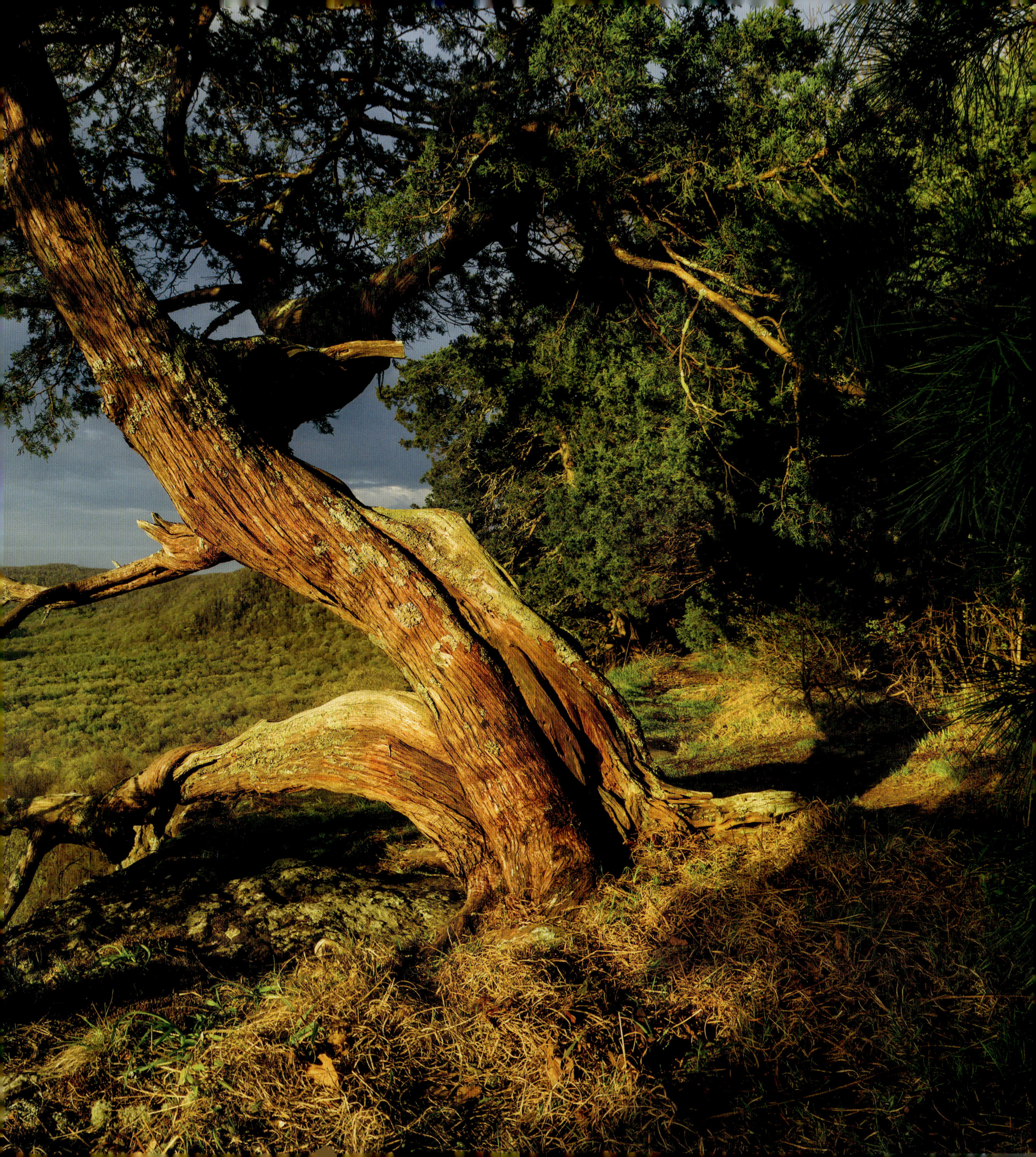

Afternoon clouds from the back deck of our Cloudland cabin

Needless to say, we love clouds at Cloudland! We can see 180 degrees from the back of our cabin looking south. We get a lot of weather systems that arrive from Oklahoma and march across the scene, or boil up from Louisiana directly overhead like these clouds were doing. Sometimes we can see giant thunderheads 100 miles away.

There are a lot of lightning storms too. Amazing how much time one can spend just sitting and waiting for the next bolt to come out of the clouds and light up the wilderness.

We also get clouds covering the canyons below. The front cover photo of this book is basically the same view off of our back deck. I've photographed this scene thousands of times for the daily "deck cam" as part of our Cloudland Cabin Online Journal, which is the longest-running journal of its kind on the internet. Baby clouds that are born down there move around and join together, then form a sea of clouds that can rise up and cover the entire wilderness. Sometimes the sea will simply evaporate. Other times it will dance and move around and do all sorts of crazy things—like chase each other around! Eventually the clouds move on to become shade somewhere else and put smiles on other faces.

Here's a note from John Muir's journal My First Summer In The Sierra—I think he enjoyed clouds as much as we do...

"Another midday cloudland, displaying power and beauty that one never wearies in beholding, but hopelessly unsketchable and untellable. What can poor mortals say about clouds? While a description of their huge glowing domes and ridges, shadowy gulfs and canons, and featheredged ravines is being tried, they vanish, leaving no visible ruins. Nevertheless, these fleeting sky mountains are as substantial and significant as the more lasting upheavals of granite beneath them. Both alike are built up and die, and in God's calendar difference of duration is nothing."

Twisted cedar at dawn, Buffalo River Wilderness (previous pages)

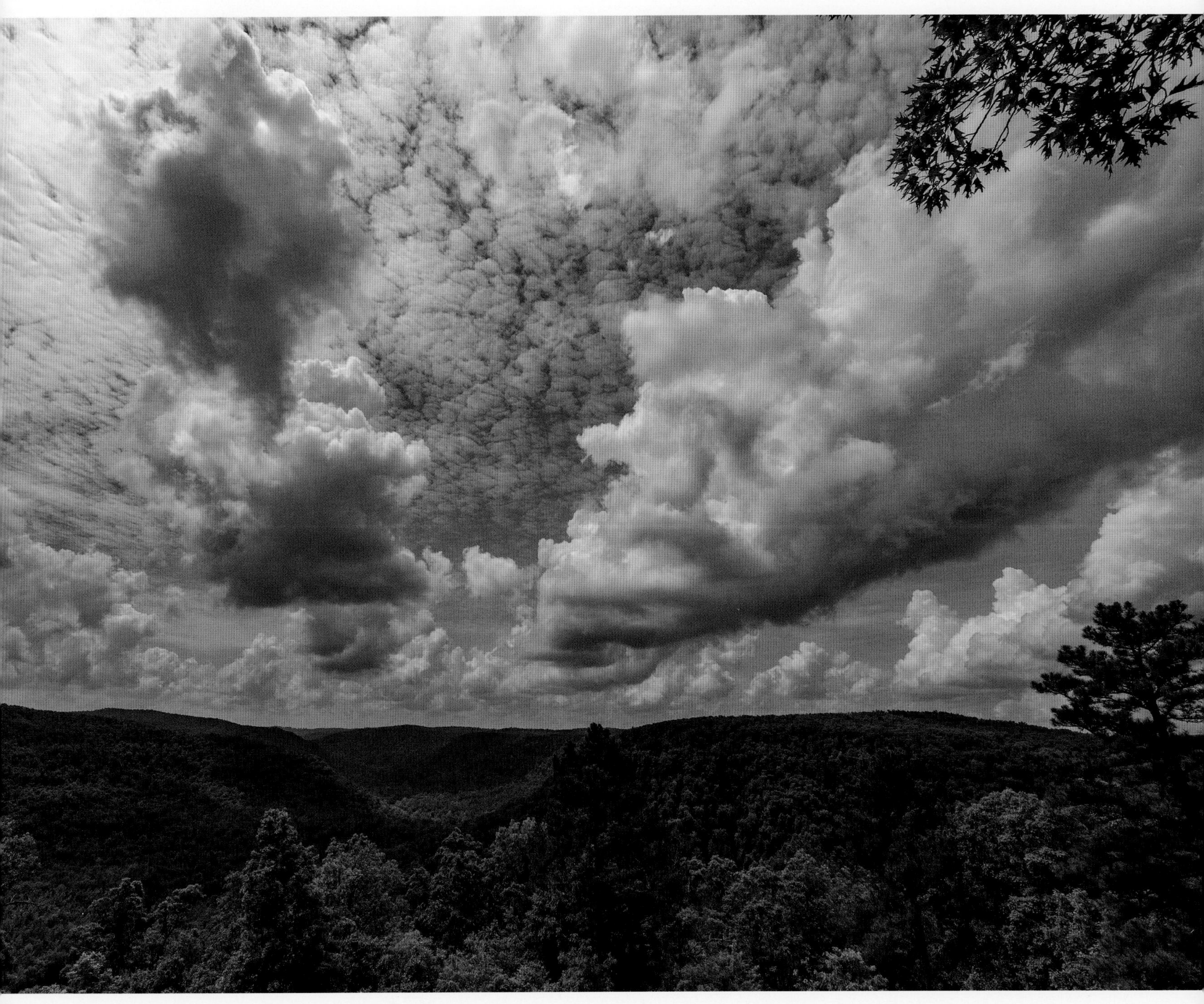

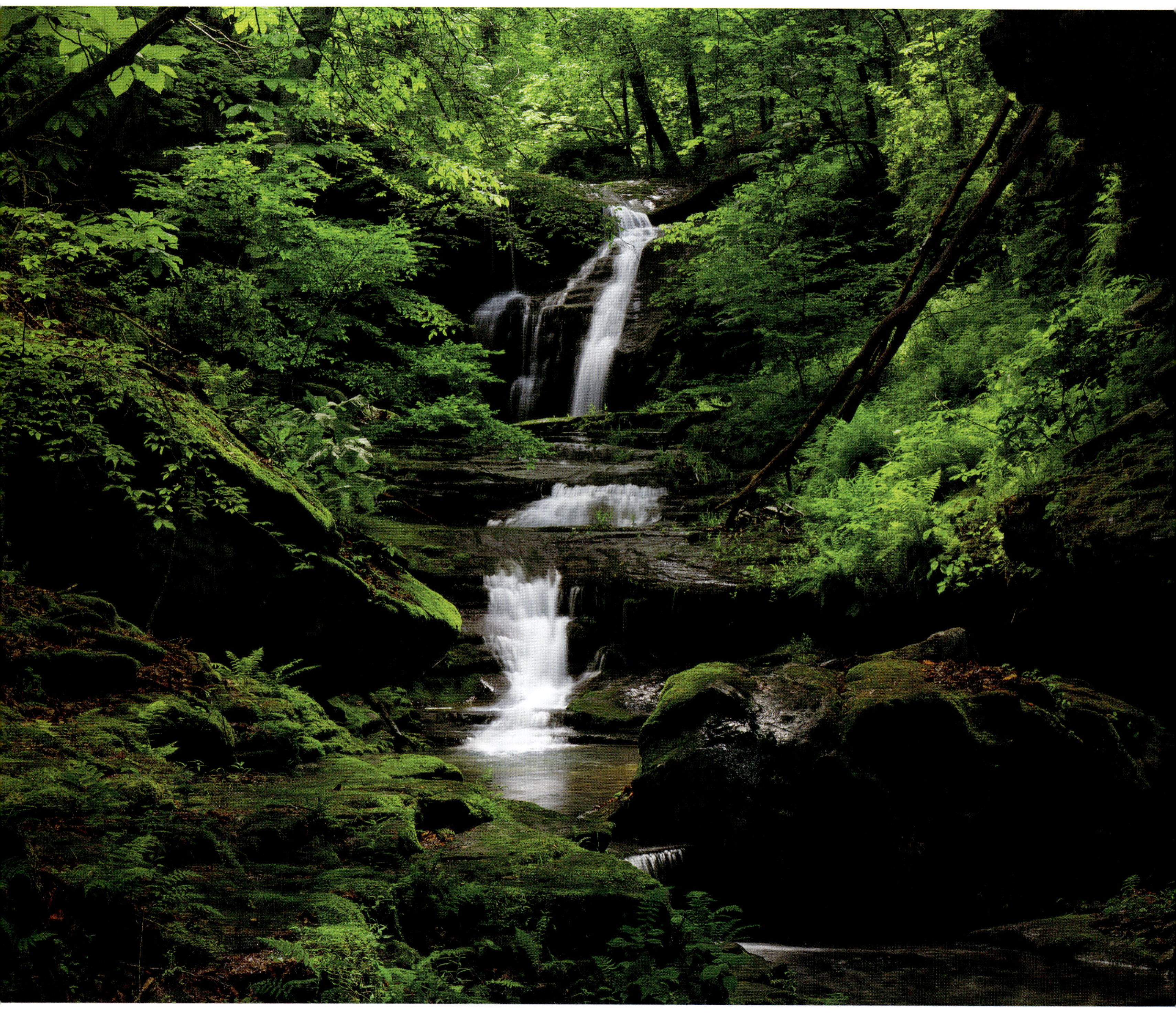

Four Drop Falls, Dismal Hollow Special Interest Area

The Milky Way rises above "Beaver" Jim Villines pioneer cabin, Boxley Valley Historic District

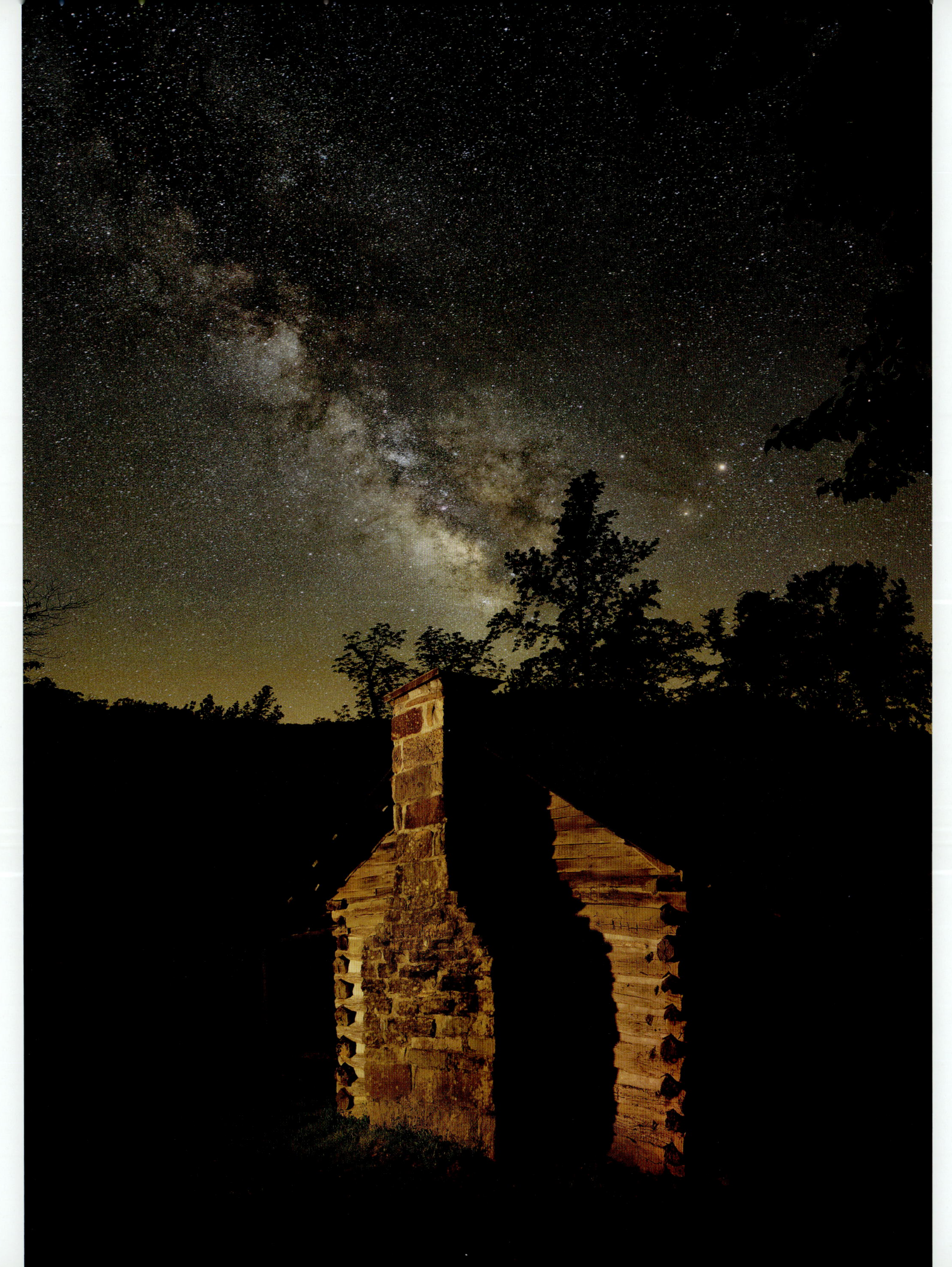

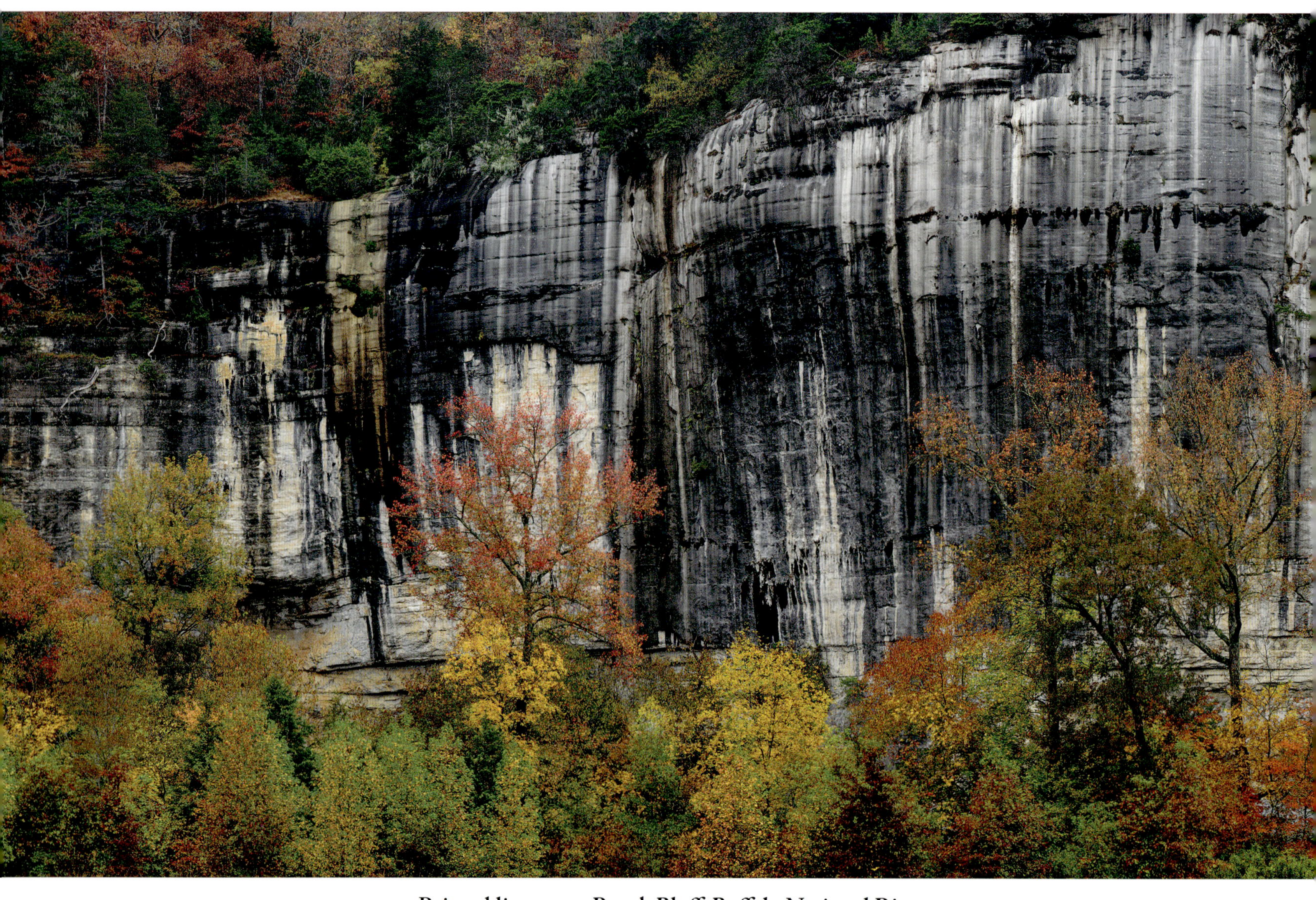

Painted limestone Roark Bluff, Buffalo National River

Yellow coneflowers, part of a lush wildflower display at the Elk Info Center in beautiful downtown Ponca

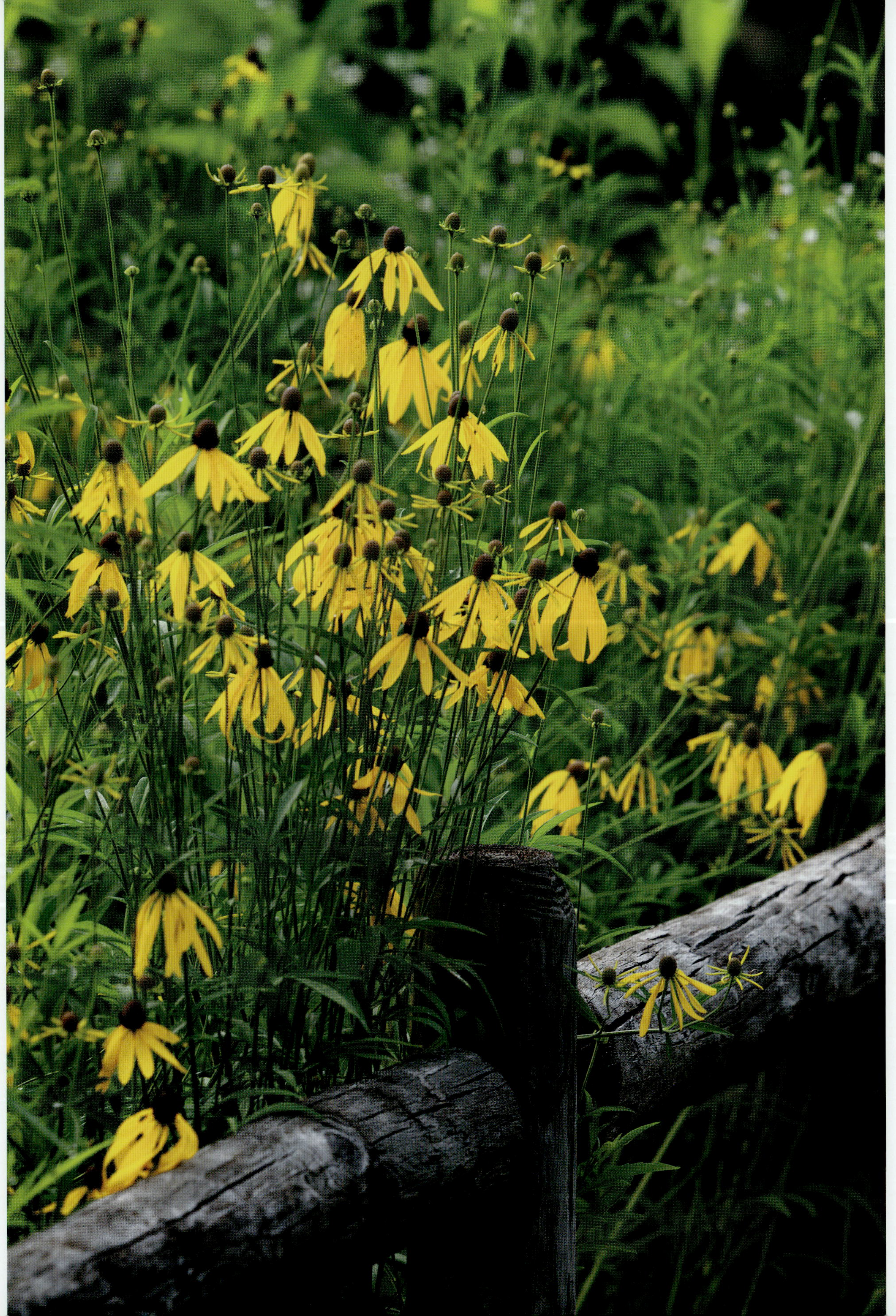

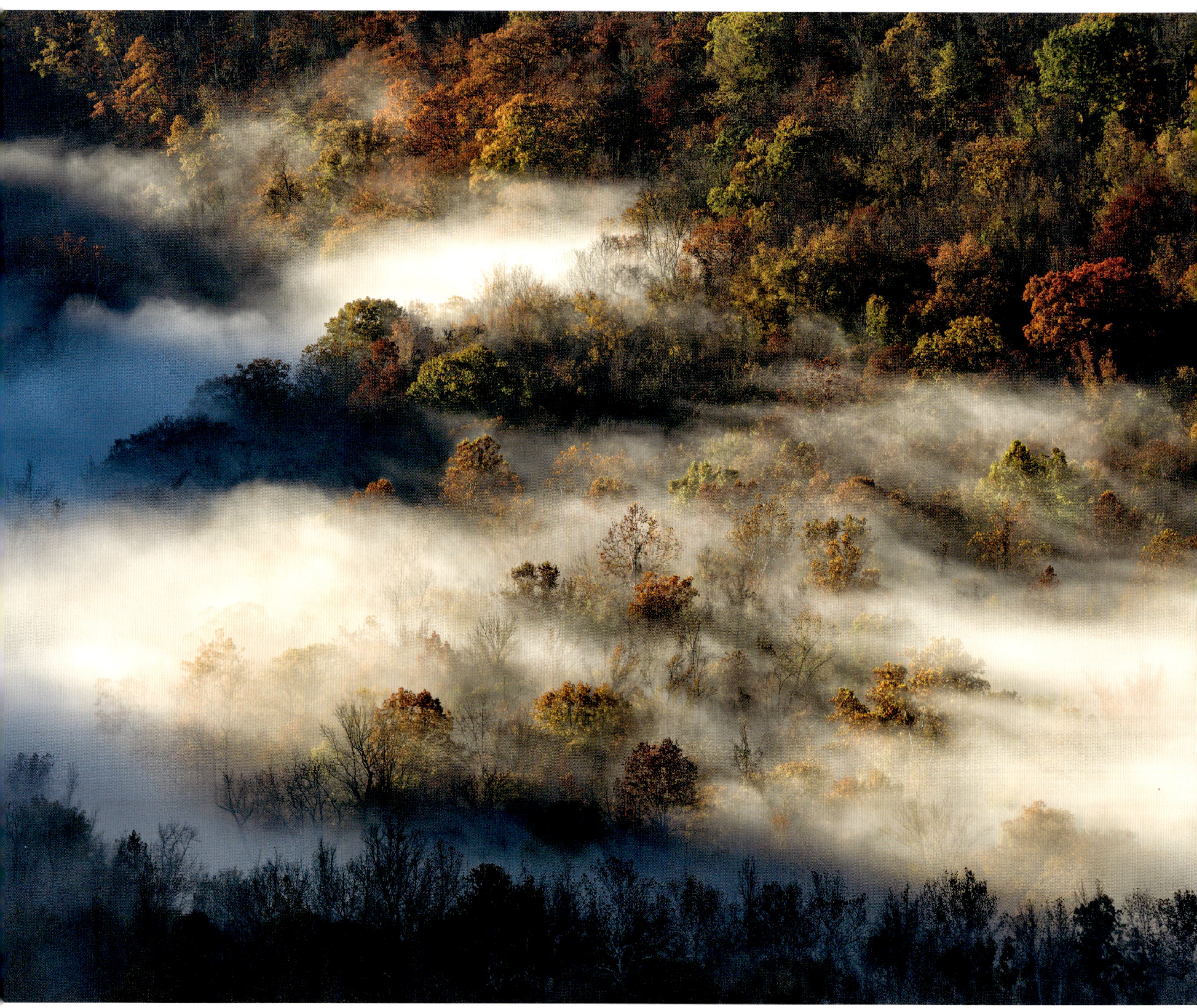

Fog swirls through the last of the autumn color deep in the canyon behind our cabin

Hickory tree and winter stars after a fresh snowfall

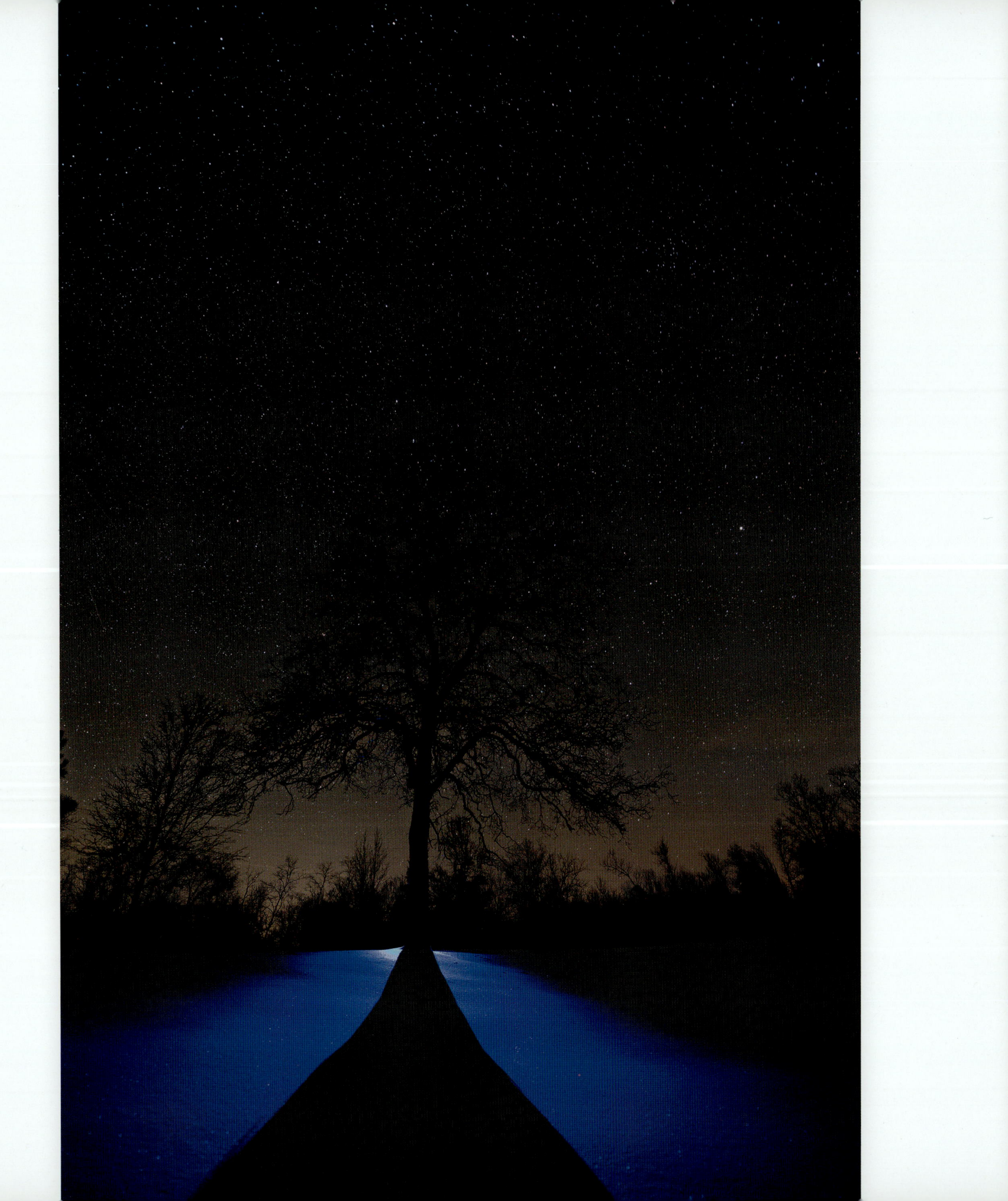

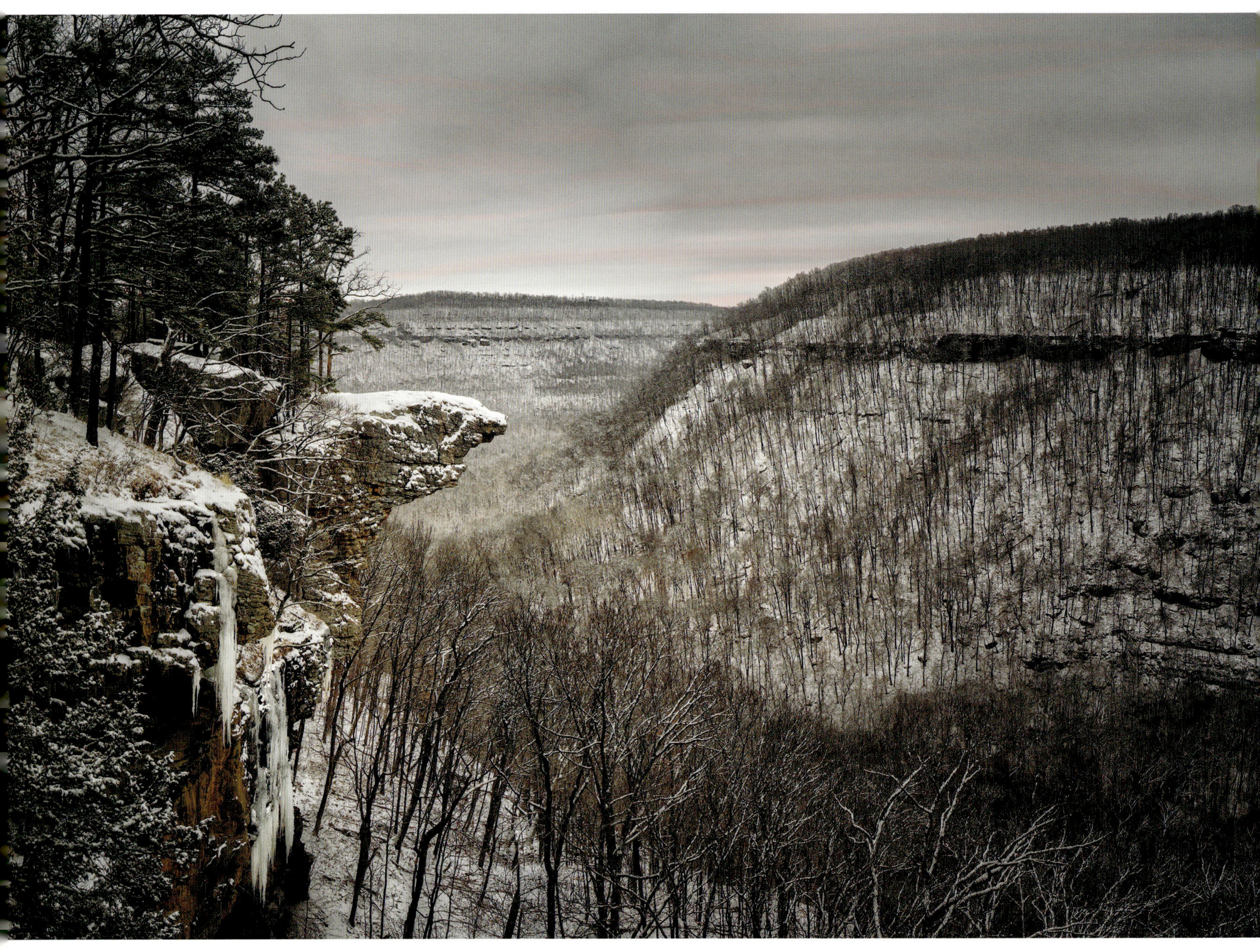

Snow and ice on Hawksbill Crag at dawn, Upper Buffalo Wilderness Area

Butterfly weed bouquets line roadways in summer

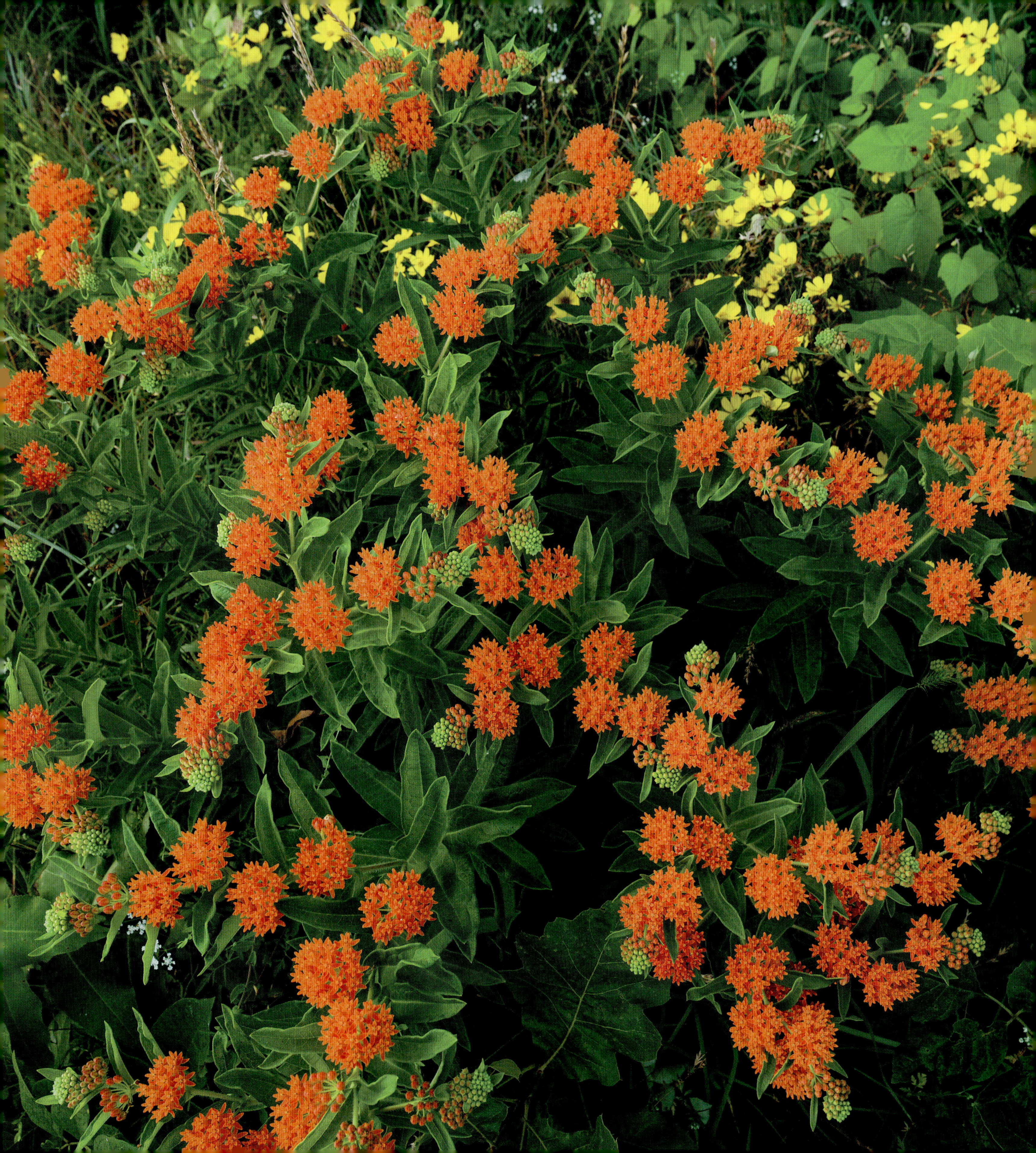

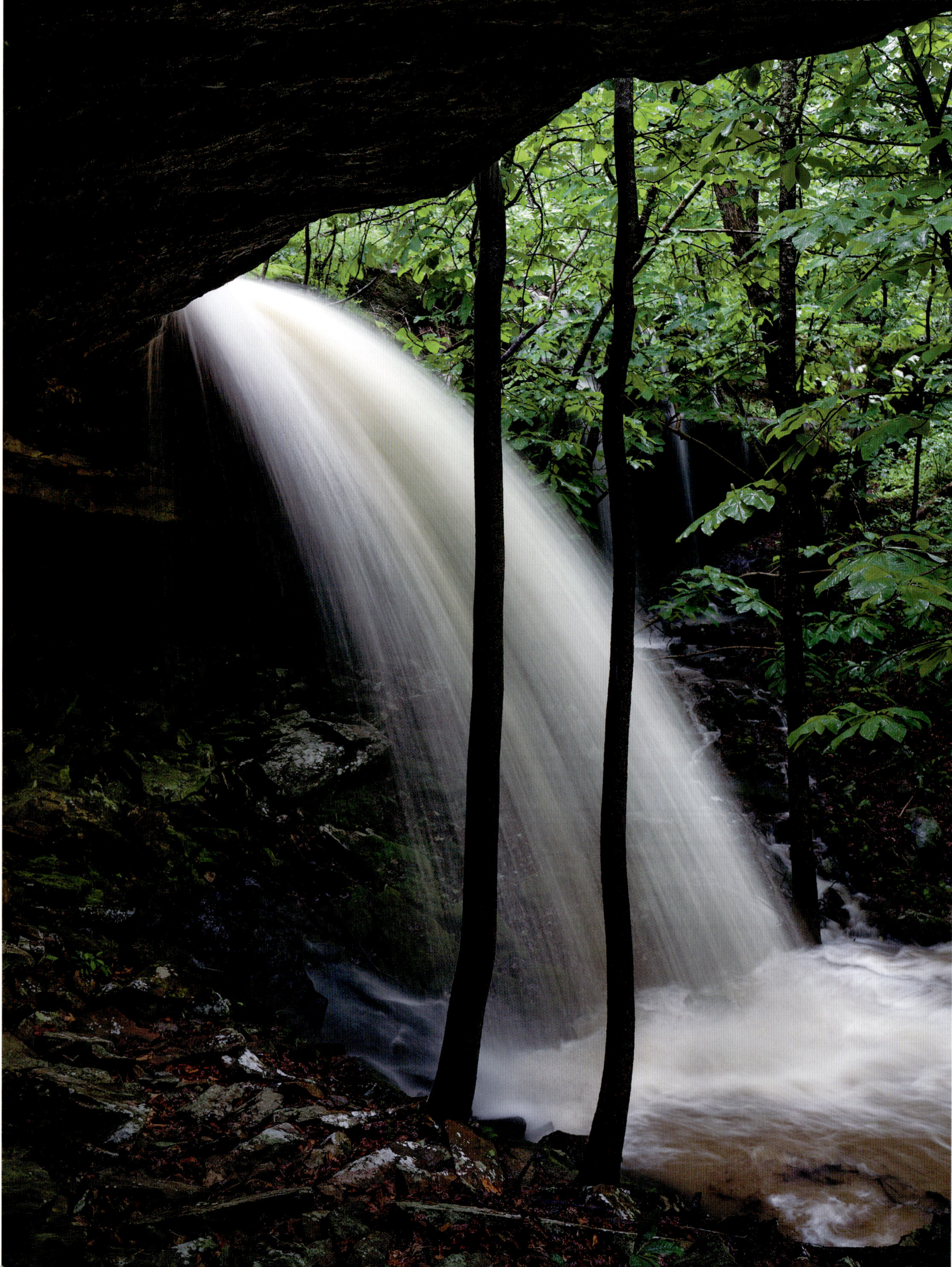

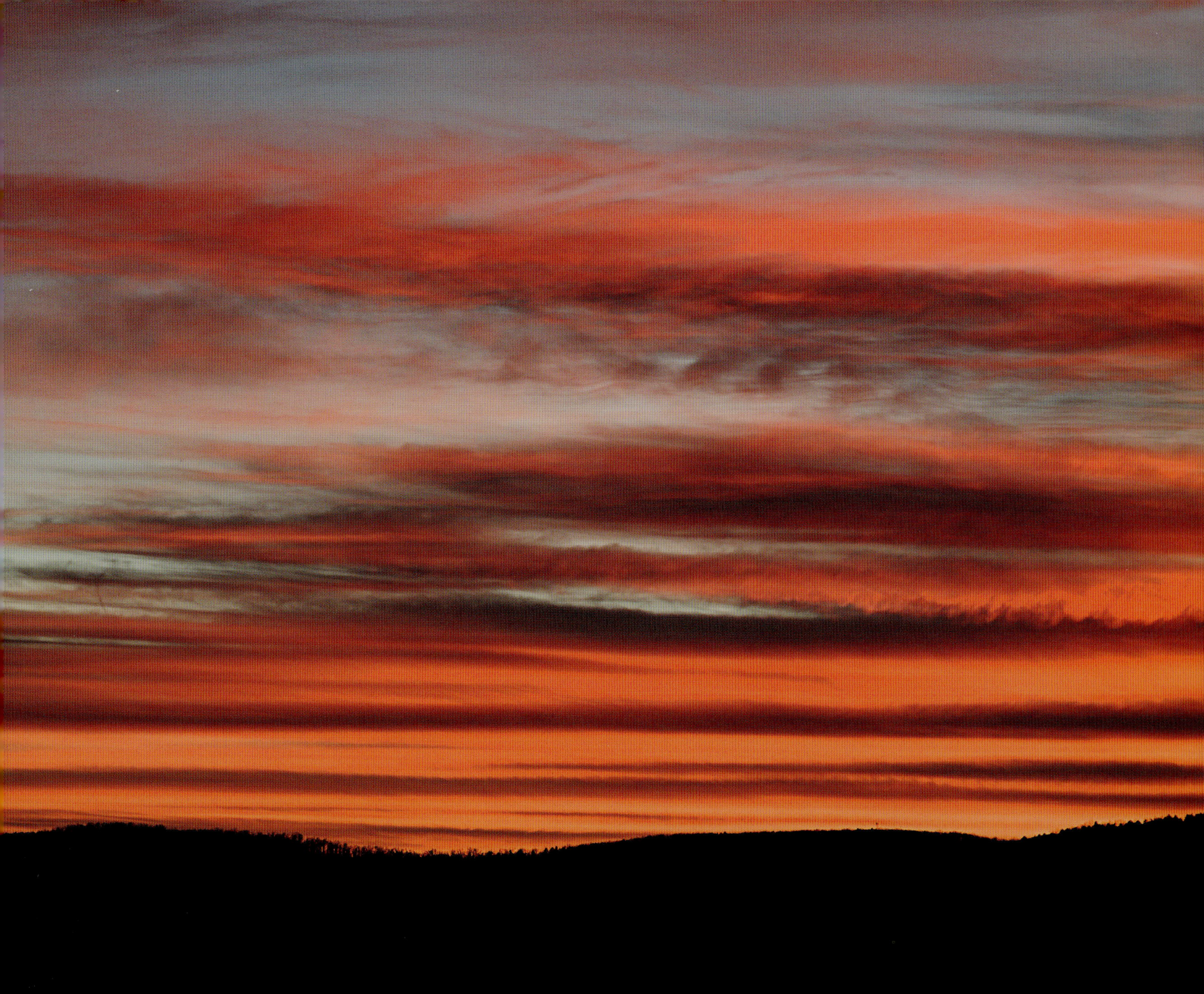

A colorful winter sunset from the back deck of our cabin (look for the tiny Buffalo Fire Tower on the horizon)

A very flooded Little Pine Hollow Falls, Upper Buffalo Wilderness Area

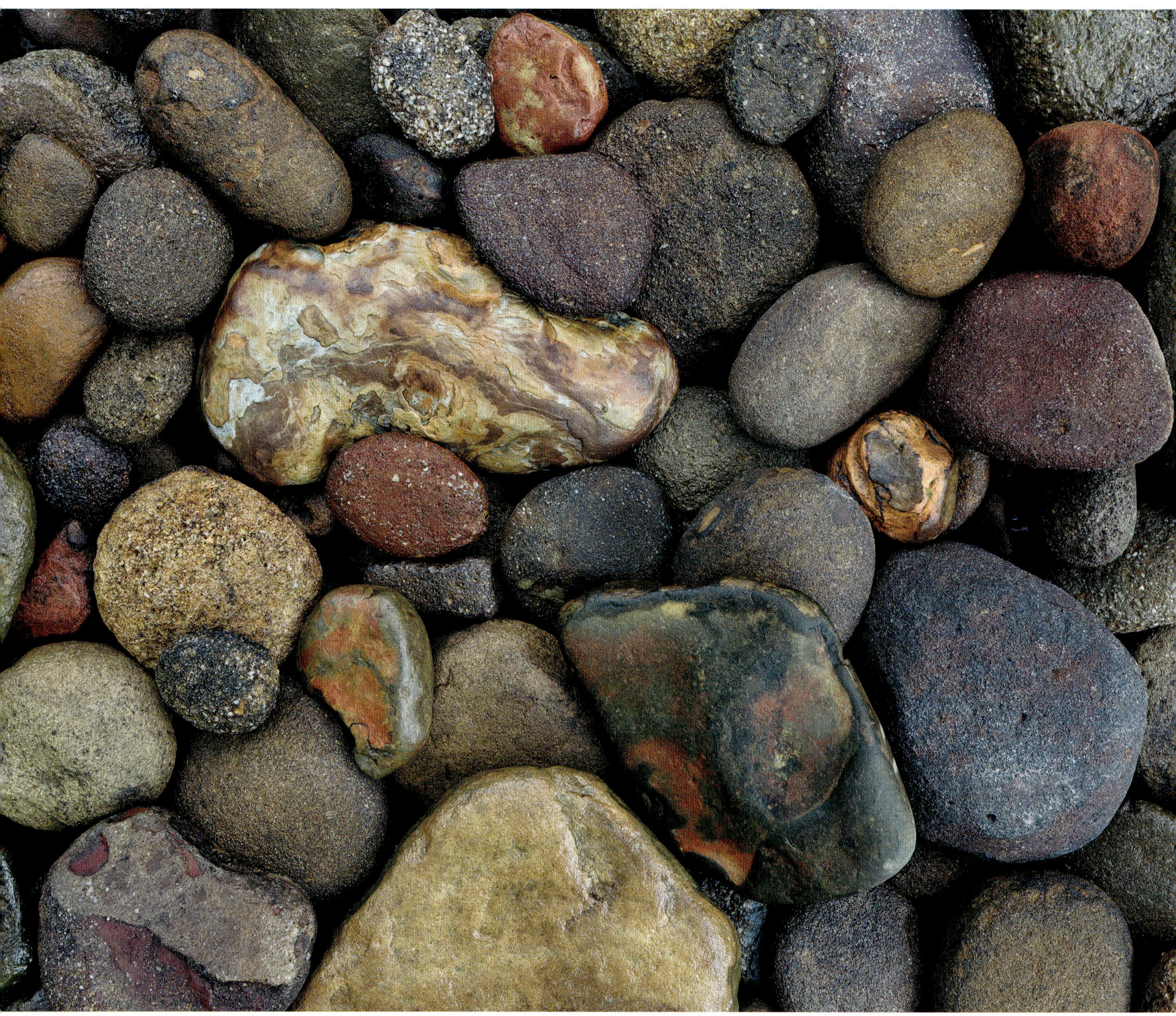

Polished river rocks, Kings River

Brilliant sunshine, maple trees, and blue sky—must be autumn in Arkansas!

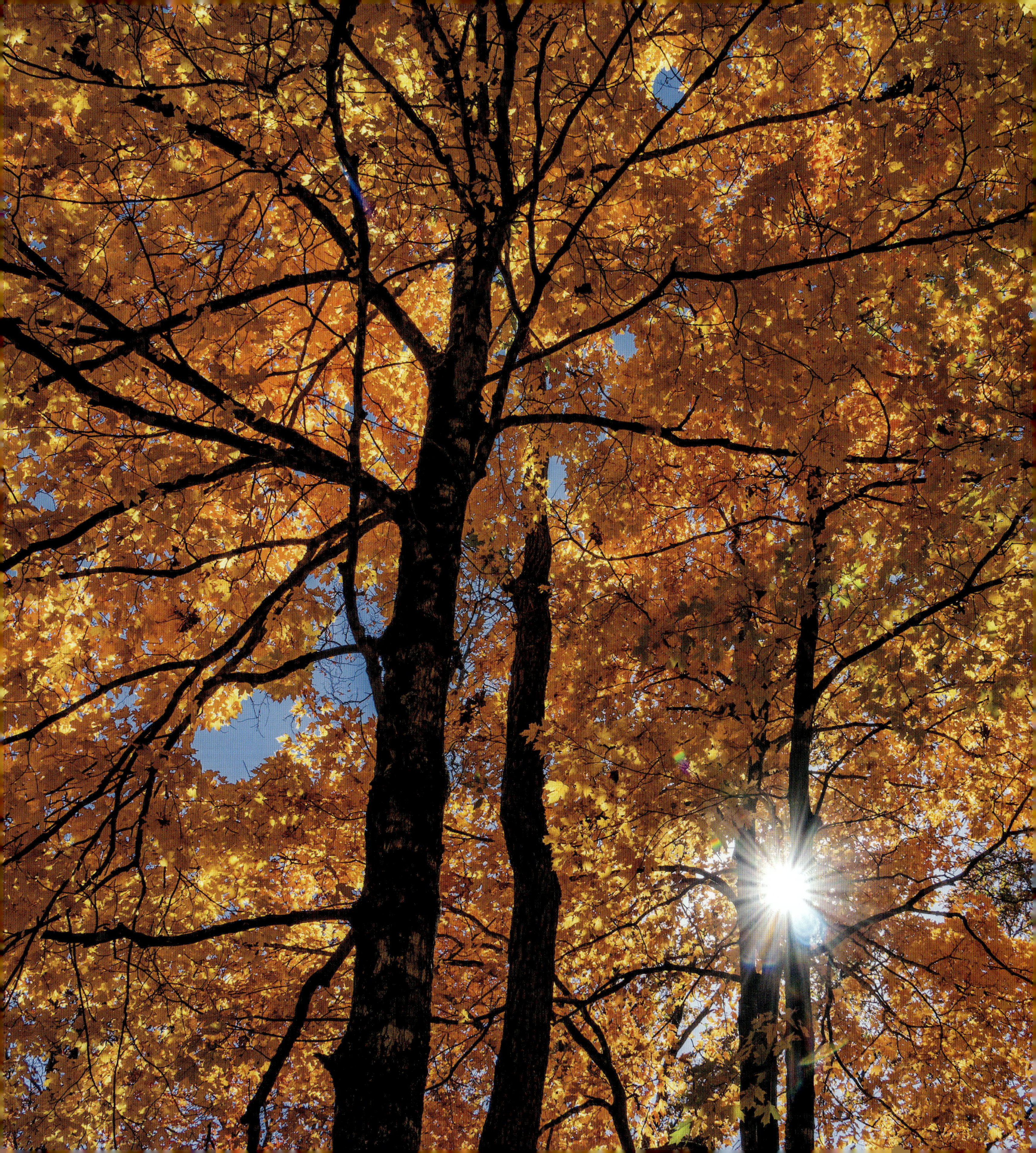

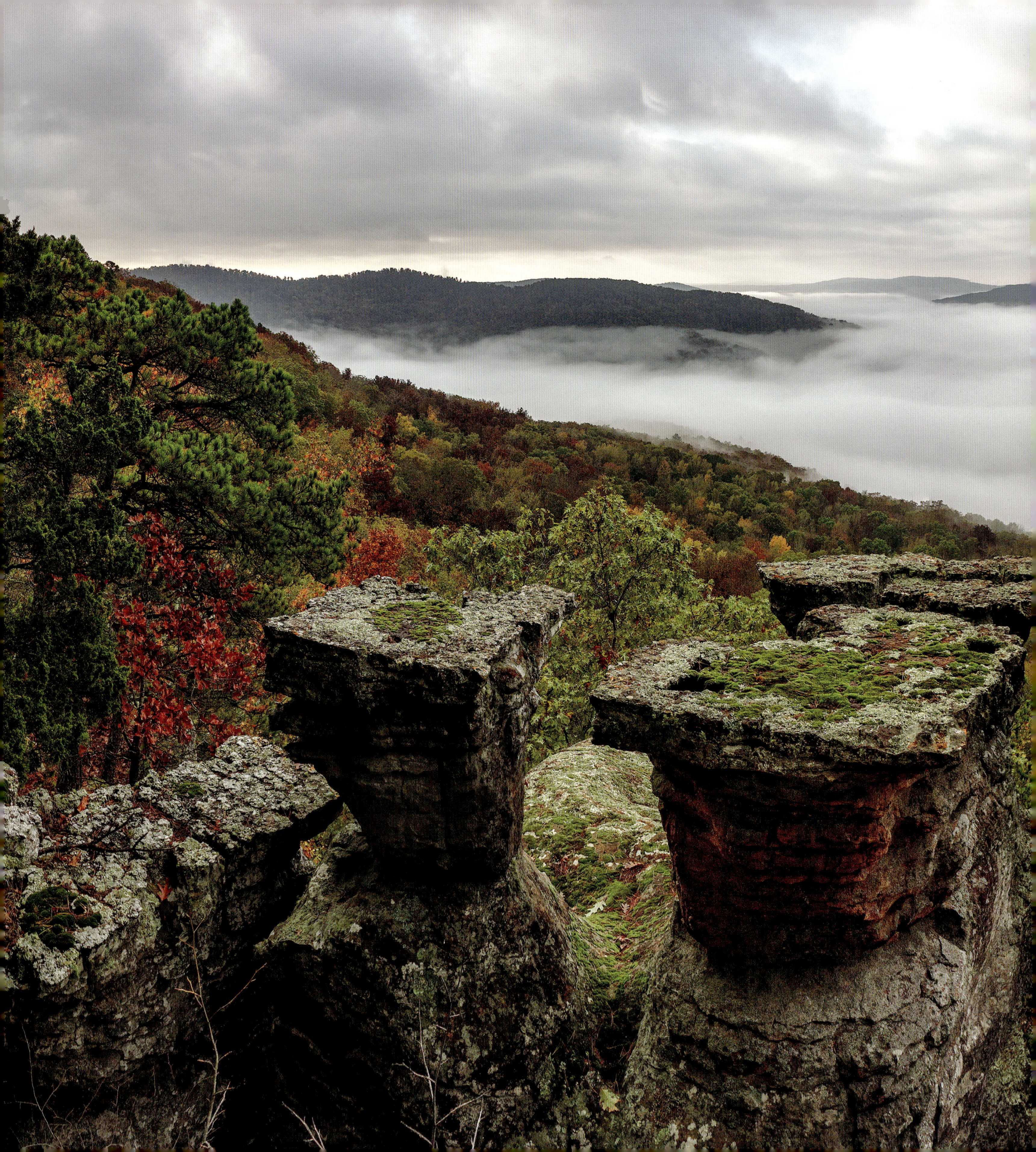

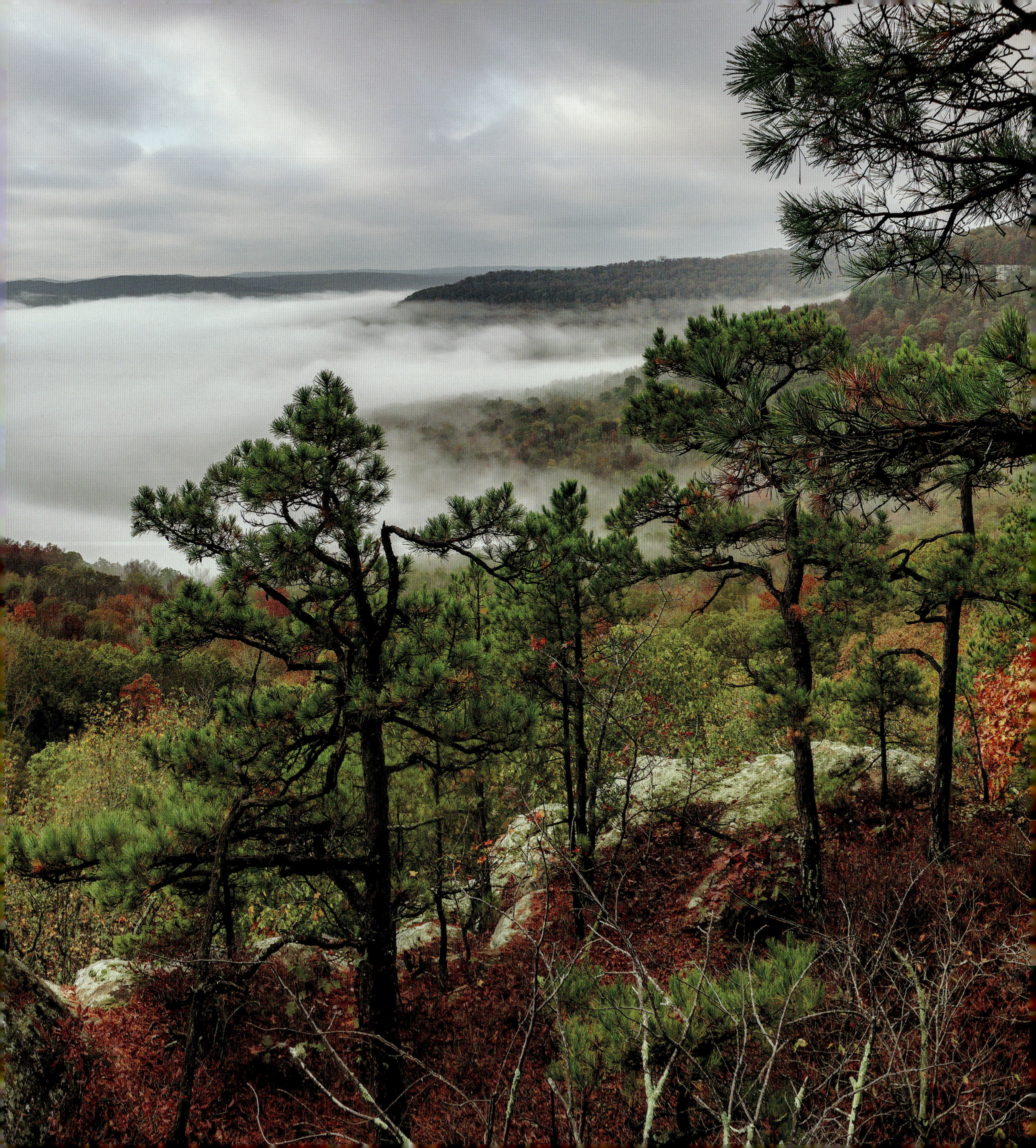

Rustic barn and the Milky Way, Boxley Valley Historic District

Rustic barns are as much a part of the scenic landscape as anything, and we still have lots of them in our area, like this beauty in the heart of Boxley Valley. Don't give me barn wood frames on the wall—I would much rather see the real thing, especially beneath a starry sky!

These old barns are also a rich part of our cultural history—some date back to the 1800's—and it is great to see them still a part of everyday farm life.

A sea of fog beneath Tea Table Rocks, Ozark National Forest (previous pages)

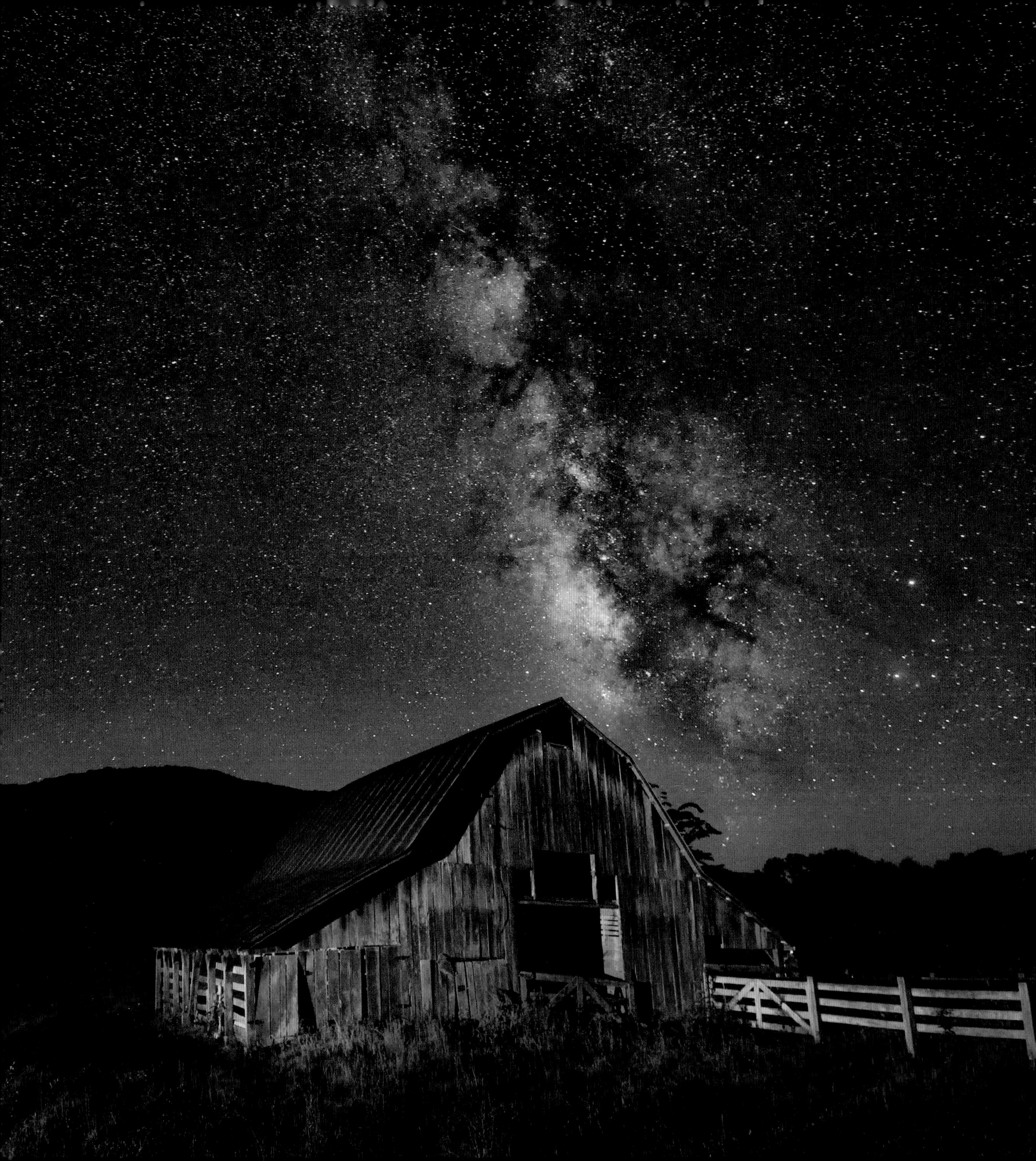

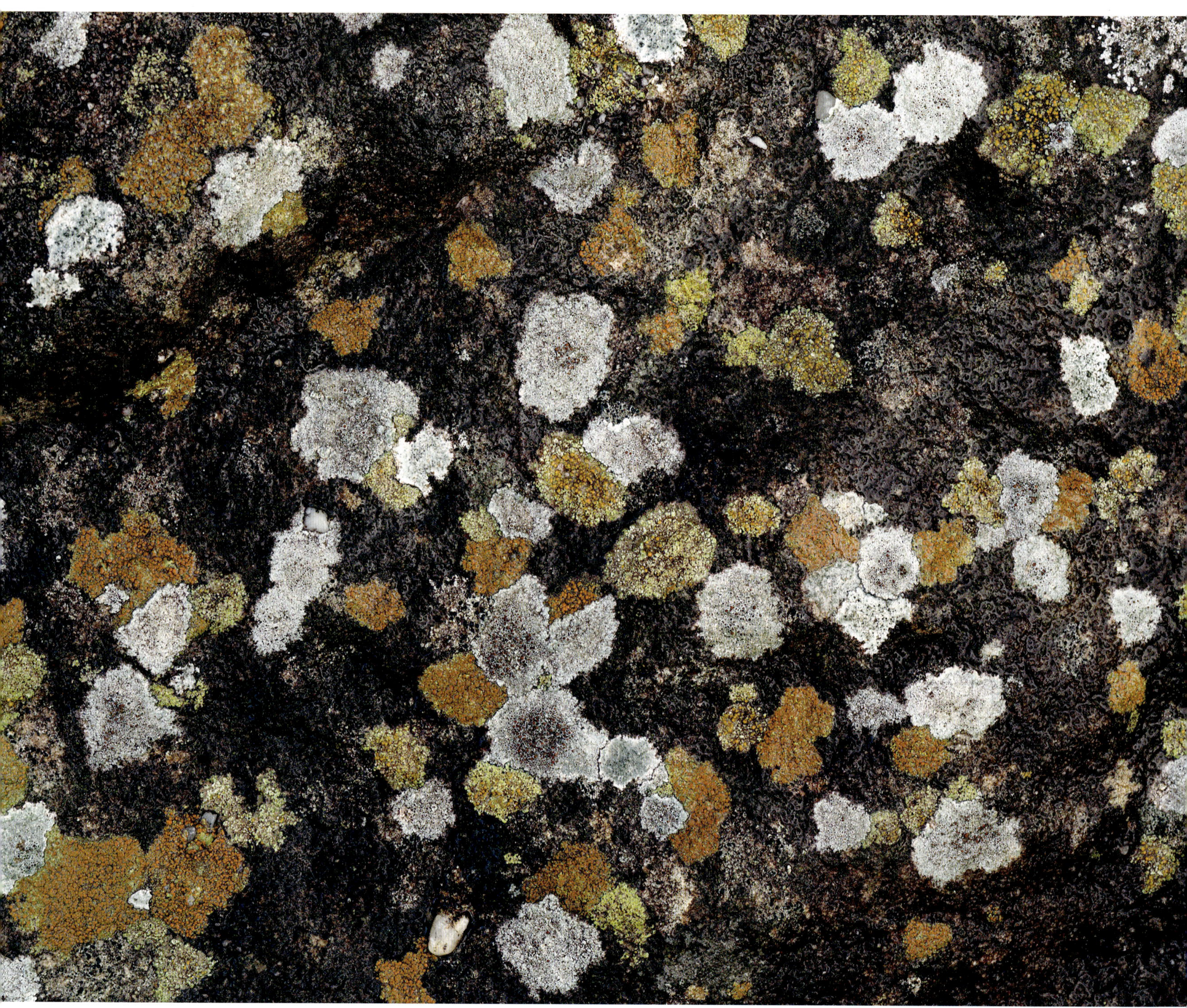

Lichens on sandstone

Nuckles Falls on Nuckles Creek, Ozark National Forest

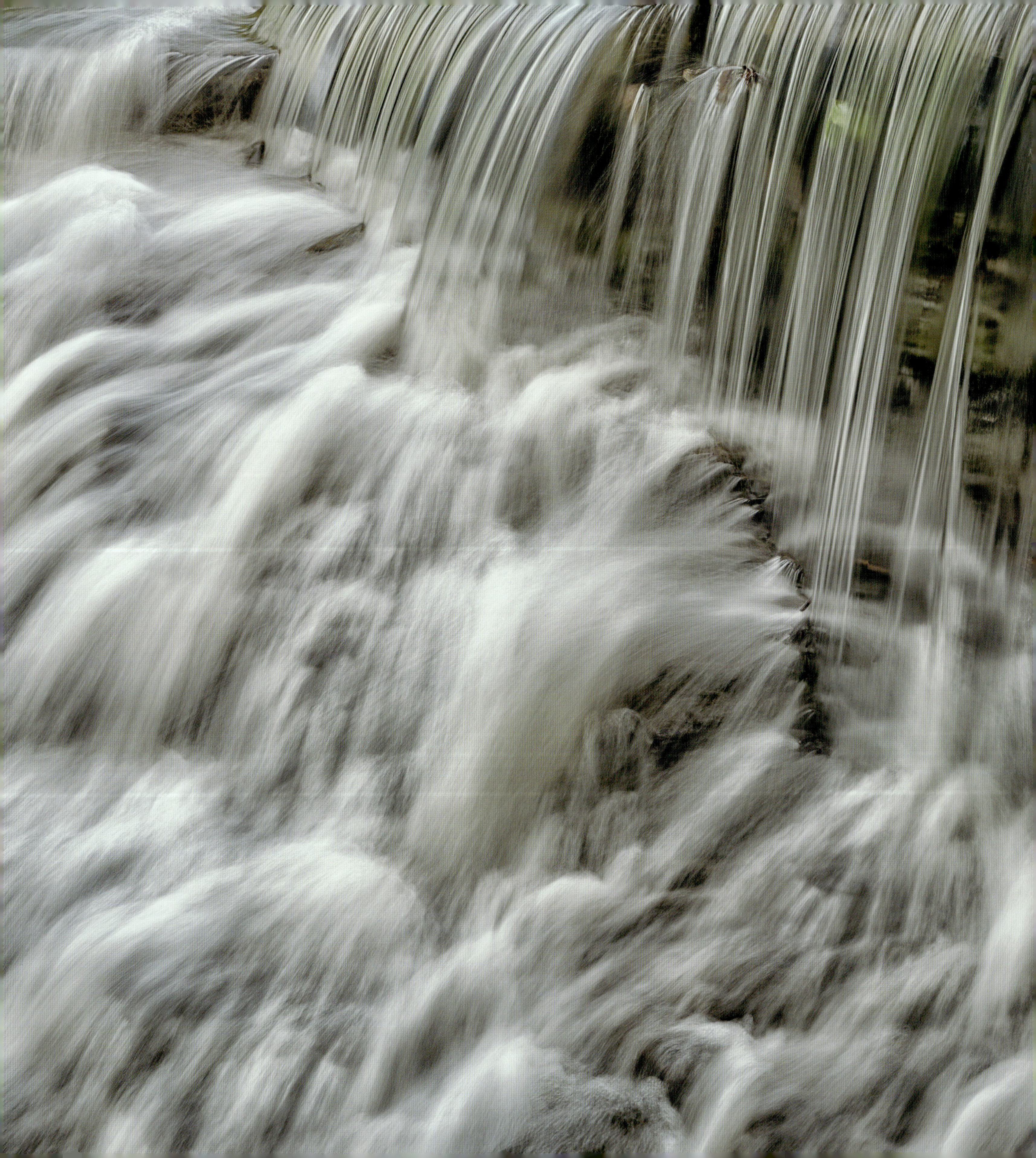

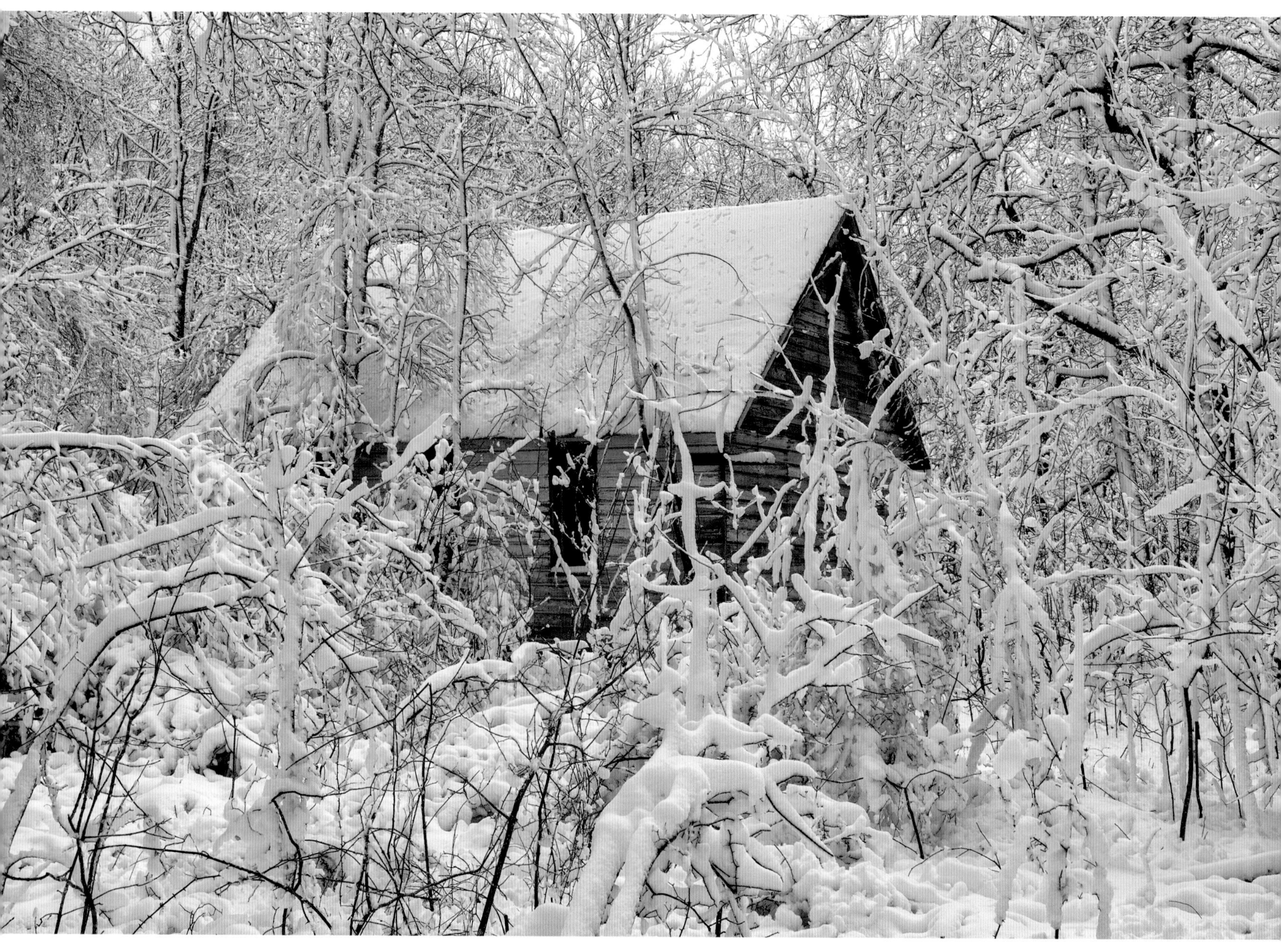

Historic church and one-room schoolhouse at Roberts Gap, Ozark National Forest

Crescent moon and walnut tree at dawn

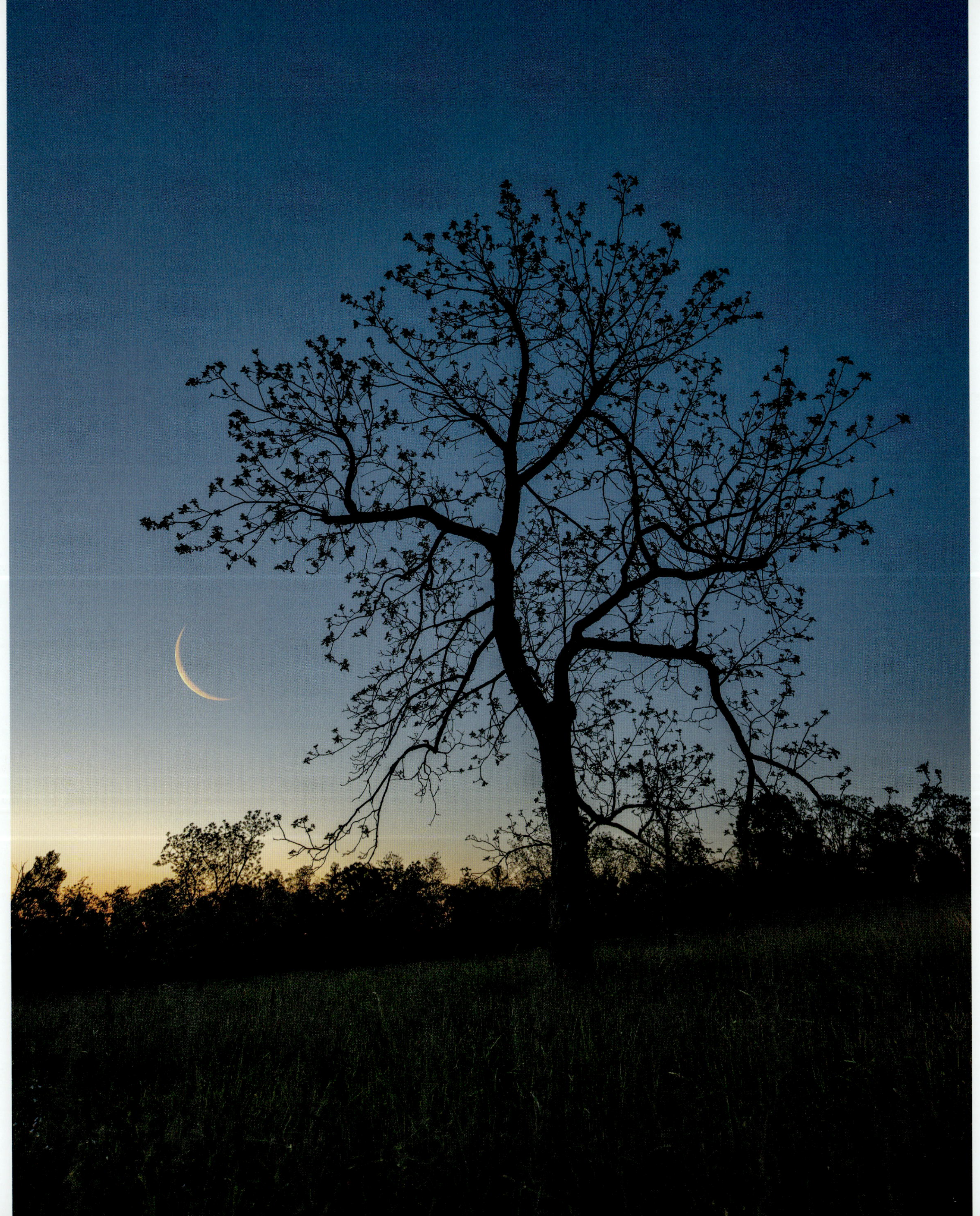

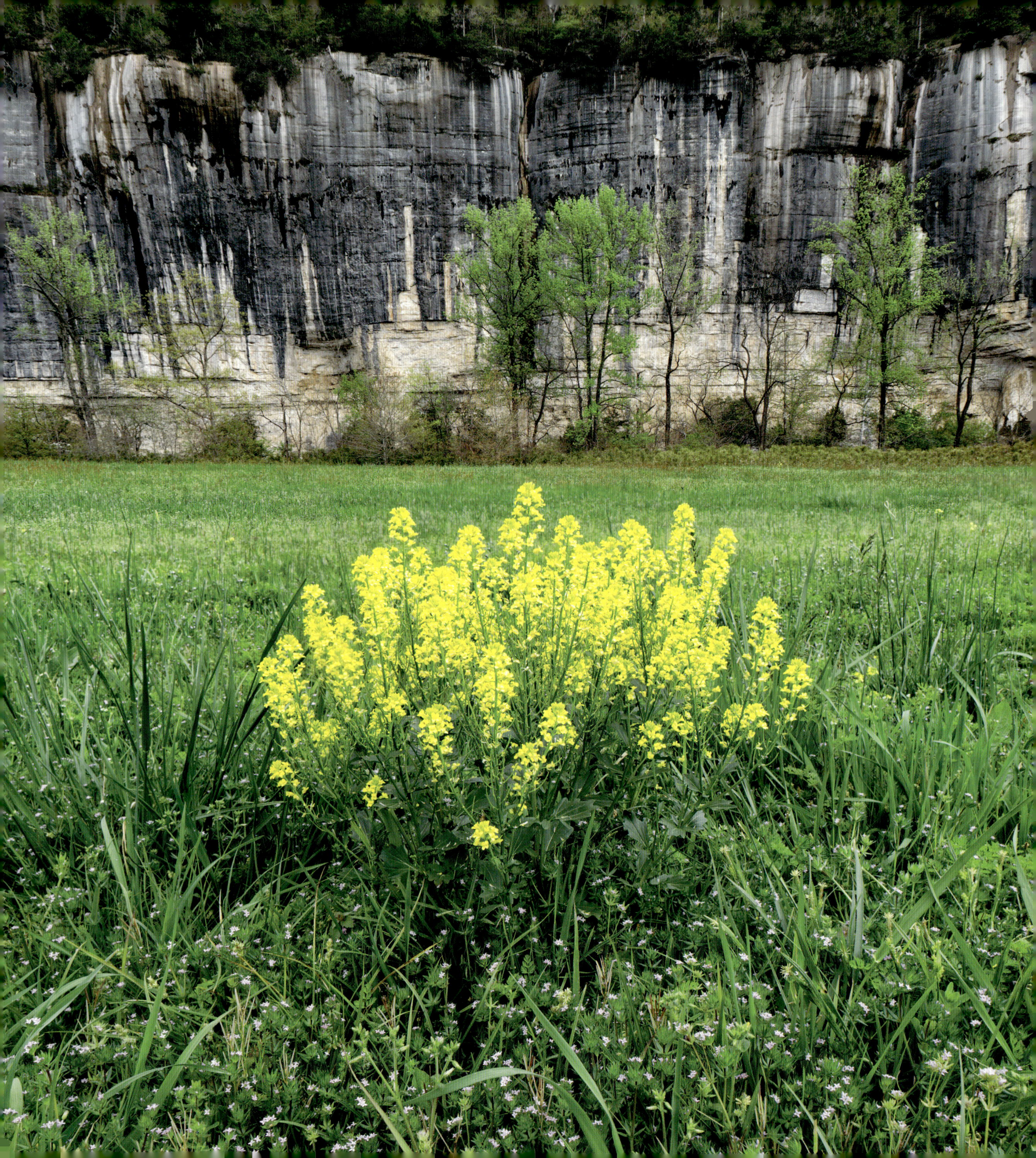

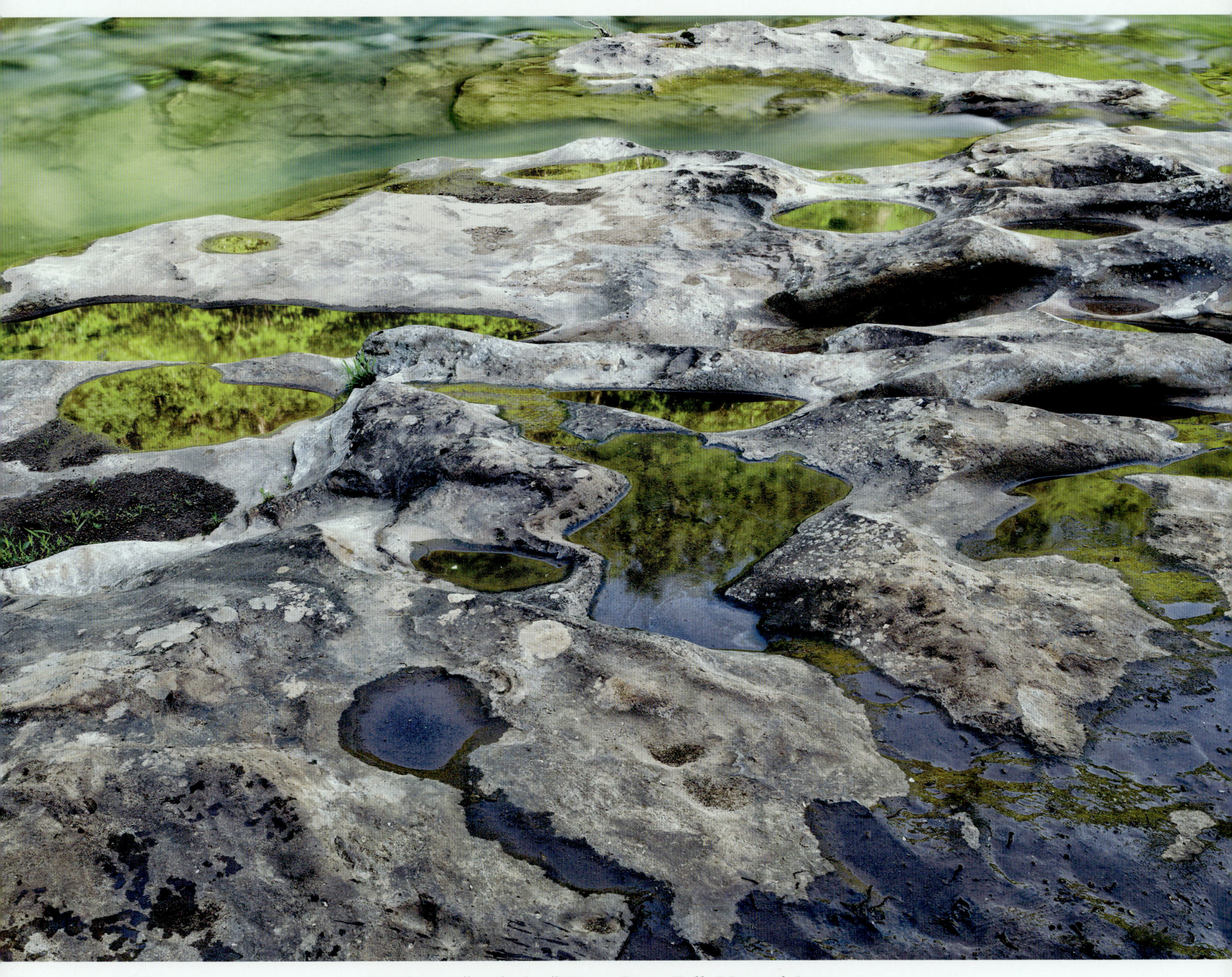

Sandstone "potholes," Kings River Falls Natural Area

Yellow rocket and tiny bluet wildflowers in the meadow beneath the towering Roark Bluff, Buffalo National River

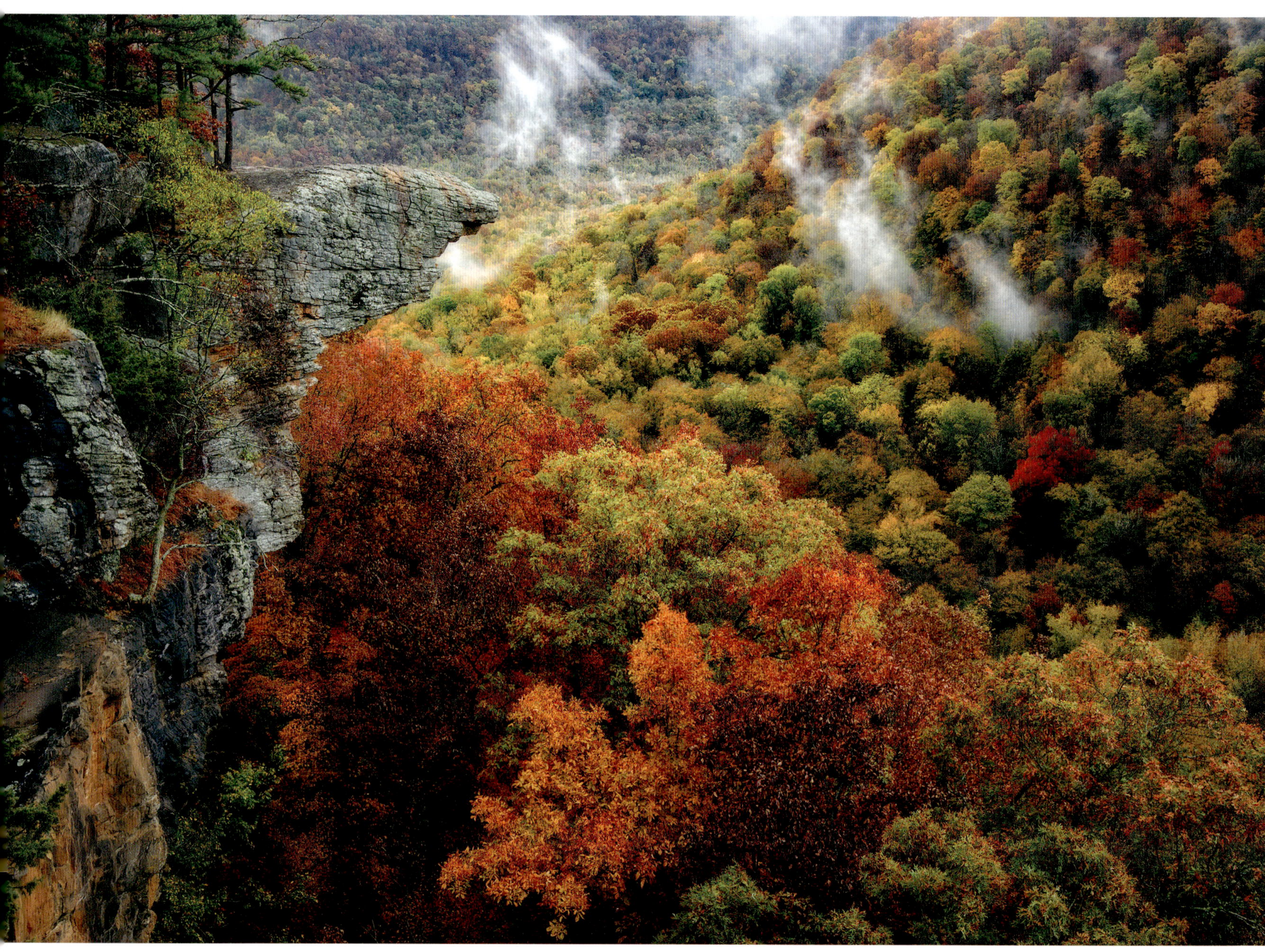

Hawksbill Crag in the mist, Upper Buffalo Wilderness Area

A chorus of daisies sing to the sky

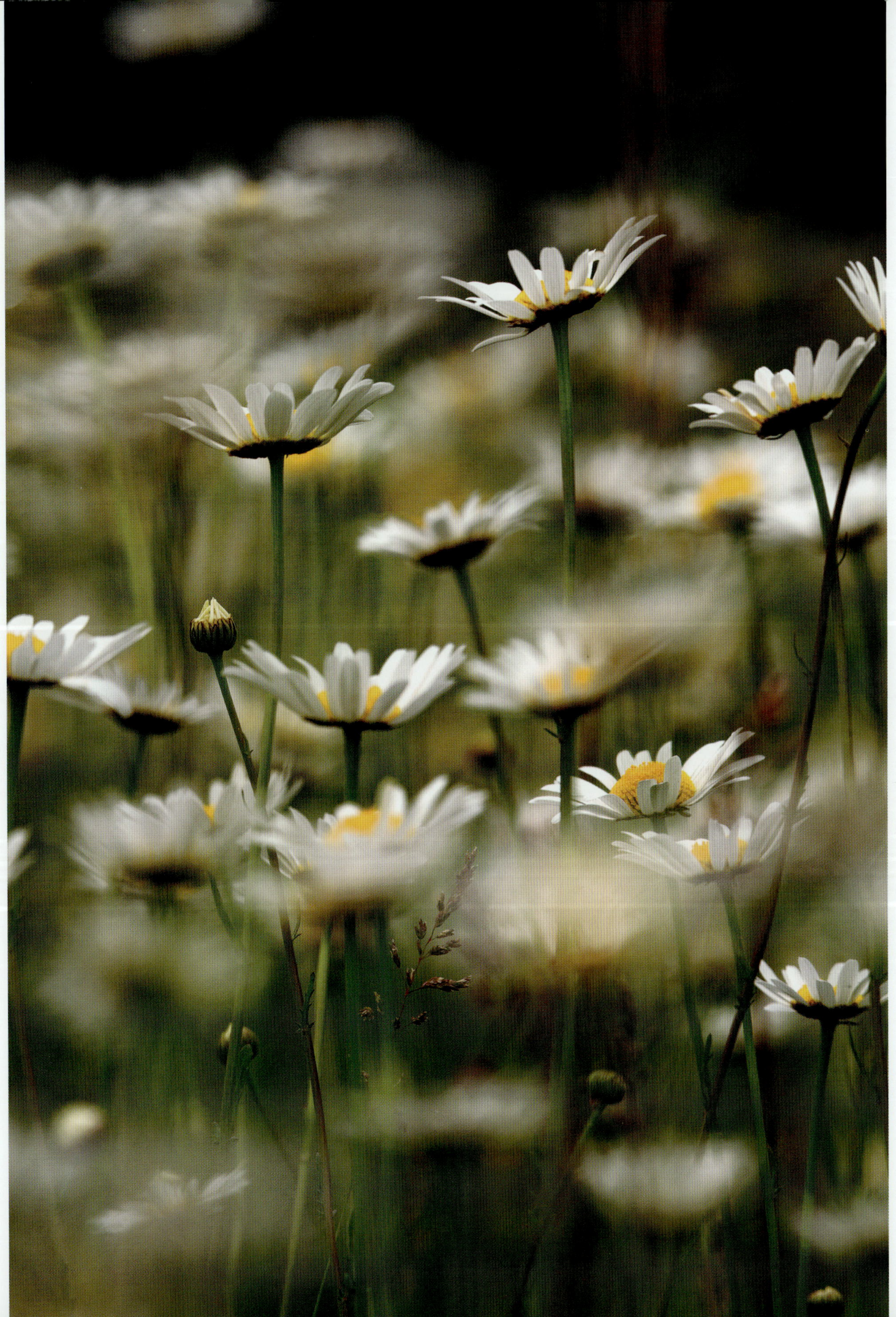

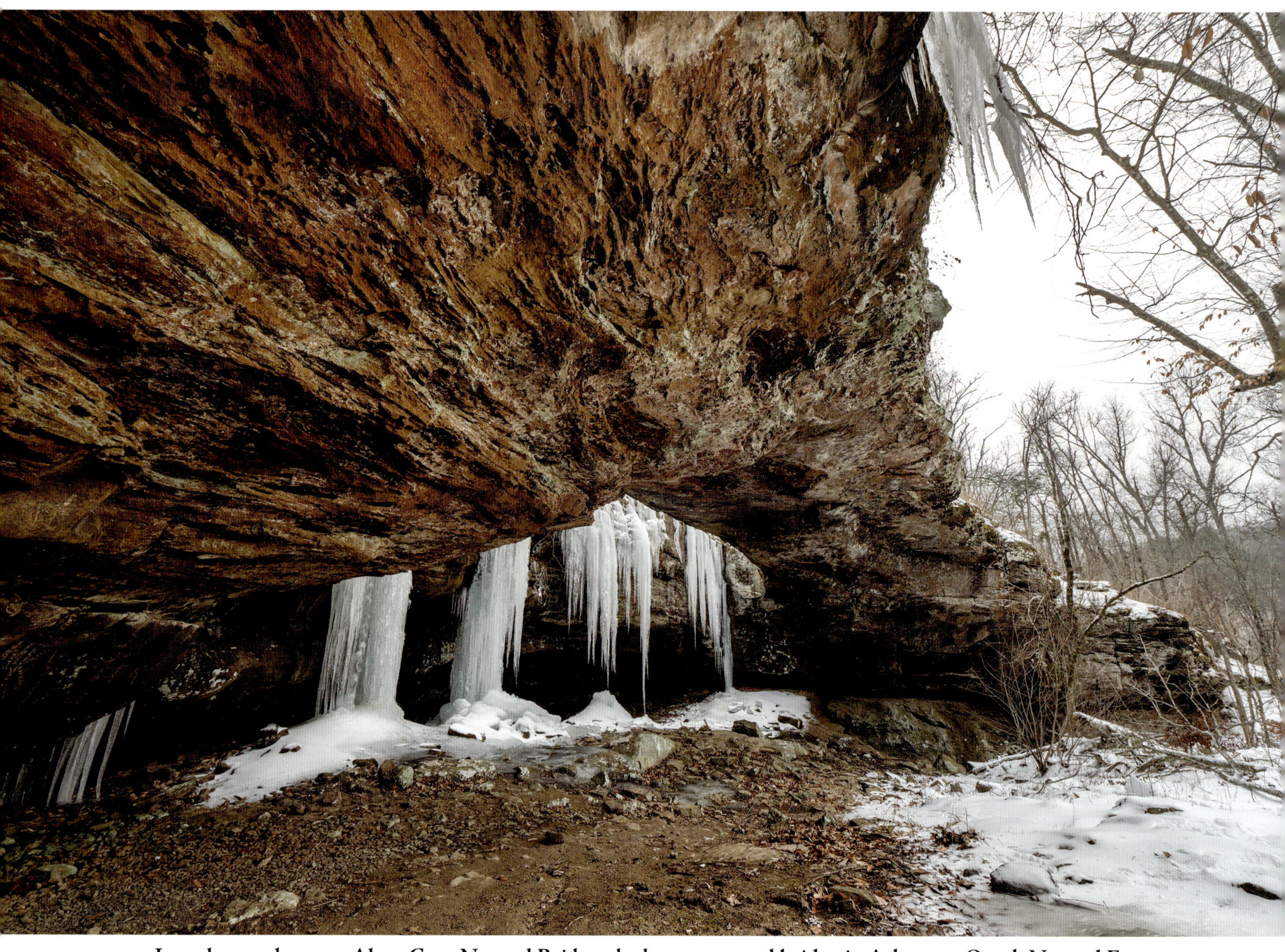

Ice columns decorate Alum Cove Natural Bridge, the largest natural bridge in Arkansas, Ozark Natural Forest

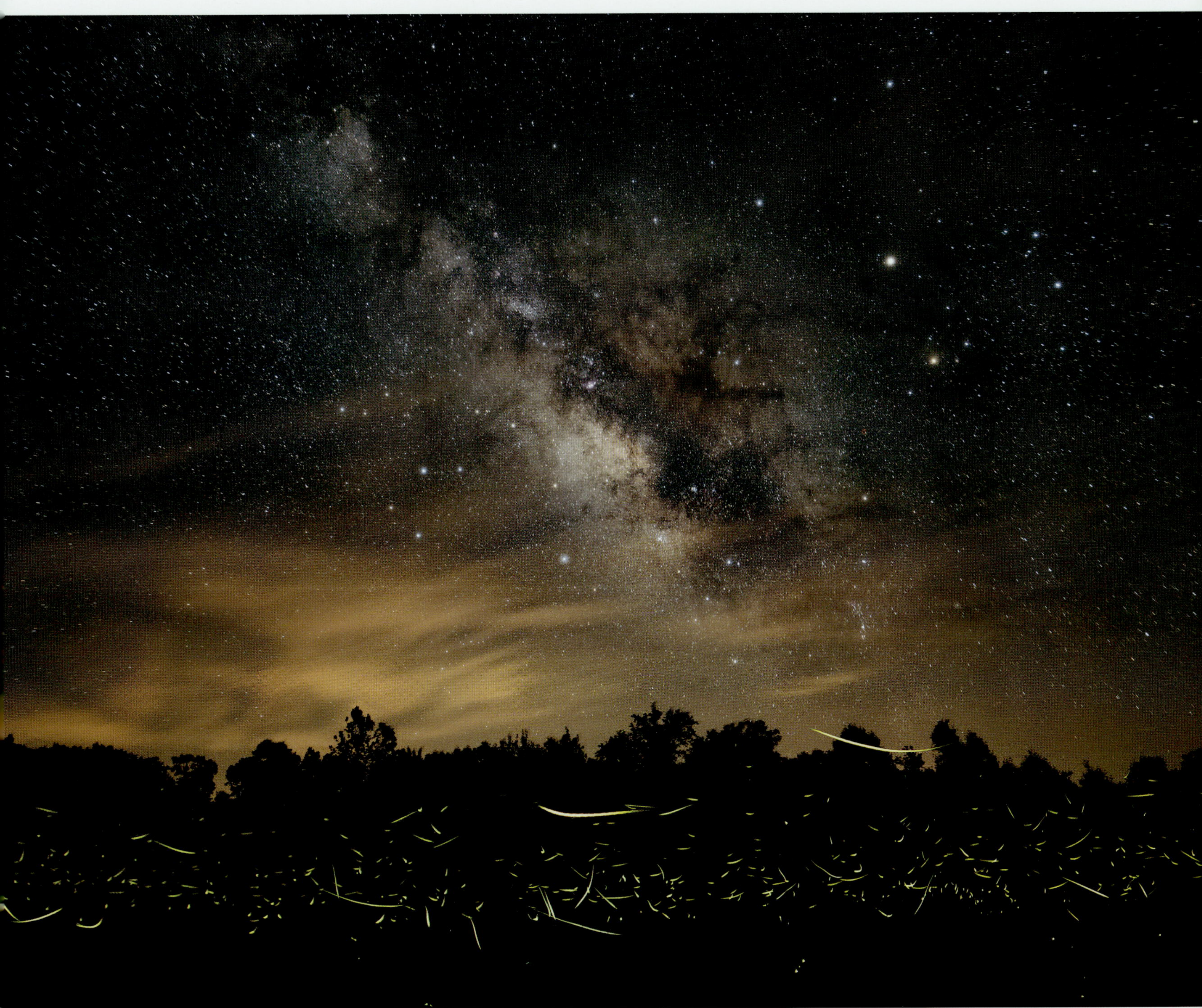

Lightning bugs dance and play beneath the rising Milky Way

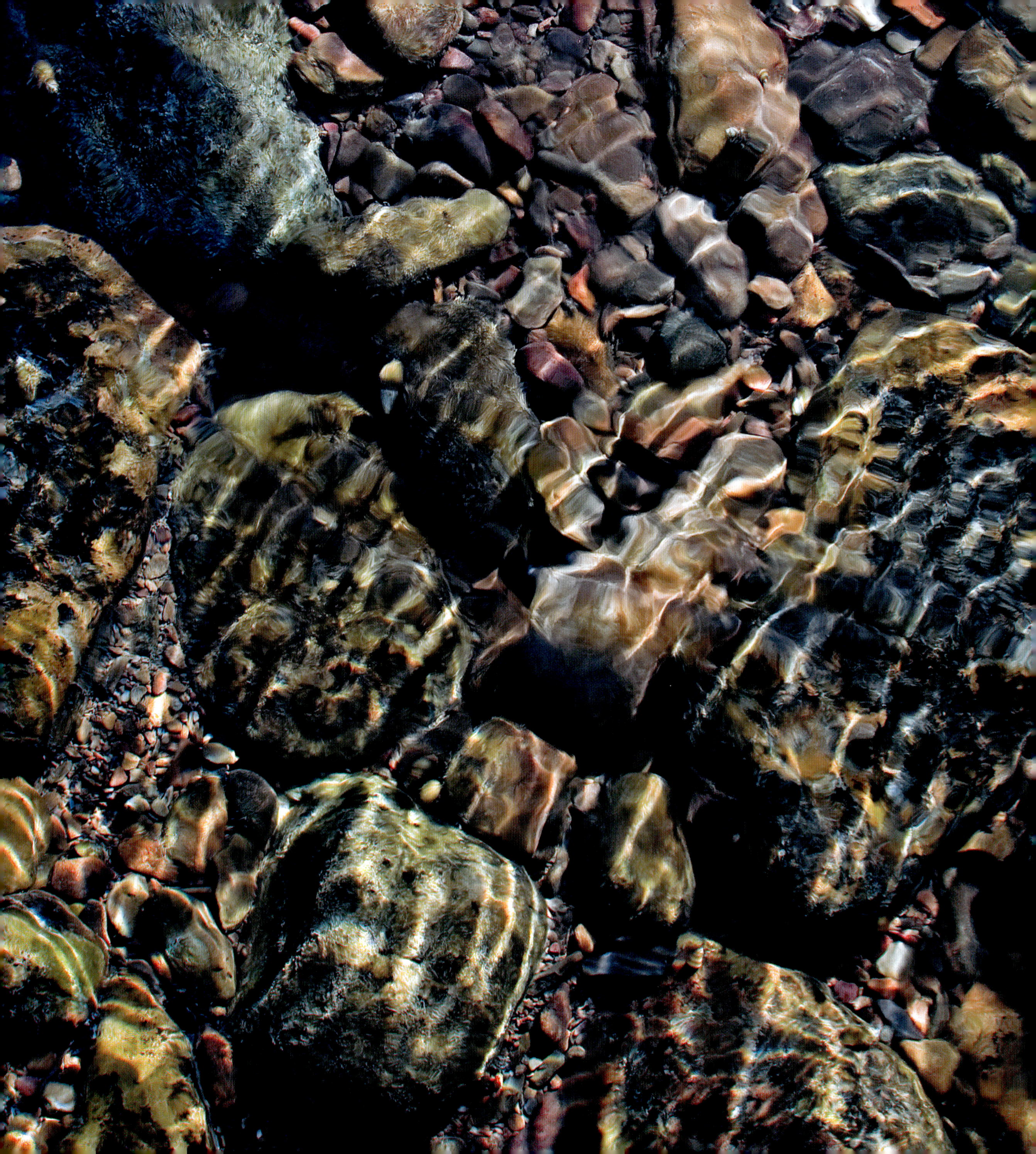

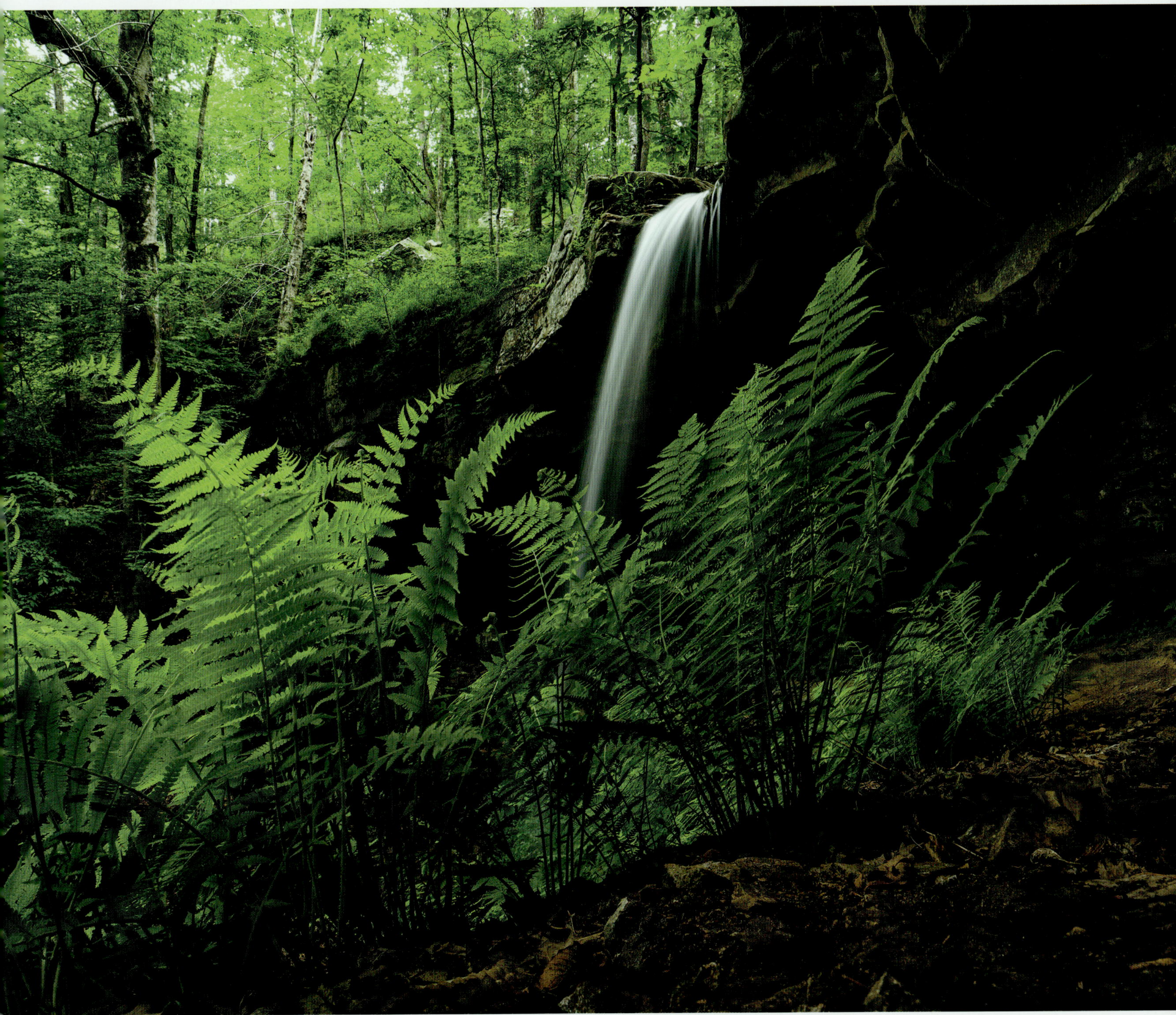

Ferns applaud Mule Trail Falls, Upper Buffalo Wilderness Area

Sunlight ripples shine through the crystalline waters of the Buffalo River to the polished stones below

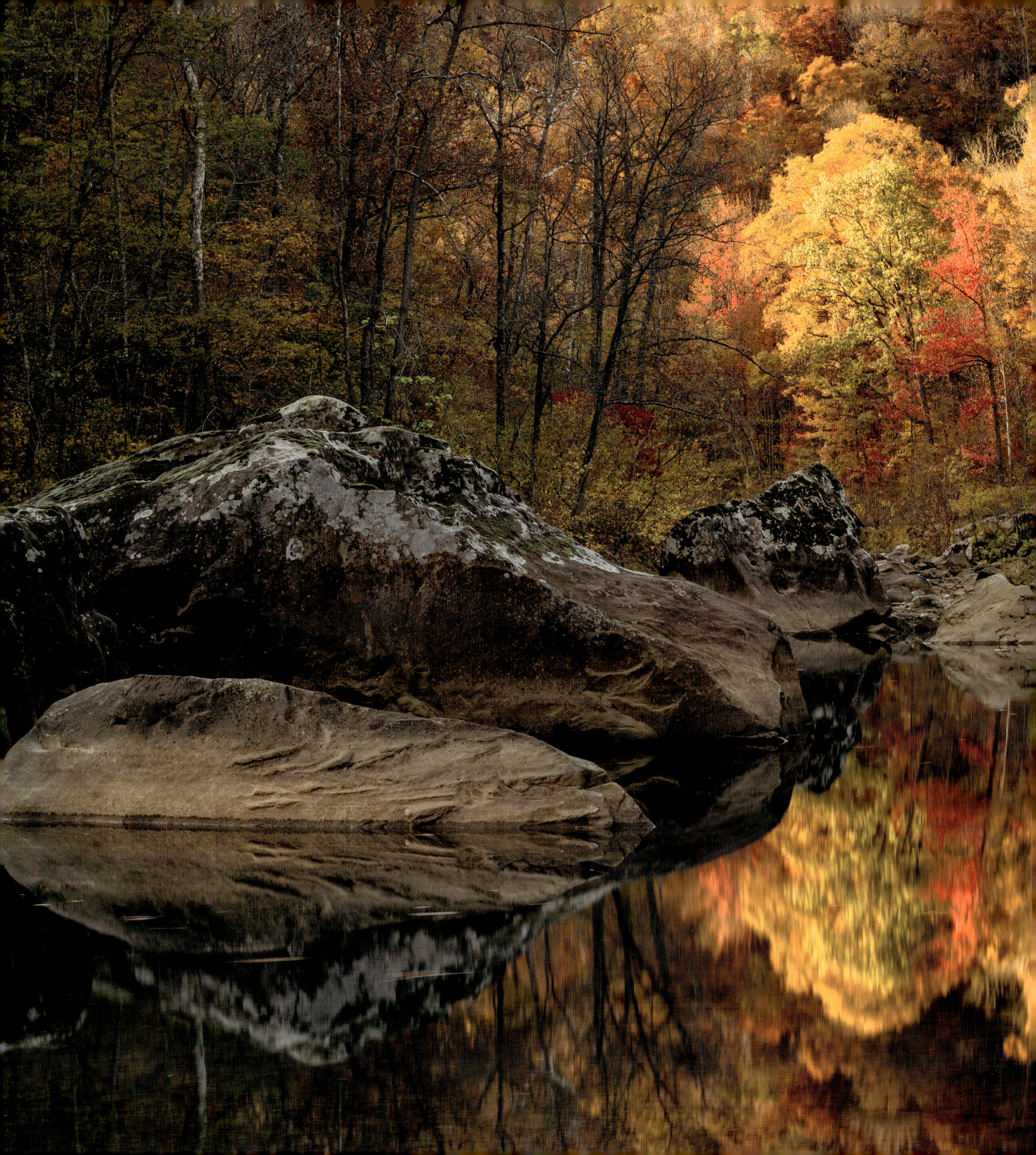

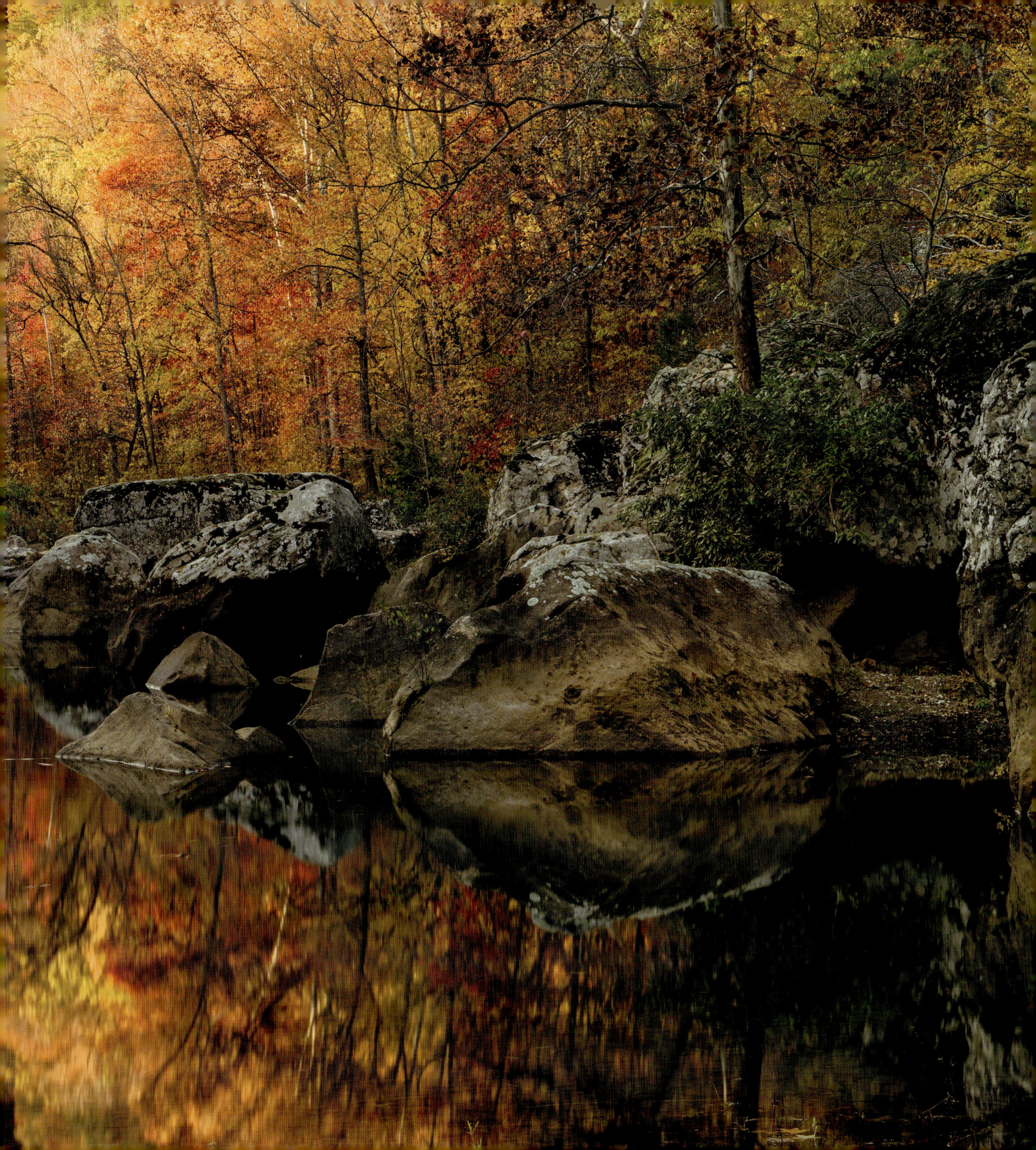

Looking out from a grotto waterfall on Leatherwood Creek, Buffalo National River

There seem to be a lot of overhangs or grottos behind waterfalls in our part of Arkansas. They tend to draw me into them, back there where the water thunder is loud and resonates through your bones.

Some of these overhangs are wide, tall, and deep, the sort of place where Native Americans or pioneers lived. Others are very shallow or tight, with just enough space to squeeze past without getting wet. I've been known to crawl on my belly to get way back under a low-roof in order to photograph a view like this one—where the bluff wraps completely around the scene. I know of four different waterfalls that have even drilled a hole right through the roof—The Glory Hole Falls is one example (page 56).

Many times a large branch or tree falls across or is washed down and hangs in the waterfall. I named one of these waterfalls "Leaning Log Falls" but the namesake log rotted and washed away—a new log soon took its place so the name is correct again!

See page 50 to see this waterfall and log from the front taken on the same day. Amazing how the view changes!

Evening light and the last color of the season, Upper Buffalo Wilderness Area (previous pages)

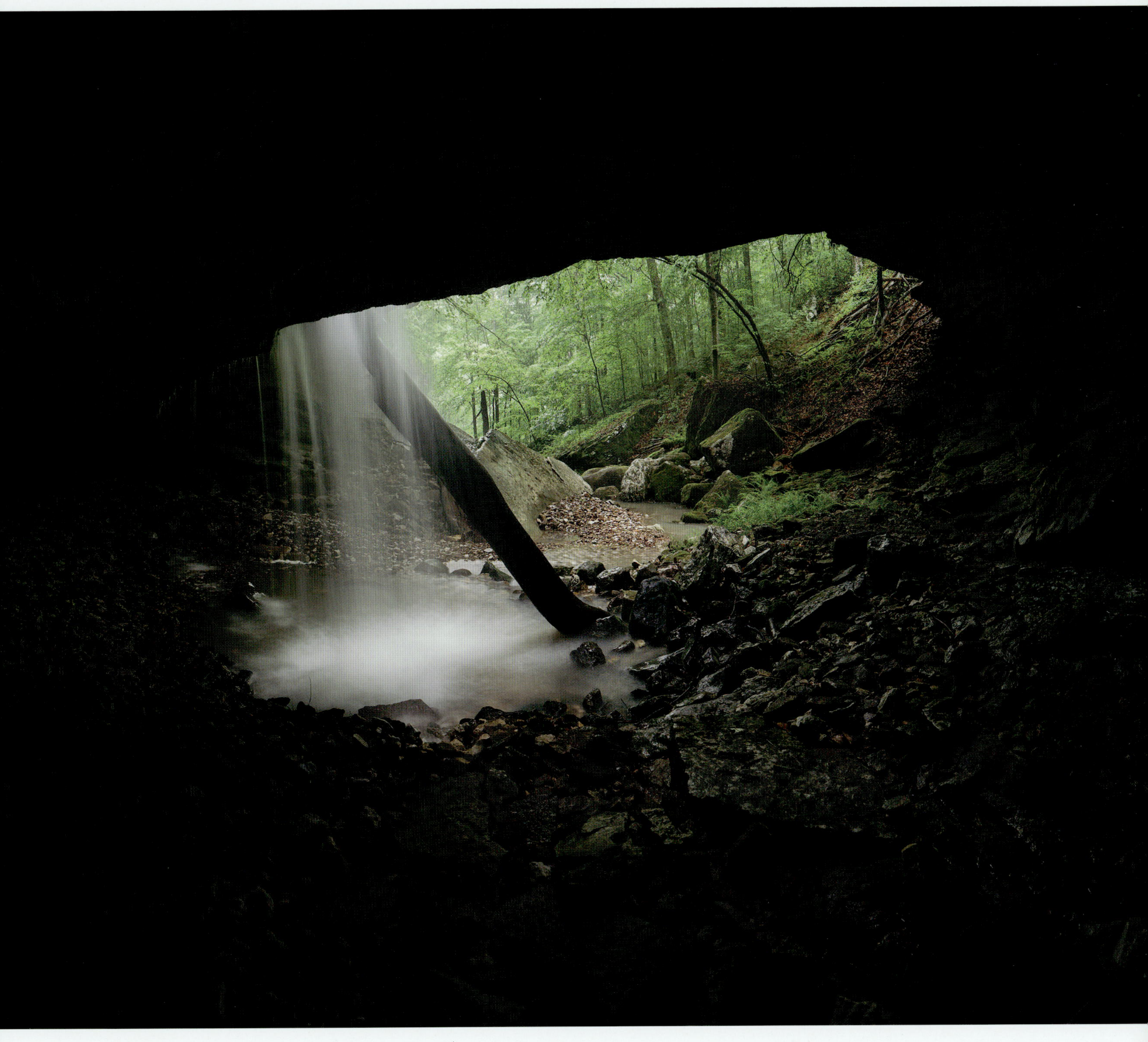

PHOTOGRAPHY NOTES

The pictures in this book were made within the past year or two and have never been published in book form before. We've long since passed the day when the equipment was more important than technique or location—most any digital camera can produce amazing pictures. I'm not funded or supported by any brand or company, so I use whatever camera will get the job done—or sometimes whatever camera I happen to have with me when a memorable moment presents itself.

I will confess that sometimes I buy a particular camera just because it is supposed to do something cool or innovative, and since someone else is using it and making big bucks it must be the camera—but the new fancy system usually doesn't improve my photos any and I end up sending it back and sticking with some old favorites.

The cameras I've used most often lately have been a small Sony A6000 mirrorless with a Hasselblad 16-70mm lens, which is with me most of the time and is what I use whenever I can't use a tripod; for star photos my favorite has been a Nikon 810 with a 14-24mm lens; and for the important, serious photos my first choice is a Pentax 645Z medium-format camera with a couple of 40-year old film-era lenses.

The tripod and tripod head are as important to me as the camera and lens, and my favorite is a 20-year-old Velbon tripod with a cube-style geared head—both have gone crashing down their share of hillsides and spent considerable time underwater (on purpose and otherwise), and it's a wonder they still function. But I guess, like me, being able to withstand the elements and abuse required to be in position to see and photograph many of these scenes is a prerequisite—good looks and shine don't matter!

A lot of these images were taken at the edges of daylight—that magical time before sunrise and after sunset when the light is fleeting yet can be brilliant and beautiful. I tend to push exposures to suit the available light (meaning long exposures of many seconds to several minutes long), and often the color and character of that light is mixed and surreal, and sometimes I can hardly believe what the camera has recorded. At night I have no idea what colors are there until the camera thinks it through and presents me with a photo.

I don't use "creative" filters—only a polarizing filter now and then to cut glare. And I hope I've never said *"I'll fix it later in Photoshop."* Photoshop can't sharpen an out-of-focus picture nor create beautiful light the way Momma Nature made it. I want to capture the scene as close to perfect as possible, although cameras and people don't see the same things the same way, so this can be a difficult task.

All digital photos ever taken in history have been processed by software though—first inside the camera, and then later, hopefully by a photographer who cares. I use Photoshop to process my RAW files with two basic goals in mind: to produce the very best possible image quality; and to reproduce as close as possible the scene that I saw and felt before me. If I've done my job as a competent photographer correctly, processing an image only takes a couple of minutes. I'd much rather be outside than at a computer screen.

Sometimes I photograph emotion, atmosphere, a feeling of calm or anticipation that has swept over the landscape—peace and tranquility when I find it. But I also want sharp detail in my images—individual leaves on trees, grains of sand, an ant crawling across the log at the back of the forest. I want to be able to look deep into a large print and see all that was there in real life.

Some of the images in this book were quick snapshots made with my little Sony camera, taken on a moment's notice. Many others were made after long hours or days of difficult work under demanding conditions—seems like those are the ones I enjoyed making the most. All of them involved a bit of luck, but sometimes that tends to follow a fella around. Far and away the most important part of it all is being there when something important happens. The rest is really pretty easy.

I'm beginning my 42nd year as a professional nature photographer, and still have a lot to learn. Come shoot with me and I'll share—I've been teaching photography workshops for 30+ years—www.TimErnst.com.

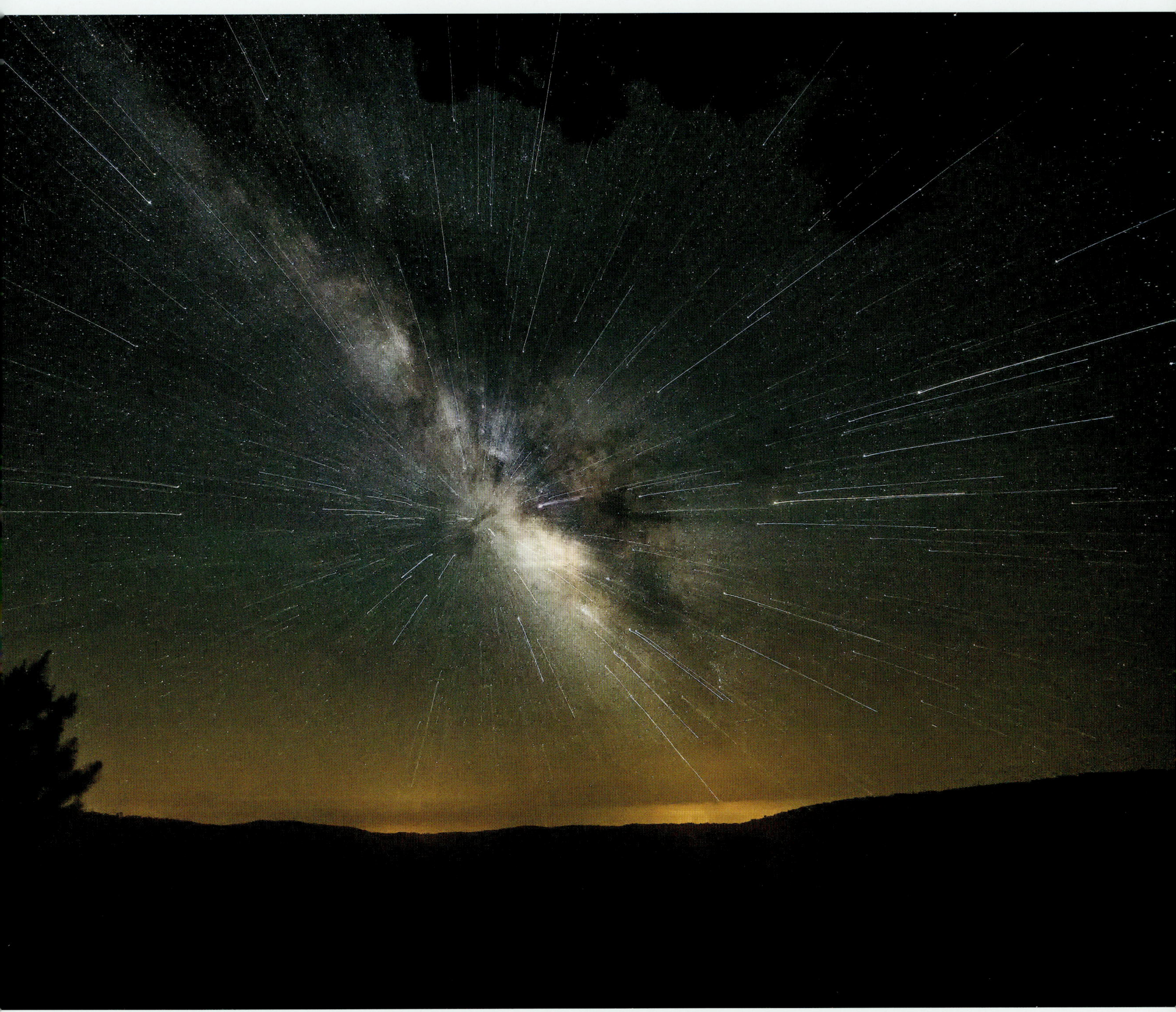

This is what happens when you accidently zoom the lens during a long exposure of the Milky Way. Oops...

ABOUT THE AUTHOR

Tim Ernst, 60+ (inching towards 70), lives in a log cabin called Cloudland in the middle of the Buffalo River Wilderness in Newton County, Arkansas, with his lovely bride, Pam.

I've been a professional nature photographer for more than 40 years with images published in most of the major nature publications from ***National Geographic*** on down, including hundreds of national, regional, and local magazines, books, and calendars. This is my 17th coffee table picture book. I have written a couple dozen guidebooks to outdoor Arkansas destinations that will lead you to waterfalls, hiking trails, and special scenic locations. My lovely bride and I own and operate a small publishing business, **Tim Ernst Publishing**, now in its 35th year. I also sell fine art prints on traditional photographic paper, metal, or on gallery-wrapped canvas to businesses and individuals around the country via our online galleries, and through our Tim Ernst Photography Canvas Gallery location that serves as gallery, digital darkroom, and print studio (open to the public on special days, and by appointment). And I've been teaching nature photography workshops to photographers of all skill levels for 30 years.

To see or order any of our products, view a schedule of our slide programs, get more information about photo workshops, view online galleries with thousands of photographs, or to keep up with life in the wilderness via our ***Cloudland Cabin Journal*** (online since 1998), go to www.TimErnst.com.

Other books by Tim Ernst
Arkansas Portfolio picture book
Wilderness Reflections picture book
Buffalo River Wilderness picture book
Arkansas Spring picture book
Arkansas Wilderness picture book
Arkansas Portfolio II picture book
Buffalo River Dreams picture book
Arkansas Waterfalls picture book
Arkansas Landscapes picture book
Arkansas Wildlife picture book
Arkansas Autumn picture book
Arkansas Portfolio III picture book
Arkansas Landscapes II picture book
Buffalo River Beauty picture book
Arkansas Nightscapes picture book
A Rare Quality Of Light picture book
Arkansas Nature Lover's guidebook
Arkansas Hiking Trails guidebook
Arkansas Waterfalls guidebook
Ozark Highlands Trail guidebook
Buffalo River Hiking Trails guidebook
Ouachita Trail guidebook
Arkansas Dayhikes guidebook
The Search For Haley
The Cloudland Journal

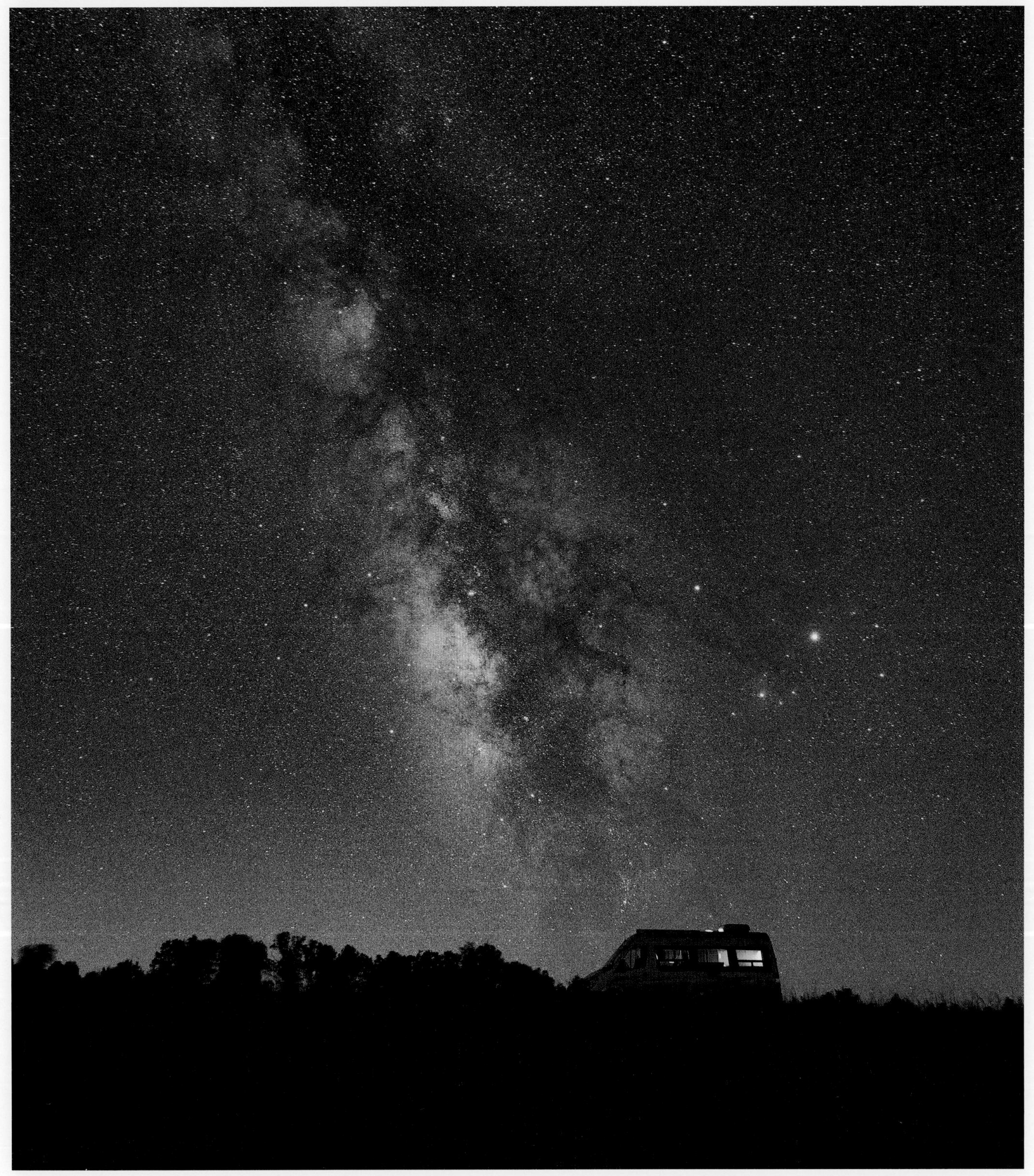

That's me inside our mobile office checking critical focus of some star photos via a laptop computer.
Our Roadtrek sprinter van makes a great tent too!

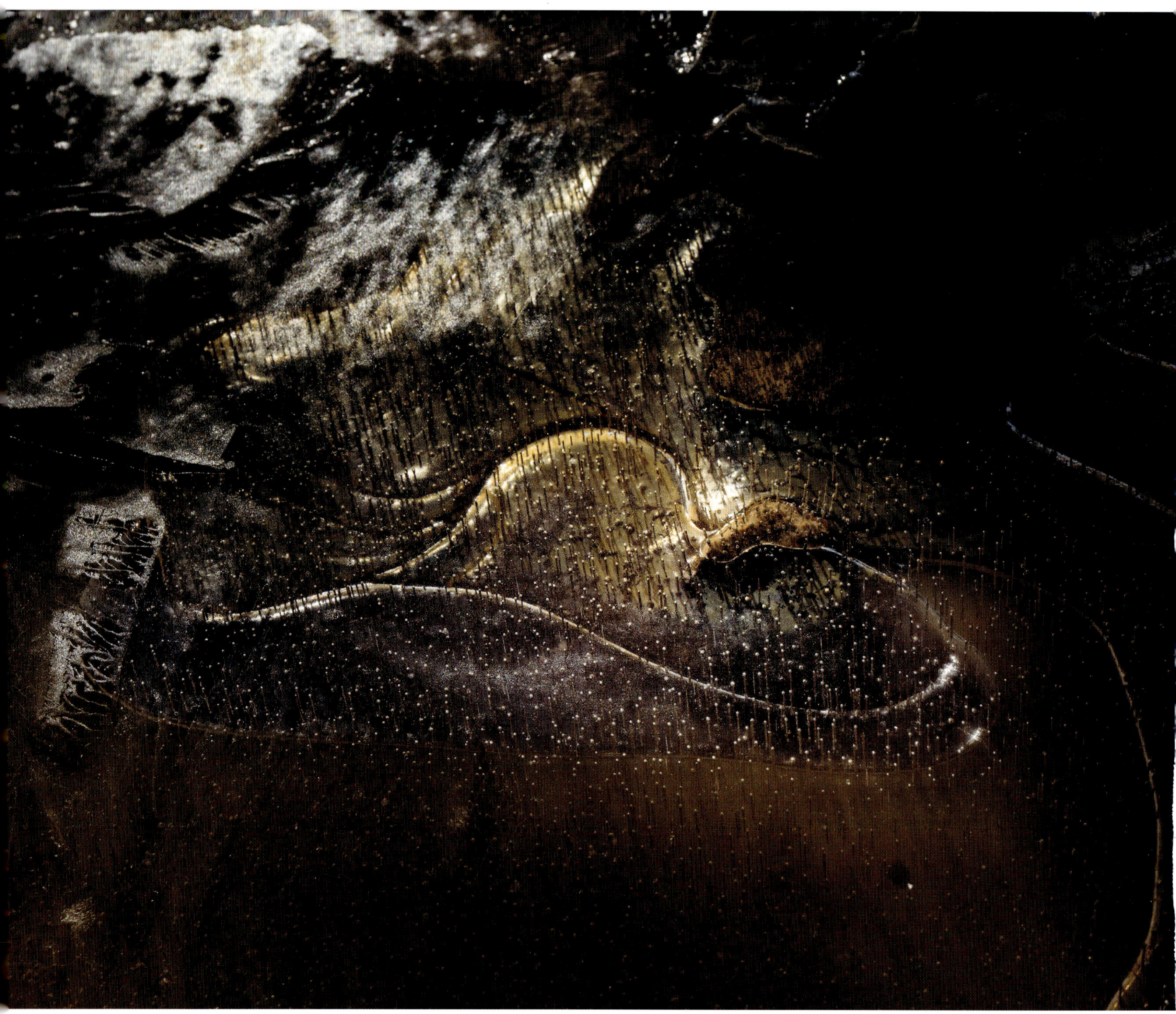

Ice formation along the trail to our home in the wilderness.